SECOND EDITION

Fitness Education for Children

A Team Approach

Stephen J. Virgilio, PhD

Adelphi University, Garden City, NY

Human Kinetics

Library of Congress Cataloging-in-Publication Data

Virgilio, Stephen J.
  Fitness education for children : a team approach / Stephen J. Virgilio. -- 2nd ed.
    p. cm.
  Includes bibliographical references and index.
  ISBN-13: 978-1-4504-0255-2 (soft cover)
  ISBN-10: 1-4504-0255-0 (soft cover)
  1. Physical fitness for children--Study and teaching--United States. 2. Physical education for children--Study and teaching--United States. 3. Curriculum planning--United States. 4. Teaching teams--United States. I. Title.
  GV443.V54 2012
  613.7'042--dc22
                              2011015255

ISBN-10: 1-4504-0255-0 (print)
ISBN-13: 978-1-4504-0255-2 (print)

The web addresses cited in this text were current as of August 2011, unless otherwise noted.

Acquisitions Editor: Cheri Scott; **Developmental Editor:** Ray Vallese; **Assistant Editor:** Derek Campbell; **Copyeditor:** Patsy Fortney; **Indexer:** Bobbi Swanson; **Permissions Manager:** Dalene Reeder; **Graphic Designer:** Fred Starbird; **Graphic Artist:** Denise Lowry; **Cover Designer:** Keith Blomberg; **Photographer (cover):** Neil Bernstein; **Photographers (interior):** Neil Bernstein and Jason Allen, unless otherwise noted; photos on pp. 1 and 153 © Human Kinetics; photo on p. 59 © Monkey Business; **Photo Asset Manager:** Laura Fitch; **Visual Production Assistant:** Joyce Brumfield; **Photo Production Manager:** Jason Allen; **Art Manager:** Kelly Hendren; **Associate Art Manager:** Alan L. Wilborn; **Illustrations:** © Human Kinetics; **Printer:** McNaughton & Gunn

Printed in the United States of America   10 9 8 7 6 5 4 3 2 1

The paper in this book is certified under a sustainable forestry program.

Human Kinetics
Website: www.HumanKinetics.com

United States: Human Kinetics, P.O. Box 5076, Champaign, IL 61825-5076
800-747-4457
e-mail: humank@hkusa.com

Canada: Human Kinetics, 475 Devonshire Road Unit 100, Windsor, ON N8Y 2L5
800-465-7301 (in Canada only)
e-mail: info@hkcanada.com

Europe: Human Kinetics, 107 Bradford Road, Stanningley, Leeds LS28 6AT, United Kingdom
+44 (0) 113 255 5665
e-mail: hk@hkeurope.com

Australia: Human Kinetics, 57A Price Avenue, Lower Mitcham, South Australia 5062
08 8372 0999
e-mail: info@hkaustralia.com

New Zealand: Human Kinetics, P.O. Box 80, Torrens Park, South Australia 5062
0800 222 062
e-mail: info@hknewzealand.com

E5323

To my sons, Stephen and Joseph

*It has been a dream come true to see you
develop from childhood into adults.
You have both far exceeded my greatest expectations as men.*

In memory of my father, Joseph

Contents

CHAPTER **9** **Collaborating With the Classroom Teacher . . 109**

CHAPTER **10** **Getting Parents
and Your Community Involved 135**

PART **III** **FITNESS ACTIVITIES 153**

CHAPTER **11** **Developmental Exercises 155**

CHAPTER **12** **Active Games 183**

Preface

If aggressive steps are not taken now to reduce childhood obesity throughout the world, we will be facing the first generation of children who will have shorter life spans than their parents or grandparents.

Elementary physical educators are deeply concerned about this frightening situation and have every intention of reversing this negative trend in children's health. I have revised the first edition of *Fitness Education for Children: A Team Approach* to specifically address childhood obesity and the promotion of active, healthy lifestyles from a physical education teacher's perspective.

Physical educators need to assume a leadership role in bringing the home, school, and community together in the fight against childhood obesity. Therefore, this book goes far beyond the typical class meeting twice per week for about 30 minutes within a traditional physical education curriculum. As educators, we must recognize that merely asking our students to run, jump, do push-ups, or maneuver through an obstacle course is not enough if we expect them to develop lifetime patterns of physical activity.

As professionals we can—and must—do more. I have written this edition as a resource for your elementary physical education program. This book provides a comprehensive approach to combating childhood obesity while developing in students an appreciation of an active, healthy lifestyle—whether you are an experienced teacher, a beginning teacher, or a student in a physical education teacher education institution.

If you are an undergraduate student studying to become a physical educator, *Fitness Education for Children: A Team Approach, Second Edition*, provides the necessary philosophy, instructional strategies, assessments, and pedagogical models to help you incorporate physical activity and fitness education into a well-balanced physical education program. If you are an experienced teacher, you will find this book a refreshing change from the traditional activities or games books, which normally have a short-sighted, narrow approach to the curriculum and leave you looking elsewhere in your efforts to modify your current school wellness program.

Furthermore, this book will expand your view of physical education and show you how to develop a school-based comprehensive team approach to address the obesity issues currently plaguing our youth. Specifically, it goes beyond the typical fitness games and activities found in many other books by including the following:

- Sample physical activity lesson plans for various developmental levels
- Contemporary teaching techniques
- Creative activities for teaching fitness concepts
- Strategies for involving parents and community members
- Ideas for integrating the curriculum with those of classroom teachers
- Fitness games
- Rhythmic activities
- Developmentally appropriate exercises
- Fitness education strategies for children with disabilities
- Reproducible instructional materials

The following are new and exciting features in this second edition:

- Up-to-date research and statistics on childhood obesity
- Approaches to childhood obesity intervention
- New physical activity guidelines
- Information about the new dietary guidelines and website (www.ChooseMyPlate.gov)
- A school wellness approach
- A discussion of the physical educator as physical activity director
- Updated Activitygram/Fitnessgram procedures

- A section on the Presidential Active Lifestyle Award
- A discussion of SMART goals
- A section on teaching children with autism spectrum disorder
- Additional exercise activities
- Updated cardiovascular health thematic lessons for classroom teachers
- Activities for integrating your curriculum with the classroom curriculum
- Information on school fitness breaks
- New fitness games
- Pedometer activities
- New rhythmic activities such as Zumba for children
- New websites for further information
- A brand-new chapter on yoga for children

Physical education teachers can't combat childhood obesity alone; a team effort is required. For many years physical educators have been planning and teaching in isolation, with little or no connection to other faculty members or the core curriculum within the school. This book will help you make physical education an integral part of the school's central focus. School administrators, classroom teachers, school volunteers, parents, school lunch personnel, health service professionals, and the community can all help create a healthy school environment.

Should you change your physical education curriculum completely? No! You can promote physical activity and develop healthy fitness levels within a balanced, high-quality program of physical education. This book, however, offers a personalized approach by showing you how to address children's developmental needs rather than their athletic ability or their ability to compete for individual fitness awards. Physical activity should be fun and enjoyable for every child—not just the physically gifted. To this end, I have designed the activities in this book to include all children, giving everyone the opportunity to succeed and reap the health benefits of an active lifestyle.

This book is divided into three parts. Part I, Developing a Foundation, describes the current status of childhood obesity and the role elementary physical educators can play to address this major health epidemic. The chapters in part I address the comprehensive team approach in schools and how you might assume the role of physical activity director for the school. Also addressed are behavior change and motivational strategies, the principles of physical activity, and health-related physical fitness as well as fitness education for children with physical disabilities.

Part II, Planning and Teaching Fitness Education, includes teaching strategies, sample lesson plans, strategies for teaching fitness concepts, ways to collaborate with the classroom teacher, and a plan for getting parents and the community involved in fitness education.

Part III, Fitness Activities, offers a number of practical, developmentally appropriate exercises; active games; dance and rhythmic activities; yoga poses for children; and schoolwide events to incorporate into your physical education program.

Children in elementary schools are at varied levels of physical, mental, social, and emotional development. To make planning your lessons easy, I have organized the health-related physical fitness concepts and activities into the following three developmental levels:

- Developmental level I (Beginner: Kindergarten and first grade)
- Developmental level II (Intermediate: Second and third grade)
- Developmental level III (Advanced: Fourth through sixth grades)

Keep in mind, however, that within each grade level you may have children at different levels of development. This supports the rationale for a fitness education program with a focus on choice, decision making, and self-directed learning.

In light of the obesity epidemic, the need for a high-quality elementary physical education program has never been greater. This innovative fitness education resource was developed to help complement an existing physical education curriculum, adding the needed zest and change to help combat childhood obesity and sedentary lifestyles in children. I hope this book helps in your day-to-day lessons, freeing you to concentrate on the challenging task of interacting with and guiding children throughout the most important years of their lives.

Acknowledgments

I would like to express my heartfelt gratitude to my wife, colleague, and best friend, Irene. We've come a long way since 1972, when we met at Woodbridge Elementary school in Tampa, Florida. Special thanks for her assistance in developing the cardiovascular thematic unit and for her unwavering support, patience, and love throughout my career.

Thank you to the students I have worked with at Adelphi University—you have been a constant source of inspiration over the last 20 years. Special thanks to students Katy DiLapi, Joseph Virgilio, Nicole Losito, and Stephanie Dunn for your help researching the activities in this edition and to my colleague Connie McKnight for her review of the yoga chapter.

I would like to thank all the children from Human Kinetics who served as models for this edition of the book: Cecilia Allen, Nate Allen, C.J. Brown, Grace Chariya, Katie Cole, James Hall, Lillian Hall, Robert Hall, Lauren Henderson, Olivia Hicks, K.J. Logue, Alex Maloney, Kelly Maloney, Madelyn Ronk, Olivia Ronk, Ethan Ruhlig, Estella Samii, Miranda Sellers, and Delaney Vallese. You all worked very hard.

I would like to extend my deepest appreciation to the professionals at Human Kinetics. Ray Vallese, my editor, was a pleasure to work with. His skill and eye for detail have made this edition a much improved resource for teachers and students. Additional thanks to Cheri Scott for getting this project up and going; the foundation you helped develop for this edition opened a clear pathway to the final product. Thanks to Derek Campbell and Kim Vecchio for their professional contributions and noteworthy insights. I appreciate the support of Scott Wikgren, division director of HPERD at Human Kinetics, whose vision of a renewed perspective of physical education is reflected in this book.

Finally, this book would not have been possible without the love and confidence of my parents, Marianne and Joseph, who have always supported my passion for physical activity.

Developing
a Foundation

A New Perspective in Elementary Physical Education

> If we are serious about combating the childhood obesity epidemic and improving child nutrition, then everyone must chip in—parents, schools, and, yes, even Congress.
>
> —Tom Harkin

In the first edition of this book, published in the late 1990s, I alerted readers to the seriousness of the childhood obesity crisis in the United States. The message was simple: if we didn't intervene and change the eating and physical activity behaviors of children, we would have one of the most critical health problems that has ever plagued the United States.

Now, more than a decade later, childhood obesity has grown into a serious national health problem. Obese Americans are draining the economy. Experts estimated that obesity in the United States cost approximately $147 billion in weight-related medical bills in 2008, which was double the cost of a decade ago. In 2010, obesity accounted for about 9.1 percent of medical spending in the United States. If Americans continue to gain weight, obesity will cost the country about $344 billion in annual medical-related expenses by 2018, consuming up to 21 percent of health care spending (Finkelstein, Trogdon, Cohen, and Dietz 2009).

The percentage of American children who are obese has doubled, and among adolescents the rates have more than tripled since 1980 (Ogden,

Carroll, and Flegal 2008). Currently, over 32 percent of school-aged children in the United States are either overweight or obese. Approximately 15 percent are overweight, and almost 17 percent are obese. That's one out of every three children with a weight issue! Obesity is categorized as a body mass index (BMI) of 30 or more, or body fat of 30 percent or more. Overweight is categorized as a BMI of over 25.

I am writing this edition because I am sensing a renewed awareness of urgency for this issue and renewed hope that something can be done. Studies have already shown that the obesity levels have stabilized and that physical activity levels among children are on the rise. But my primary reason for writing this edition is that I can't give up on the children of this world. Children are our most treasured possessions. They are the key to our future and have every right to lead long, healthy, and productive lives. Therefore, it is up to us as professionals to take a leadership role in the fight against childhood obesity.

We don't have a choice. Studies have shown that if we do not take action now, youngsters in the current generation will be the first to have shorter life spans than their parents had. Did you know that between 70 and 80 percent of the children who are currently overweight or obese will also have a weight problem when they are adults?

Obesity raises the risk for the following:

- Cancer
- Coronary heart disease
- Type 2 diabetes
- Hypertension
- High cholesterol
- Stroke
- Liver and gall bladder disease
- Respiratory problems
- Osteoarthritis
- Gynecological problems
- Social and emotional problems

HEART DISEASE BEGINS IN CHILDHOOD

Despite significant reductions in heart disease mortality rates during the last decade, cardiovascular heart disease remains the major cause of death, disability, and disease in the United States. Adults exhibiting an active lifestyle develop less coronary heart disease (CHD) than their inactive counterparts do, and when they do develop CHD, it occurs at a later age and tends to be less severe.

According to the American Heart Association (2010b) the major risk factors for CHD are as follows:

- Cigarette smoking
- Sedentary lifestyle
- Hypertension (elevated blood pressure)
- High cholesterol
- Diabetes
- Obesity

Studies have documented that close to 30 percent of American children already have elevated cholesterol levels (over 170 mg/dl), and adult-onset diabetes is now being seen more frequently in teens and young adults. Estimates have indicated that the number of deaths and incidents of disability associated with sedentary lifestyles will soon equal or exceed that associated with cigarette smoking (American Heart Association 2010a).

Physical activity and exercise can play a major role in controlling heart disease by mitigating hypertension, obesity, elevated cholesterol, and diabetes. Did you know that cardiovascular disease begins in childhood?

For more than 30 years, a team of doctors, nurses, and researchers led by Gerald S. Berenson, MD, studied more than 20,000 children in Bogalusa, Louisiana, compiling the world's largest data bank of heart disease risk factors in children: the Bogalusa Heart Study (Freedman, Mei, Srinivasan, Berenson, and Dietz 2007). Following are the results of this study:

- Adolescent Caucasian boys experienced a dramatic rise in LDL and HDL (bad to good) cholesterol ratios from childhood to adolescence, which may predispose them to developing heart disease early in life.
- Kidney factors predispose African American children to high blood pressure.
- Cardiovascular risk factors are interrelated in most children, as they are in adults (e.g., obesity and high blood pressure).
- More than 50 percent of children consume high levels of salt, fat, and sugar.
- Overweight children have a 70 percent chance of becoming overweight adults.
- Sedentary children are more likely to become sedentary adults.
- Most school-aged children possess one or more CHD risk factors.
- Families with a history of heart disease have children with higher risk factors.

The Bogalusa Heart Study is a long-term scientific study that has provided clear evidence that we must begin intervention at the early stages of life if we are to reverse the obesity crisis plaguing our children.

What does all of this research mean to you? It simply means that you can begin to identify children at an early age who are likely to have serious health problems later in life. As an elementary physical educator, you can have a significant impact on the lifestyle choices made by children, thereby affecting their entire lives. What an exciting time to be an elementary physical education specialist!

This book addresses the roles and responsibilities of elementary physical educators. The contents of this resource, however, go far beyond the traditional physical education curriculum;

they reach out to include a child's entire school environment through a home, school, and community model approach.

As a physical educator, you must consider expanding your role and look to reform and supplement your current program goals. This book offers a vision to help you accomplish your goals and place children on the track to active, healthy lifestyles. Many educational experts now agree that school is our best opportunity to reverse the downward trends in the general health of youth.

PHYSICAL ACTIVITY AS A KEY FACTOR

It appears that one of the major contributors to overweight in children is lack of physical activity. Eating trends indicate that children are consuming about the same types of foods they did 25 years ago; however, children are not as active as they once were. We could say that we are in the middle of a childhood physical inactivity crisis rather than a childhood obesity crisis.

Ironically, children are the most active segment of our population. Most children love to play, run, dance, and learn new skills. Yet in upper elementary grades and continuing into middle and high school, activity levels begin to decline, resulting in too many children carrying excess weight. What happens in that time?

Many children by the age of 11 are sitting behind some sort of screen for more than 7.5 hours per day—smart phones, computer screens, TVs, or tablet computers. Moreover, younger children (ages 5 to 10) are beginning to model this behavior. Advancements in technology have been remarkable over the last decade, and children should take advantage of the latest learning tools to develop their academic skills. However, we need to impose guidelines and restrictions so that children are not using screen time at the expense of their current and future health.

At 10, 11, or 12 years old, many children discover new interests that pull them away from play and general physical activity. Moreover, because they no longer want to be considered children, they may stop playing childhood games. During this period, too often, parents and teachers convey the message that physical activity must have a purpose; they encourage children to join athletic teams to compete for honors and awards or to take karate lessons to become black belts. Children who are not motivated by these adult goals tend to become inactive because they feel incompetent and unsupported. We must stop treating 10-year-olds like miniature adult athletes and start letting them develop naturally as children who need to move freely, play, have fun, and express their physical selves.

When children in middle schools were asked why they stopped participating in physical activity and sports, most said, "I didn't care for the competition" and "It wasn't fun anymore." Let's listen carefully to what our children are saying and modify our approach to physical activity to meet their needs.

Participating in regular physical activity is one of the most powerful things people can do for their general health regardless of age. Just think how healthy children would be if they started at a very young age on a pathway of lifetime physical activity. The benefits of physical activity include the following:

- Weight control
- Controlled blood pressure
- Reduced risk of heart disease
- Reduced risk of some cancers
- Reduced cholesterol levels
- Reduced risk of type 2 diabetes
- Improved quality of life and psychological well-being
- Strong bones and muscles
- Improved ability to perform daily activities
- Increased chance of living longer

NATIONAL PHYSICAL ACTIVITY PLAN

In 2010, a committee consisting of U.S. organizations at the forefront of physical activity and public health launched a groundbreaking document to bring awareness to the problem of inactivity and create an action plan to help increase physical activity among children, adults, and senior citizens.

The National Physical Activity Plan's primary vision is that one day all Americans will be physically active and will live, work, and play in environments that facilitate regular physical activity (2010). The plan includes a comprehensive set of policies and program initiatives to help increase physical activity in all segments of the American population. The plan is a collaborative effort of the public and private sectors to support change in communities throughout the United States. The intention is to create a national culture that encourages an active, healthy lifestyle. The major purposes are to improve health, prevent disease and disability, and enhance the quality of life.

The U.S. National Physical Activity Plan is organized into eight sectors:

- Business and industry
- Education
- Health care
- Mass media
- Parks, recreation, fitness, and sports
- Public health
- Transportation, land use, and community design
- Volunteer and nonprofit

Within these sectors are strategies that outline specific approaches that communities, organizations and agencies, and individuals can use to promote physical activity.

In developing the plan, the coordinating committee relied on a number of guiding principles such as including all sociodemographic groups; directing the action at local, state, federal, and institutional levels; encouraging the involvement of diverse stakeholders; grounding the plan in the ecological model of health behavior; and presenting the plan as a living document that is consistently updated and revised to meet the needs of an ever-changing society.

For additional information, go to www.physicalactivityplan.org.

NASPE PHYSICAL ACTIVITY GUIDELINES FOR CHILDREN

Two very important documents by the National Association for Sport and Physical Education (NASPE) were developed to serve as guidelines when planning for children's physical activity. *Active Start: A Statement of Physical Activity Guidelines for Children From Birth to Age 5* (2009a) provides recommendations for early childhood, and *Physical Activity for Children: A Statement of Guidelines for Children Ages 5-12* (2004b) offers suggestions for elementary school–aged children.

Active Start

NASPE's position statement *Active Start* (NASPE 2009a) provides guidance to parents, caregivers, teachers, and child care administrators regarding the physical activity capabilities and needs of infants, toddlers, and preschoolers. Because children at these ages vary widely in developmental levels, the document described physical activity at each stage—infants, toddlers, and preschoolers. For our purposes, I've listed the guidelines for preschoolers.

General Position Statement

All children from birth to age 5 should engage daily in physical activity that promotes movement skillfulness and foundations of health-related fitness.

Guidelines for Preschoolers

1. Preschoolers should accumulate at least 60 minutes of structured physical activity each day.

2. Preschoolers should engage in at least 60 minutes—and up to several hours—of unstructured physical activity each day, and should not be sedentary for more than 60 minutes at a time, except when sleeping.

3. Preschoolers should be encouraged to develop competence in fundamental motor skills that will serve as the building blocks for future motor skillfulness and physical activity.

4. Preschoolers should have access to indoor and outdoor areas that meet or exceed recommended safety standards for performing large-muscle activities.

5. Caregivers and parents in charge of preschoolers' health and well-being are responsible for understanding the importance of physical activity and for promoting movement skills by providing opportunities for structured and unstructured physical activity.

Reprinted from NASPE 2009.

Physical Activity for Children

NASPE's position statement *Physical Activity for Children* (2004b) is an extension of the *Active Start* guidelines and addresses the needs of children ages 5 to 12.

1. Children should accumulate at least 60 minutes, and up to several hours, of age-appropriate physical activity on all or most days of the week. This daily accumulation should include moderate and vigorous physical activity with the majority of the time being spent in intermittent activity.

2. Children should participate in several bouts of physical activity lasting 15 minutes or more each day.

3. Children should participate each day in a variety of age-appropriate physical activities designed to help them achieve optimal health, wellness, fitness, and performance benefits.

4. Extended periods (i.e., of two hours or more) of inactivity are discouraged for children, especially during the daytime hours.

Reprinted from NASPE 2004.

PHYSICAL ACTIVITY PHILOSOPHY

My philosophy for teaching children to adopt a long-term active, healthy lifestyle is encompassed in the following five simple guidelines:

1. Teach children the health benefits of physical activity and healthy eating.

2. Make physical activity available to all children.

3. Reinforce physical activity by tapping into children's innate desire to move.

4. Make good health habits fun.

5. Teach children as children, not as miniature adults.

First, children should be taught the health benefits of physical activity and proper eating habits. Chapter 2, as well as the numerous activities in this book, will help you do this.

Second, you need to make physical activity available to everyone. All children are entitled to the healthful benefits of physical activity, play, games, dance, and sport. Children with disabilities, including obese children, are often ignored and are not provided the same opportunities to move as other children.

Third, physical activity should be reinforced by tapping into children's innate desire to move. All children begin life with an innate need and desire to play and move. Teachers and parents should continue to promote this need in a positive, non-competitive environment on a daily basis.

Fourth, good health habits should be fun. Physical activity and eating with friends, classmates, and family should take place in a relaxed, safe, supportive environment. Children should have fun when they are physically active—laughing, singing, moving, and exploring. Positive experiences will promote a continued desire to move. Children should also have fun when they are eating. Make meals colorful, create food designs, and make eating a family affair.

Fifth, children should be taught appropriately. They are not miniature adults. Many of the approaches and techniques adults identify with are inappropriate for young children, such as maintaining a workout schedule or routine and measuring weekly gains. For many years, we taught children based on the premise that their motivations to move were similar to those of adults. Children are physically active because they enjoy play, need to interact with their peers, want to develop new motor skills, and need to express themselves through physical activity. Furthermore, their eating habits are quite different from those of adults. For example, school-aged children should normally eat about every two and a half hours throughout the day, which means that they should have five or six smaller meals per day.

COMPONENTS OF HEALTH-RELATED PHYSICAL FITNESS

Children need a wide variety of physical activity choices. You should encourage them to make decisions and support their individual interests while also making sure they are getting a balance of all the health-related physical fitness components (figure 1.1). Those components are as follows:

- Cardiorespiratory endurance
- Muscle fitness
- Flexibility
- Body composition

Cardiorespiratory Endurance

Cardiorespiratory endurance is the ability to participate in large-muscle physical activity for relatively long periods of time at moderate to vigorous levels of intensity. It is the capacity of the

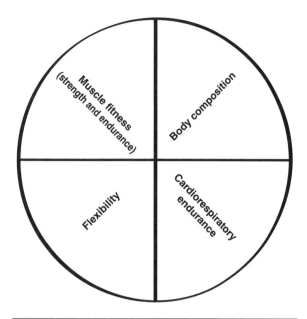

Figure 1.1 Components of health-related physical fitness.

heart, blood vessels, and lungs to deliver nutrients and oxygen to the tissues to provide the energy needed for endurance exercise. Jogging, dancing, and swimming are three popular activities that build cardiorespiratory endurance (see figure 1.2).

Figure 1.2 Jogging for cardiorespiratory endurance.

Muscle Fitness

The contemporary term *muscle fitness* is used in this book to convey the combination of muscular strength and muscular endurance for children. When using the muscle fitness exercises in this book, make sure your students use a submaximum level of resistance as well as body support activities (see figures 1.3 and 1.4).

Figure 1.3 *(a)* Pull-up for dynamic strength and *(b)* hand push for static strength.

Figure 1.4 *(a)* Repeatedly throwing a softball or *(b)* doing curl-ups can help build muscular endurance.

Flexibility

Flexibility is the ability to move joints in an unrestricted fashion through the full range of motion to bend, stretch, twist, and turn. Properly stretching muscles, ligaments, and tendons promotes good body alignment as well as reduces stress in the neck and back area. The seated hamstring stretch and other stretching exercises require and develop flexibility (see figure 1.5).

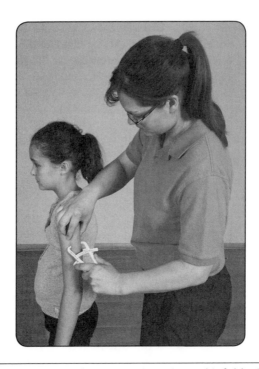

Figure 1.6 Teacher measuring triceps skinfold with calipers.

Figure 1.5 Seated hamstring stretch for flexibility.

Body Composition

Body composition is the ratio of body fat to lean body tissue. Teach children the dangers of excessive body fat and the role exercise plays in controlling body weight (see figure 1.6). When you talk about nutrition, discuss body composition as well.

SPORT-RELATED PHYSICAL FITNESS

Sport-related physical fitness (sometimes referred to as skill-related physical fitness) includes agility, speed, power, balance, and coordination. Although these components are not absolutely necessary for maintaining physical health, it is still important to include them in your physical education program so that your students can apply them to games, sports, and recreational activities.

Agility

Agility, often called quickness, is the ability to quickly change direction or body position accurately while moving through space. Agility is essential in sports such as basketball and soccer.

Speed

Speed is the ability to perform a movement in the shortest possible time. It is essential in most sport-related activities and movements, including track, basketball, baseball, and soccer.

Power

Power is the product of strength and speed. Activities that require power, such as the standing broad jump and shot-putting, involve explosive movements in short periods of time.

Balance

Balance is the ability to maintain equilibrium and body position whether moving or stationary. Tumbling, gymnastics, balance beam activities, in-line skating, and snow and water skiing demand a high degree of balancing ability.

Coordination

Coordination, the ability to integrate a number of motor skills into a smooth, efficient motor pattern, is vital in most sport-related activities. Contrary to popular opinion, nearly everyone can develop and improve coordination with proper instruction and adequate practice. Hitting a softball, shooting a basketball, and juggling are examples of advanced motor skills that require a high degree of coordination.

FITNESS EDUCATION

Fitness education involves promoting general physical activities such as walking the dog, playing sports, and going on a bike ride, as well as promoting exercises that facilitate the health-related physical fitness components. It should also include nutrition education for maintaining healthy body composition. Physical activity and exercise can complement each other and should be interspersed throughout a child's experiences both in and out of school in a fun, age-appropriate manner.

Fitness education is viewed as a comprehensive, multidisciplinary approach to help children acquire the knowledge, attitudes, beliefs, and behaviors for the promotion of long-term active, healthy lifestyles within a quality physical education program. For this approach to work, the school, home, and community must share the responsibility of promoting healthful habits in students.

Your physical education program should be the foundation on which the other influences in your students' lives can build. It should include a balance of general physical activity, health-related physical fitness, motor skills, content knowledge, and personal and social development activities. In 2004 the National Association of Sport and Physical Education (NASPE) established the following six key standards to develop a framework for quality physical education:

- **Standard 1:** Demonstrates competency in motor skills and movement patterns needed to perform a variety of physical activities.
- **Standard 2:** Demonstrates understanding of movement concepts, principles, strategies, and tactics as they apply to the learning and performance of physical education.
- **Standard 3:** Participates regularly in physical activity.
- **Standard 4:** Achieves and maintains a health-enhancing level of physical fitness.
- **Standard 5:** Exhibits responsible personal and social behavior that respects self and others in physical activity settings.
- **Standard 6:** Values physical activity for health, enjoyment, challenge, self-expression, and/or social interaction.

Reprinted from NASPE 2004.

This book shows how fitness education can complement and enhance your overall elementary physical education program.

Characteristics of a Quality Fitness Education Program

As you plan the fitness education component of your program, consider that physical educators in high-quality programs usually do the following:

- Plan, communicate, and cooperate with classroom teachers, administrators, health service professionals, school lunch personnel, and parents.
- Choose noncompetitive, developmentally appropriate physical activities, including a wide variety of exercises and movement experiences for general body development.
- Make sure children have the opportunity to be physically active at least 60 minutes per day, five days of the week.
- Teach children the benefits of an active lifestyle and of staying active throughout their lives.
- Design activities to include every child regardless of physical abilities.
- Emphasize rewards, not awards, using incentives, positive reinforcement, and intrinsic value to motivate children rather than giving awards for particular levels of fitness.
- Encourage children to accept responsibility for their own physical activity and fitness progress by teaching them how to monitor their progress and by giving them opportunities to make decisions related to their own health and fitness goals.
- Make fitness activities fun, allowing children to enjoy fitness activities with friends, family, or alone in a safe, supportive environment.
- Integrate fitness education throughout the school year and throughout other classroom subject areas.
- Teach fitness activities using a wide variety of teaching strategies, recognizing that how children learn about their bodies will have a lasting impact on their values related to physical activity.
- Model positive physical activity behaviors, remembering that actions speak louder than words.

How do you include every important aspect of a high-quality fitness education program? I'll give you tips and suggestions throughout this book.

Physical Education Reform

It is important to provide children with a balanced curriculum that includes movement education, motor skills, rhythms, dance, tumbling, developmental games, sport education, and fitness education. Each component is critical to developing an active, healthy lifestyle. However, in light of the existing research on childhood obesity and low activity levels, physical educators have moved from a skills and sport curriculum model to one that emphasizes increasing physical activity levels, health-related fitness components, and personal and social skills to encourage students to adopt behaviors that will result in active and healthy lifestyles in the long term (see figure 1.7).

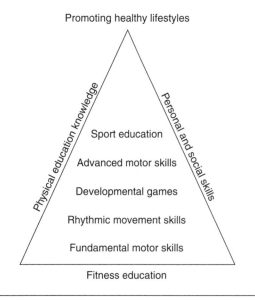

Figure 1.7 A balanced elementary physical education curriculum.

Remind children continually that the general purpose of learning motor skills and participating in sports is to stay physically active, develop lifetime skills, and enjoy playing with their friends—not to compete or earn awards. To join the reform movement, you need not throw out your existing program—simply modify your focus to meet the demands of a changing society.

SUMMARY

The time has arrived to modify the traditional elementary physical education curriculum to promote long-term active, healthy lifestyles in our students. The childhood obesity problem has become an epidemic, and serious action is necessary to revise this downward trend in the health of children throughout the world.

Physical activity can play an instrumental role in helping control weight issues and fight many of the most serious diseases that affect our lives as adults. Integrate fitness education throughout your curriculum. Concentrate on the health-related components of physical fitness while increasing students' general physical activity levels through a fun, developmentally appropriate approach. Teach concepts related to healthy lifestyles along with a high-quality, well-balanced program of physical education.

Your own attitudes, actions, and instruction will teach your students that the purpose of physical education is not to create elite athletes for future sport competition, but to establish positive physical activity attitudes, beliefs, and behaviors for a lifetime of health and enjoyment.

You are not going to be doing this alone. Develop a team approach through a comprehensive school wellness program with strategies for intervention at home, at school, and in the community.

A Team Approach to Fitness Education

> Two stonecutters were asked
> what they were doing. The first said,
> "I'm cutting this stone into blocks."
> The second replied, "I'm on a team
> that's building a cathedral."
>
> —*Unknown*

Over 97 percent of the children in the United States ages 5 through 12 attend private or public elementary schools. This creates a tremendous opportunity for schools to serve as the primary place to reverse the downward trends in children's health behaviors. Unfortunately, many children are not getting enough physical education in school to foster a significant change.

At the elementary school level, children on average have physical education twice per week for about 30 to 40 minutes. This is clearly not enough time to develop long-term positive health behaviors in children. According to the National Association for Sport and Physical Education (NASPE 2003), elementary school children should accumulate a minimum of 150 minutes of quality physical education weekly, and middle and high school students should accumulate 225 minutes weekly.

According to the *School Health Policies and Programs Study (SHPPS)* (Centers for Disease Control and Prevention [CDC] 2006), only 3.8 percent of elementary schools, 7.9 percent of middle schools, and 2.1 percent of high schools reported

meeting NASPE's minimum number of minutes of physical education. At the time of this study, only two states met the recommended NASPE minute requirements for elementary schools of 150 minutes per week—Louisiana and New Jersey. The study also indicated that 43.6 percent of elementary schools provided regular physical activity breaks, and more than 57.1 percent scheduled daily recess.

NASPE (2003) believes that every student, from preschool through 12th grade, should have the opportunity to participate in a high-quality physical education program. The four components of a high-quality physical education program are as follows:

- Opportunity to learn
- Meaningful content
- Appropriate instruction
- Student and program assessment

High-quality programs are important for developing the following primary goals of physical education:

- Health-related fitness
- Physical competence
- Cognitive understanding
- Positive attitudes about physical activity

NASPE believes that these goals will facilitate an active lifestyle in students.

MIXED MESSAGES

High-quality physical education may not be enough to turn around the mind-set of policy makers. For many years, parents, administrators, and teachers have given children mixed messages about the value and importance of physical activity and physical education. Consider the messages our children receive from the following:

- Physical education is a part-time subject, meeting only two or three days per week.
- Classroom teachers often allow students to attend physical education class only if they have finished their classroom assignments.
- Teachers sometimes take away physical education for misbehavior in the classroom.
- Physical education teachers often include fitness activities without teaching students about the content, value, or importance of the activity to their health.
- Many administrators and teachers regard physical education classes as a way to let off steam or give the children a break from class.
- Teachers and parents often give children snacks that are loaded with fat, sugar, and sodium.
- Physical education teachers might provide physical activities without regard to individual differences (e.g., having everyone run a mile).
- Funds for equipment, space, or additional physical education faculty are limited.
- School and organization fund-raising campaigns often include selling candy, cookies, or cupcakes.
- The average school lunch includes foods that are high in fat, sodium, and sugar.

Make it your goal as a physical educator to address these mixed messages and help establish new guidelines and policies within your school or district. You can accomplish this by creating a multidisciplinary school wellness plan for your school.

MULTIDISCIPLINARY TEAM APPROACH

The responsibility for developing positive health behaviors within the school should not lie entirely with you, the physical educator. To achieve your goals, begin to incorporate a multidisciplinary team approach, enlisting the help of parents, professionals, and resources in both the school and local communities. For example, the Heart Smart Program was developed as a comprehensive cardiovascular health and physical activity model for school-aged children in New Orleans, Louisiana (Downey et al. 1987). This model modified and built on existing educational components such as school health assessment, the classroom curriculum, the school lunch program, school health services, parent and community involvement, and schoolwide events. It included a fitness education component titled SuperKids-SuperFit that was integrated into a traditional physical education program (Virgilio and Berenson 1988). This model approach was funded by the National Institute of Health (NIH) and served as the springboard for many programs and national documents.

In 1997, the U.S. Department of Health and Human Services (USDHHS) and the Centers for Disease Control and Prevention (CDC) published "Guidelines for School and Community Programs to Promote Lifelong Physical Activity Among Young People." The general theme of this document was to bring the home, school, and community together to address the health of young children. The guidelines included the following 10 recommendations:

1. **Policy:** Establish policies that promote lifelong physical activity among children.
2. **Environment:** Provide physical and social environments that enable safe and enjoyable physical activity.
3. **Physical education:** Implement a curriculum that emphasizes physical activity and helps students develop the knowledge, attitudes, motor skills, behavioral skills, and confidence to lead active, healthy lifestyles.

4. **Health education:** Implement a health education curriculum to help students develop the knowledge, attitudes, behavioral skills, and confidence needed for adopting and maintaining active, healthy lifestyles.

5. **Extracurricular activities:** Provide extracurricular activities that meet the needs of all students.

6. **Parental involvement:** Include parents and guardians in physical activity instruction and in extracurricular programs, and encourage them to support their children's participation.

7. **Personnel training:** Provide education to school and community personnel to effectively promote enjoyable lifelong physical activity among young people.

8. **Health services:** Assess physical activity patterns among young people, counsel them about physical activity, and refer them to appropriate programs and services.

9. **Community programs:** Provide a range of developmentally appropriate community sport and recreation programs that are attractive to young people.

10. **Evaluation:** Regularly evaluate school and community physical activity instruction, programs, and facilities.

From USDHHS/CDC

In 2004, the U.S. Congress recognized that schools play a critical role in promoting student health, preventing obesity, and combating issues related to poor nutrition habits and sedentary lifestyles. Congress passed legislation titled the Child Nutrition and Women, Infants and Children (WIC) Reauthorization Act of 2004 and PL-108-265 to address the health issues of children. The act required schools to establish wellness policies by school year 2006. This legislation placed the control of developing wellness policies at the local level, to include the following:

- Goals for nutrition education, physical activity, and other school-based activities
- Nutrition guidelines
- Guidelines for reimbursable school meals
- A plan for measuring implementation of the local wellness policy
- Community involvement

As a result of this legislation, schools have taken a more serious view of childhood wellness and have begun to incorporate specific strategies to help address the eating and physical activity levels within the structure of the school setting.

COMPREHENSIVE SCHOOL PHYSICAL ACTIVITY PROGRAMS

To meet the minimum requirements of 60 minutes of physical activity each day, NASPE (2008) published a document with guidelines and recommendations for implementing a comprehensive school physical activity program (CSPAP). The program includes several approaches to add physical activity time throughout the course of the school day. The additional opportunities are not designed to take the place of physical education but rather to supplement the time needed to reach a minimum of 60 minutes of physical activity per day. NASPE has endorsed the use of physical activity breaks as one strategy to increase physical activity time. At the elementary school level, NASPE has taken the position that all children should be given a minimum of 20 minutes of recess with ample opportunity for general physical activity.

In 2009, NASPE supported the use of Kid Fitness breaks during classroom time. This school-based approach was developed from the characters of the *Kid Fitness* TV show, which airs on over 28 public television (PBS) stations throughout the United States and Puerto Rico. The Kid Fitness school physical activity breaks are endorsed and financially supported by the United Way and currently used in over 10,000 classrooms throughout the United States. The Kid Fitness program comes packaged as a kit with instructional materials, subject matter integration (reading, language arts, science), flash cards, a DVD and CD of the activity breaks, and supplemental games and an activities booklet for the teacher to use on the playground. The physical education teacher serves as a partner to help the classroom teacher implement the physical activity breaks throughout the school year.

To establish a comprehensive school physical activity program (CSPAP), schools should take the following steps:

1. Appoint a CSPAP committee to oversee physical activity opportunities and establish policies and procedures.

2. Assess current opportunities, needs, barriers, and so forth.

3. Create an action plan addressing each of the following component areas:
   - High-quality physical education
   - Before-school strategies
   - After-school strategies
   - Staff personal wellness
   - School employees' wellness and involvement in the CSPAP
   - Family and community involvement
   - Physical activity integrated into the classroom
   - Physical activity breaks
   - Recess
   - Intramurals
   - Walk and bike to school programs

4. Implement the plan.

A key factor in developing a CSPAP is to designate a teacher (preferably the physical education teacher) to serve as the physical activity director. The director assumes responsibility for the implementation of the plan and facilitates each of the aforementioned components.

LET'S MOVE AND LET'S MOVE IN SCHOOL

In 2010, first lady Michelle Obama announced an ambitious national goal to combat childhood obesity: Let's Move. This campaign takes a comprehensive approach to mobilizing both public and private sectors and includes strategies to address the various factors that lead to childhood obesity. Let's Move brings together leaders from government, medicine, science, business, education, athletics, and community organizations to provide strategies to help children be more active in and out of school, to eat better, and to develop healthier lifestyles. (For further information, go to www.letsmove.gov.)

To support Michelle Obama's campaign, NASPE launched the Let's Move in School initiative. This initiative urges parents, school administrators, policy makers, and concerned citizens to take action steps to help schools implement the major components of the comprehensive school physical activity program.

Let's Move in School provides tools to support instructional physical education and enhanced opportunities for physical activity. It also offers sources of funding; recognition for outstanding physical education teachers and programs; and information on federal, state, and local policy efforts. The brochure "Active Kids and Academic Performance: The Positive Impact of School-Based Physical Education and Physical Activity" (available at www.aahperd.org/letsmoveinschool), designed for parents and administrators, details the importance of daily physical activity.

SCHOOL WELLNESS PLAN

Getting the picture? It appears the team approach is the best way to address childhood obesity. But as I mentioned, you can't do it alone. The components of a comprehensive school wellness plan will take shape only if the major stakeholders are brought together in a well-organized approach under a unified theme. For example, one school used the theme The Health of Children—Now and Tomorrow. A theme can give a school added direction.

This book will help you be a team player in a coordinated school wellness initiative. Remember, physical education and physical activity are an important piece to the overall plan, but other factors need to be addressed. Let's take a brief look at the critical components of a school wellness plan (figure 2.1).

Figure 2.1 Components of a school wellness plan.

- Wellness committee
- Health assessment
- Classroom curriculum
- School lunch and food services
- School health services
- High-quality physical education
- School physical activity programs
- Staff development
- Parent and community involvement

Wellness Committee

The first step in a comprehensive wellness plan is to formulate a wellness committee. The committee should consist of people from a wide variety of areas of expertise and backgrounds. Administrators, such as the principal or assistant principal, should provide guidance to the committee when administrative questions or concerns arise throughout the school year. The committee might consist of the following:

- Health and physical education teachers
- School nurse
- School psychologist or guidance counselor
- Parents or guardians
- School food service personnel
- Director of health and physical education
- Classroom teachers (primary and intermediate)
- Community members
- Outside health professional (university professor, medical doctor, physical therapist, registered nurse)
- School physical activity director

This coalition can serve as a powerful force to help establish new policies and create exciting changes within the total home, school, and community environment.

Health Assessment

General health and physical fitness screening is a schoolwide responsibility, but how do you undertake a comprehensive screening program? Once again, use a team approach and establish a schoolwide health committee in your school, including teachers, parents, health care professionals, university faculty, and community members. You may

be able to enlist the help of volunteer professionals or students from a local medical school, university, or wellness institute to help you establish baseline health evaluations for the children at your school. The team may choose to measure height, weight, blood pressure, vision, hearing, posture, cholesterol, health-related physical fitness, and physical activity behaviors.

You may even identify children who are at risk for heart disease or other health-related problems. If you lack support, screen only the third- and fifth-graders each year and monitor their progress by keeping a health portfolio or file on a data disk.

Classroom Curriculum

Enlist the help of classroom teachers. First, educate them about the benefits of physical activity and proper nutrition by doing the following:

- Distribute brochures and articles about exercise and general health.
- Arrange to have guest speakers at faculty meetings.
- Establish a school staff wellness room that includes DVDs, exercise equipment, a spring water cooler, cookbooks, reading materials, and magazines.
- Teach an exercise class for staff members after school one or two days a week.

Second, give classroom teachers ideas for new and creative activities. Show them ways to integrate health-related fitness and nutrition into other subject areas, such as math, science, and reading. In addition, help create thematic units in which students study various aspects of a topic. For example, cover cardiovascular health from a fitness perspective at the same time the students are learning about the cardiovascular system in science class. (See chapter 9 for more information on working with the classroom teacher.)

Finally, help teachers incorporate activity breaks into the school day. Use published programs such as Kid Fitness (see page 15 for additional information), or design an activity break of your own. Practice the breaks in physical education so that students are aware of the routine and how to perform the exercises correctly.

School Lunch and Food Services

The school lunch program and school parties give children opportunities to practice making healthy choices. To improve the fare available at school, establish a subcommittee of the wellness program, involving homeroom parents, the school nurse, a classroom teacher, a member of the school lunch staff, a consultant such as a university professor, and yourself.

The committee should establish school policies regarding the use and distribution of food within the school and during school events. Ask the question, How can we reduce fat, sodium, and sugar in our school lunches? In addition, create and label heart-smart choices on the menu so children can make their own decisions about what they are eating. Educate parents about the importance of healthy snacks and about how the school is trying to help children develop positive eating habits. Encourage parents and classroom teachers to make sure that all parties include heart-smart choices, such as frozen yogurt, fruit, bottled water, and vegetables with low-fat dip.

School Health Services

Make professionals such as the school nurse, guidance counselor, and psychologist your allies. As a representative of the medical profession, the school nurse adds credibility to the concept of prevention. A counselor or psychologist can help you understand human behavior by outlining techniques to help change health attitudes.

High-Quality Physical Education

Physical education is a pivotal component of the multidisciplinary wellness approach. Plan a yearlong curriculum that gives students the knowledge, skills, and behaviors that reinforce active, healthy lifestyles. Integrate health-related fitness concepts and activities into each module to constantly remind students of the need for physical activity and the many health benefits it confers. (See also chapter 4.)

School Physical Activity Programs

The school should designate a physical activity director. Remember, creating opportunities for additional physical activity is neither physical education nor a replacement for physical education classes. The primary responsibility of the physical activity director is to ensure that all children are getting a minimum of 60 minutes of physical activity within the school day, or during before- and after-school activities. NASPE has supported this approach as a part of the comprehensive school physical activity program (CSPAP).

Staff Development

Staff development should include all personnel on the school campus. The two primary approaches are staff education and staff wellness.

In staff education, you are trying to educate all school personnel about the benefits of an active, healthy lifestyle through newsletters, blogs, seminars, guest speakers, and so on. You are also educating them about the instructional materials, curricula, and learning activities that may be used within the total wellness approach.

Staff wellness is directed at the personal health and well-being of everyone on the elementary campus. Show staff members how to monitor their eating and physical activity behaviors. The school may also offer special exercise classes, before school or directly after school. Redesign the teacher's lounge into a wellness room. This effort will help invite the staff to form a common bond related to a recognition of the importance of good health.

Parent and Community Involvement

As the most important aspect of a child's life, the family must participate in teaching, modeling, and reinforcing a healthy lifestyle. You can engage the support of parents and the community by educating them through newsletters, workshops, PTA demonstrations, and health fairs; by involving them as volunteers, teacher aides, and committee members; and by including them in home-based activities, such as family exercise, homework help, and family contract programs. (See also chapter 10.)

HEALTH-RELATED PHYSICAL FITNESS TESTING

For many years, physical educators viewed fitness testing as an end in itself. The goal was simply to increase the number of curl-ups or push-ups children could do in one minute. The typical pre- and posttest measures that many teachers used may have indicated marked improvement by the end of the school year, yet researchers are convinced that a large percentage of those increases could be attributed to genetics and children's physical growth and development (Bouchard, Shephard, Stephens, Sutton, and McPherson 1990). Unfortunately, when you emphasize fitness testing, children get the message that they should exercise only to get an award or to compete against their classmates.

In contrast, a high-quality fitness education program emphasizes education, prevention, and intervention with health-related physical fitness testing playing a minor, yet valuable, role. I encourage you to use physical fitness testing to help children monitor their own progress and plan individual goals. In addition, use the physical data to help your students improve their performances in the various components of health-related fitness (Virgilio 1996). A high-quality fitness education program includes authentic assessments in addition to standardized fitness test results to evaluate individual students' progress. Student participation, effort, knowledge, and personal feelings can also indicate progress.

Review the following guidelines as you plan ways to include fitness testing in your physical education program:

1. **Test for a purpose.** Know why you are testing. What are your major objectives? How will you use the data?

2. **Test to teach.** Perform each assessment component in association with a health-related fitness concept. For example, teach children the health benefits of performing curl-ups: stronger abdominal muscles keep the internal organs intact, reduce stress on the low back, and develop core stability and muscular endurance.

3. **Focus on individual progress.** Base your standards on students' personal goals and improvement rather than on established national test standards. Aim for healthy fitness zones.

4. **Create a humanistic environment.** Keep testing as private and confidential as possible. Never announce or post class fitness scores or embarrass students. For example, never gather 25 students around the flexibility box to watch each student perform.

5. **Limit testing time.** If you are spending six class periods both in the fall and spring testing, you are squandering too much class time! If necessary, reduce the number of items on the fitness test, or request

extra class periods from the principal to complete the assessments.

6. **Allow students time to prepare for the tests.** Provide exercise classes and time to practice actual test items. Teach safety precautions and exercise principles as well.

7. **Allow students to test themselves.** Monitoring their own progress and accepting the responsibility for their personal development will help them develop long-term values.

8. **Communicate test results.** Help students interpret the meaning of their fitness scores. Communicate your testing philosophy and the results to parents. Consider a computer-assisted report card system such as Fitnessgram or Activitygram (Cooper Institute 2010).

9. **Offer feedback.** After sharing test results with students, recommend strategies, activities, and specific exercises to help them improve. For example, give a student at the 20th percentile in flexibility a set of stretches to practice seven days per week both at home and in school.

10. **Reward effort and achievement.** Be certain that goals are attainable for all students. Children who improve their scores, complete a program, or demonstrate increased physical activity levels should be individually acknowledged and commended for their efforts. We all need encouragement and support, and when it comes from the teacher, it is a powerful message!

YOUTH FITNESS TESTS

Let's look now at several common fitness test items. The most widely used youth fitness tests are Fitnessgram and Activitygram (Cooper Institute 2010).

Fitnessgram

Fitnessgram is a comprehensive fitness assessment for youth. It includes assessments of health-related physical fitness areas such as cardiorespiratory fitness, muscular strength, muscular endurance, flexibility, and body composition. The tests are based on criterion-referenced standards in each of the health-related physical fitness components.

Let's look at several fitness assessments contained in Fitnessgram:

- For cardiorespiratory endurance: the one-mile run-walk and the PACER
- For body composition: skinfold measurements of the triceps and calf to determine the percentage of body fat
- For muscular strength and muscular endurance: the push-up, curl-up, and pull-up tests
- For flexibility: the back-saver sit-and-reach and the shoulder stretch

As you read this section, think about which test(s) you'd like to include in your curriculum. Keep in mind that measuring fitness components is only one aspect of a complete assessment approach within a high-quality fitness education program.

To learn more about the Fitnessgram software, see (www.fitnessgram.net).

Cardiorespiratory Endurance

The two basic tests discussed in this section measure cardiorespiratory endurance, or aerobic capacity. The one-mile run-walk is normally administered outdoors on a carefully measured route; the PACER can be administered indoors or outdoors on a hard, flat surface.

One-Mile Run-Walk

Have students run for one mile as fast as possible. Permit walking or jogging if a student cannot run the entire distance. Do not time students in kindergarten through third grade.

Height and weight for each student must be entered in the software, in addition to the performance time. This allows the software program to calculate aerobic capacity ($\dot{V}O_2$max) with each student's body mass index (BMI). Calculation of aerobic capacity requires a one-mile running time of less than 13:01.

Equipment: One-mile running course, one stopwatch (for you), and one scorecard and pencil per student

PACER

The PACER (Progressive Aerobic Cardiovascular Endurance Run) is a multistage aerobic capacity fitness test in Fitnessgram. Students run back and forth between two lines that are 20 meters apart at a specified pace that gets progressively faster (a 15-meter test is provided for smaller gym facilities). The early stages of the test serve as a warm-up period. Students run to the opposite line in the gym and try to touch it

with a foot before a beep sounds on the CD. At the sound of the beep, students turn around and run back to the starting line. Students who don't reach the opposite line before the beep should immediately turn around and try to get back to the starting line. If they fail to reach the opposite line by the time they hear a beep, it constitutes a fault.

Students continue in this fashion until they fail to reach the line before the beep for the second time. The results are calculated from the number of laps completed and the student's BMI. You must enter each student's height and weight in the software program. Research has indicated that differences in body size can influence oxygen uptake and the measures of aerobic capacity typically expressed relative to body weight. The new standards provide classifications in three zones: (1) the healthy fitness zone, (2) needs improvement—some health risk, and (3) needs improvement—high risk. The lowest fitness zone would provide youth and parents with an appropriate warning that this level of fitness increases various health risks.

Children in grades K-3 should experience the test and practice their pacing skills but should not be scored. Allow them to run at their own pace and strive to make the end line before the beeps as a fun jogging type of activity.

Equipment: PACER CD; safe, flat, nonslip surface (at least 15 or 20 meters long); measuring tape; marker cones; pencils; scorecards

Body Composition

Skinfold measurements are a simple yet reliable way to measure body composition. You will need skinfold calipers as well as some training and practice to do this assessment.

Measure the triceps and calf skinfolds to determine the percentage of body fat. These sites are recommended because they are easily measured and are highly correlated with total body fat. The triceps skinfold is measured on the back of the right arm over the triceps muscle midway between the elbow and the acromion process of the scapula. The calf skinfold is measured on the inside of the right leg at the level of maximal girth. An alternative assessment is the BMI, which includes a child's weight relative to height. This estimation does not consider the percentage of body fat, which is a more useful indicator of body composition. Also, portable bioelectric impedance analyzers (BIAs) are now available for body composition analysis and might be easier and less

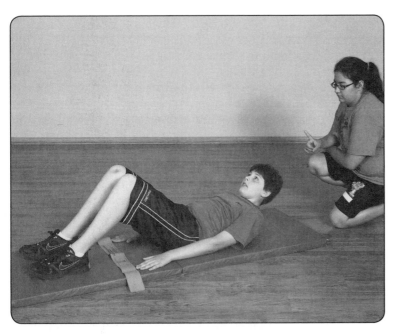

Figure 2.2 Curl-ups are a good way to measure abdominal strength and endurance.

Figure 2.3 Push-ups are a good way to measure upper-body strength: *(a)* starting position; *(b)* down position.

invasive in physical education classes than skinfold calipers.

Equipment: Skinfold calipers and one scorecard and pencil per student

Abdominal Strength and Endurance

How well a student can perform curl-ups is a good measure of abdominal strength and endurance.

Have students complete as many curl-ups as possible at a specified pace of about 20 curl-ups per minute (up to a maximum of 75). The student curls up, slowly sliding the fingers across a measuring strip on the mat under the knees. When the fingertips reach the other side of the measuring strip, the student curls back down. Place a piece of paper under the head on the mat; when it creases, you will know the student has gone fully back. Organize students into pairs. Tape the measuring strip securely to the mat. One partner performs the curl-ups and the other counts and records faults. The test ends on the second fault (see figure 2.2).

Equipment: Gym mats, one scorecard and pencil per student, one cardboard measuring strip (30 by 4.5 inches, or 76.2 by 11.4 centimeters) per two students (children 5 to 9 years old use a 3-inch-wide [7.6 cm] strip)

Upper-Body Strength

Use one of the following three tests to assess upper-body strength, choosing the test in which your students are likely to have the most success.

Push-Up Test Have students complete as many push-ups (to an elbow angle of 90 degrees) as possible at a rhythmic pace of 20 push-ups per minute to a prerecorded cadence (see figure 2.3, *a* and *b*).

Equipment: CD of cadence, CD player, one scorecard and pencil per student

Pull-Up Test Have students complete as many pull-ups as possible. (Use this test only with students who can pull up at least once.)

Equipment: Horizontal bar at a height at which the student's feet clear the floor or ground when hanging with the arms extended, and one scorecard and pencil per student

Flexed-Arm Hang Test Have students hang with the chin above the bar as long as possible.

Equipment: Horizontal bar at a height at which the student's feet clear the floor or ground when hanging with the arms extended, and one scorecard and pencil per student

Flexibility

Use one or both of the following two tests to measure flexibility. Remember, flexibility is joint specific, so try to use both assessments in your testing program.

Back-Saver Sit-and-Reach Have students sit and reach a maximum distance first on the right side of the body and then on the left (see figure 2.4). By reaching on one side of the body at a time, students can avoid hyperextending. Record the number, in inches or centimeters, on each side to the nearest 1/2 inch (or 1/2 cm), to a maximum score of 12 inches (30.5 cm) to discourage hypermobility.

Equipment: Several back-saver sit-and-reach boxes for the class and one scorecard and pencil per student. If you design your own box, be sure to use a sturdy box about 12 inches (30 cm) high. Place a measuring scale on top of the box with the 9-inch (23 cm) mark even with the near edge of the box. The zero end of the ruler is nearest the student.

Shoulder Stretch Have students try to touch their fingertips together behind their backs by reaching over the shoulder and under the elbow. To test the left shoulder, students reach with left hand over the left shoulder and down the back as if to pull up a zipper. At the same time, they place the right hand behind the back and reach up, trying to touch the fingers of the left hand. Students who can touch fingertips pass the test. They then test the right shoulder by reversing hand positions (see figure 2.5). The healthy fitness zone is reached by touching fingers on both the right and left sides.

Activitygram

Activitygram is a specific three-day recall of general physical activity levels. The assessment gives children a general understanding of their physical activity habits as well as teaches them how to include physical activity throughout their daily lives. It provides data on each student's type, intensity, and estimated duration of general physical activity. Activities are categorized as lifestyle activities, aerobic activities, aerobic sports, muscular activities, flexibility activities, and rest. Students enter the data on the software

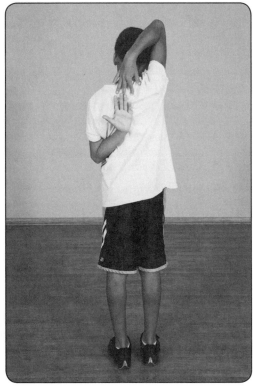

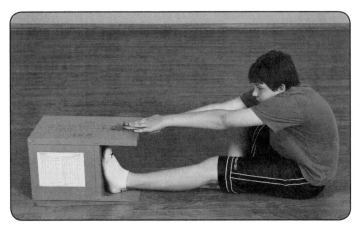

Figure 2.4 The back-saver sit-and-reach measures flexibility in the lower body, primarily the hamstrings.

Figure 2.5 The shoulder stretch is a flexibility test for the shoulders.

and rate their intensity (light, moderate, vigorous) and duration (some of the time or all of the time).

You can develop your own simple, easy-to-use activity log sheet; see appendix A for a sample. It would be a great start to get students to self-report their daily physical activity behaviors.

PRESIDENTIAL ACTIVE LIFESTYLE AWARD

Historically, Fitnessgram has not endorsed a recognition system for fitness achievement, because a significant portion of high scores are achieved by students with strong heredity factors and early maturation levels. In 2010, the President's Council on Physical Fitness and Sports (PCPFS) and the Fitnessgram/Activitygram programs established a working relationship to use the PCPFS Presidential Active Lifestyle Award (PALA) for children ages 6 to 17. Because the award is given for physical activity levels and not achievement, it was deemed motivating and educationally sound.

The award is given to students who achieve 60 minutes of activity per day, five days a week, for a six-week period. Students may also use a specific daily step total based on a pedometer reading (11,000 steps for girls, 13,000 steps for boys) completed five days per week for six weeks. Students completing this level of physical activity are recognized with a PALA patch, a certificate, or both. (For additional information, visit www.presidentschallenge.org.)

AUTHENTIC ASSESSMENT

If standardized tests are only part of a complete assessment approach, what can you do to make sure you have enough data to guide your students properly and modify your future lessons? Authentic assessment requires both teachers and students to engage in an ongoing process of evaluation, including self-evaluation. You must become as actively involved in class as your students by providing feedback and monitoring their progress with appropriate rubrics or checklists. Simply put, the better you understand your students' performances, the better you will be able to plan instruction that will help them progress.

Authentic assessment is an informal approach for gathering and interpreting useful information about students' feelings, attitudes, knowledge, physical activity levels, likes and dislikes, individual goals, personal choices, and health-related fitness levels. Ideally, students will learn to see assessments as realistic and meaningful tasks that will help them improve their personal fitness levels, resulting in their developing and maintaining their own physical activity programs because of the guidance they receive.

Have students use personal active lifestyle portfolios (see the sample in appendix A) to assist them in collecting, organizing, and analyzing their physical activity progress throughout the school year. The portfolios are individual booklets used to help both students and their teachers understand the factors that affect health-related physical fitness. If you choose, have students also use their portfolios to record their attitudes, feelings, and opinions about physical activity. Additional samples of authentic assessment you may wish to include in student portfolios are checklists for students to use (chapter 6), family fitness contracts (chapter 10), and nutrition logs (appendix A). Students should keep their active lifestyle portfolios in the regular classroom and use them throughout the school year to help integrate various learning experiences in the classroom as well as in physical education class (see chapter 9).

SUMMARY

The elementary school environment is ideal for establishing healthy lifestyles in our students. To accomplish this ambitious goal, use a multidisciplinary team effort to enhance school wellness. Enlist the support of classroom teachers, lunchroom personnel, the school nurse, special service teachers, administrators, parents, and the community to help children adopt healthy attitudes and behaviors to help them reach their health goals. Assessment should include a broader view of a child's health status. Additionally, health-related physical fitness testing should facilitate your efforts to provide a more personalized approach to help children reach their physical best.

Behavioral Change and Motivational Strategies

> It is exercise alone that supports the spirits,
> and keeps the mind in vigor.
>
> —*Marcus Tullius Cicero*

If children inherently like to move and enjoy active play, why are they becoming so unfit? Why are children getting heavier and physical activity levels dropping lower?

One answer to this question may be that we need a behavioral change plan and new motivational strategies in physical education classes. Traditionally, the physical education curriculum included a number of fitness-related activities, such as obstacle courses, active games, jogging, exercises, and aerobic dance, to increase activity levels. Many teachers presented these activities to meet the short-term needs of a particular class period, sport purpose, or fitness test without a major concern for long-term behavioral changes.

Even now, most teachers neglect to build into their curriculum behavioral skills that will help children value physical activity for a lifetime. In other words, you must motivate your students to maintain their interest in physical fitness so they will develop an appreciation for physical activity as a way of life. Doing all the developmentally appropriate fitness activities in the world will not instill in children positive long-term lifestyle habits (see figure 3.1).

Figure 3.1 Behavioral plan: the missing link.

RAINBOW TO YOUTH FITNESS AND ACTIVE LIFESTYLES

For the purposes of this book, I have developed the Rainbow to Youth Fitness and Active Lifestyles (figure 3.2). This model incorporates a developmentally appropriate sequence of stages for establishing healthy physical activity patterns in children—from fitness fun, the first stage for young children, to the final stage, active lifestyles.

Do children naturally go from depending on you to provide fitness fun to independent active lifestyles overnight? Of course not, but by gradually increasing students' opportunities to make choices and to monitor themselves, you'll be helping them reach their goals at the end of the rainbow: active, healthy lifestyles. Use the Rainbow to Youth Fitness and Active Lifestyles to guide your planning as you strive to shape positive fitness behaviors.

Fitness Fun

Young children are naturally active. They love to play and express themselves through movement. Take advantage of this to promote fitness fun. Keep in mind that if children think an activity is fun and enjoyable, they will repeat it over and over again. In this stage, children who perceive the movement environment as safe, supportive,

interactive, and exciting will develop a positive attitude toward a variety of physical activities.

Practice

Children are naturally creatures of habit. To develop positive physical activity habits, engage children in physical activity daily. Try to create a school environment that gives children frequent chances for physical activity. Recess, free play, before- and after-school physical activity programs, intramurals, and fitness breaks are all good opportunities for children to accumulate at least 60 minutes of physical activity each day. Encourage parents to be active with their children, and try to promote community opportunities at parks and recreation centers to enhance physical activity outside of school. But don't stop at this stage, assuming that ample physical activity levels will meet your program goals. Children merely participating in physical activity without sufficient knowledge and support will not develop lasting values or behaviors.

Knowledge

Knowledge is the key to teaching children to value physical activity and healthy lifestyles over the long term. Children need to understand why they are exercising and how to perform the activities correctly. They are more likely to participate in physical activity when they understand how and

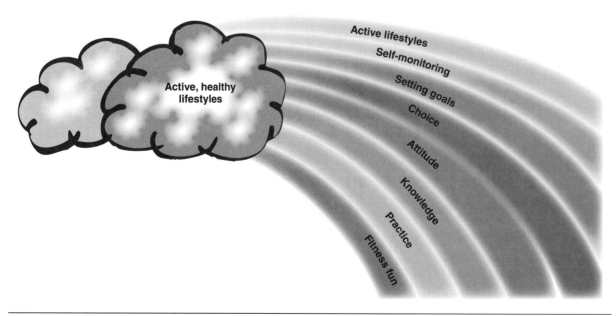

Figure 3.2 The Rainbow to Youth Fitness and Active Lifestyles.

why their bodies respond to exercise. Include a sequence of planned health-related fitness concepts throughout the elementary school physical education experience. Work with classroom teachers, parents, and special service professionals such as the school nurse, lunch director, or counselor to reinforce these concepts outside of the gym.

Attitude

Your role as the teacher is especially critical when it comes to developing positive attitudes. Once children have experienced physical activity in a fun, supportive environment, engaged in practice, and established a foundation of knowledge, they can begin to develop positive attitudes toward physical activity based on these experiences. At this stage they are ready to commit but might not be too sure about how to move forward and whether they will be successful. You are instrumental in supporting their interests and in giving them the confidence to continue. Use the motivational strategies described later in this chapter to build on children's natural inclination to enjoy movement. And remember, use a multidisciplinary team approach to design your physical education program so that your students experience a cohesive home, community, and school environment united in support of positive behavioral changes.

Choice

Would you want to do the same activity over and over? Try not to hamper children's naturally positive attitudes toward movement by failing to provide variety. Although children do enjoy repeating activities that they enjoy, a wide variety of physical activities will generate fresh interest when boredom threatens. Choice gives your students a chance to discover what they enjoy the most, and over time, they'll learn to make their own selections based on their personal preferences and individual physical needs. Therefore, allow children to select from various activities and exercises and to choose the amount of time they will spend on each choice whenever possible in your classes.

Setting Goals

At some point, student choice goes beyond just choosing from the variety you provide. This is the time to teach children how to set personal goals and make effective choices to reach those goals. By establishing goals, students discover the need

for self-direction and meaning in their physical development. Students must have practice thinking independently and making choices based on their individual needs to eventually lead physically active lives independently. Empower your students to take charge of their physical selves through goal setting.

Establishing written goals can be effective at any age. The goals can be geared to a component of health-related physical fitness (HRPF) or general physical activity. Several factors must be considered before you help students plan their activity goals:

- Age
- Developmental level
- Motivation
- Emotional status
- Current fitness and physical activity levels
- Activity interests

Once you have established a baseline of your students' current status, you are ready to help them establish SMART goals. Follow these simple goal-setting steps to ensure a successful learning experience. SMART is an easy-to-remember acronym to make sure you are planning developmentally appropriate educational goals.

Goals can be short term (within a week), intermediate (within two to four weeks), or long term (more than one month). Because most children lose interest with long-term goals, try to concentrate on short or intermediate goals.

S—Specific
M—Measurable
A—Attainable
R—Realistic
T—Time sensitive

Specific

Help your students clearly define their goal. A goal might be a component of HRPF, such as cardiorespiratory endurance, measured with the Fitnessgram test, or it might be to increase physical activity time during the day, as noted on the student's activity log (see appendix A). In any event, the goal should be a specific behavior that you and the student agree on.

Measurable

Once you have established a specific goal, you must be sure that it can be measured. An example would be to increase physical activity time by 15 minutes per day for at least five days per week for a two-week period, or to decrease the time on the one-mile run by 5 percent.

Attainable

Be sure that your students' goals are attainable. You can build success and confidence by helping students achieve easy-to-reach, shorter-term goals. Once they have established a desirable pattern, you can encourage them to expand the reach of their goals. Initially, for instance, a student may strive to increase her push-up score by one. Build in support and recommend activities to help students attain their goals.

Realistic

Goals need to be realistic. Children can begin to learn the valuable skill of self-honesty as they learn to evaluate themselves and their goals. For example, achieving a goal of 10 push-ups in a two-week period would be unrealistic for a student with a pretest score of 2 push-ups. Rather than embarrass students, help them to understand more about themselves and the need to adjust goals to their individual status.

Time Sensitive

Goals should have starting points, ending points, and fixed durations. Goals without time frames tend to get lost in the day-to-day experiences of school and home life. Deadlines can be flexible, but students who lose sight of their goals and time frames must get right back on track. Establish intermittent check points to help your students keep their goals in sight.

SMART Goal Example (Intermediate)

Johnny will be physically active at least five days per week, for a total of 60 minutes each day or 12,000 steps, during the month of November, as measured by his personal activity log and documented by his teacher or parent.

Self-Monitoring

As children move closer to independence, you can be more flexible in your teaching approach. Allow fourth-, fifth-, and sixth-graders to maintain their personal active lifestyle portfolios (see appendix A). Children at this stage should plan, self-evaluate, and track their activity patterns. Self-monitoring allows children to set goals for achieving their personal bests, make decisions

according to their activity preferences, and design their individual physical activity programs. This stage is reachable for children in grades 4 through 6.

Active Lifestyles

Students who have reached this stage exhibit a genuine commitment to physical activity. They are motivated to participate, eager to improve, happy to volunteer to help others, open to learning new activities, persistent in their efforts to reach goals, able to work independently, and happy and relaxed in the learning environment. Although they will continue to need support and reinforcement for their choices throughout middle school and high school, they have a firm foundation that will almost certainly lead to a lifetime of health and fitness.

WHAT MOTIVATES CHILDREN TO MOVE?

The word *motivation* comes from the Latin word *movere*, which means "to move." We can think of motivation as something that directs, sparks, or maintains behavior: it's what gets students moving and keeps them going. For many years we assumed that children had similar motivations to exercise as adults do.

But children are not miniature adults! Adults engage in physical activity to enhance their appearance, improve their health, and prevent disease. Children are physically active because they enjoy play, need to interact with their peers, wish to develop physical competence, and need to express themselves through various movement forms. Let's examine each of these aspects closely.

Play and Fun

Children view play as an important ingredient in their lives. When an activity is nonthreatening, success oriented, and exciting, children become very motivated. The desire to play is inherent in all human beings and is a necessary developmental stage in childhood.

Social Interaction

Children need the opportunity to relate to other children through active play. In a supportive movement environment, children develop a sense of belonging and acceptance, which helps bond them to their peers. The feelings of security experienced through group play may enhance both self-esteem and the ability to form positive relationships with others.

Physical Competence

Children have a strong desire to develop competence in physical skills. The challenge inherent in mastering physical skills motivates children to continue physical activity. The perception children have of their abilities may be determined by the amount of time, effort, and value they place on activities. When children receive support and encouragement from the important people in their lives, they gain the confidence they need to develop active lifestyles and continue in a chosen physical activity.

Self-Expression

Not surprisingly, children naturally express themselves through active movement. Physical activity is often the vehicle for children to express their feelings and emotions to friends, parents, and teachers. Children are less able than teenagers and adults to verbalize their feelings or discuss differences of opinion. As a result, they often express feelings such as happiness, anger, frustration, and excitement physically.

TYPES OF MOTIVATION

Motivation takes two general forms. Extrinsic motivation involves factors outside of the individual that are unrelated to the task being performed. Intrinsic motivation is an individual's internal desire to perform a particular task (Ormrod 2009). Intrinsic motivation promotes long-term behavioral change more effectively than extrinsic motivation does. Indeed, students who learn to rely on intrinsic motivation are more likely to develop a long-term commitment to an active lifestyle. To enhance intrinsic motivation, empower students to develop the self-confidence to believe that they are capable of accomplishing certain tasks, the self-esteem to believe that they are worthy of good health, and the self-efficacy to believe that they are in control of their own destinies.

For many years, physical educators provided children with poor and inappropriate motivation, turning them off to exercise rather than turning

them on. The following are examples of inappropriate practices and conditions:

- Boring, repetitive, drill-like fitness activities (e.g., running laps each class)
- Group exercising
- Inflexible standards
- Using fitness testing along with an award system for the top achievers
- Competition
- Traditional curriculum offerings each year (e.g., soccer, softball, volleyball)
- Low levels of activity in class
- Continual use of direct teaching techniques
- Poor equipment and sterile, dingy facilities
- Unmotivated teachers

Would you be motivated to become physically active in this type of environment?

MOTIVATIONAL STRATEGIES

What can you do to foster intrinsic motivation throughout your physical education program? Let's look at several easy-to-incorporate motivational strategies to get your program started.

Teach Basic Skills

Teach your students basic skills, such as how to jog and how to do curl-ups. When you take the time to instruct your students on the proper form and techniques, they will assume you really care about improving their physical development. Moreover, show a personal interest in each student by providing individual skill feedback in a positive, supportive way.

Choose Success-Oriented Activities

When children feel successful, they'll repeat an activity and gain the confidence to advance to more difficult activities. To motivate students, design activities at an appropriate developmental level that include challenges that students can achieve through practice. For example, students should have activity choices, such as the regular push-up, open stance push-up, push-up stance, or wall push-up, to meet their physical needs and ensure some degree of success.

Have Fun, Fun, Fun

I can't emphasize this point enough: children should laugh, sing, play, and interact while engaged in physical activity. See how fast they tune into your class objectives when they are having fun and enjoying the lesson. For example, develop arm muscle fitness using the parachute by making waves or pretending popcorn is popping (use playground balls; see chapter 11). Children will have enormous fun while developing muscle fitness.

Add Creative Equipment

Add new and exciting equipment to add spark to your classes. Many times physical educators use the same equipment year in and year out, and children become bored and tired of the same old thing. Add items such as rubberized exercise toners (figure 3.3), heavy jump ropes, heart rate monitors, and resistance balls to renew their interest in physical activity.

Add New Activities

Constantly be on the lookout for new activities to add to your program. Incorporate such lessons as

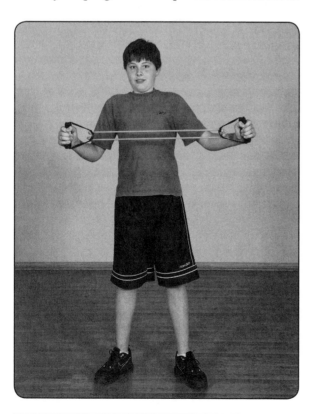

Figure 3.3 Upper-body exercise using a rubberized exercise toner.

Zumba dancing (chapter 13), in-line skating, yoga (chapter 14), outdoor education, and new fitness games such as Fitnopoly (chapter 12).

Create a Colorful Environment

Decorate the gym with colorful posters, exercise charts, and bulletin boards. Have a monthly theme. For example, February can be Heart-Smart Month. Have students in different grades take turns decorating each month along with their parents. To really add pizzazz, organize a Sport Art Show in which you display everyone's sport-related art projects in the gym.

Provide Incentives

Students need support and encouragement for their hard work in your classes. Occasionally provide children with positive, healthy incentives for active participation. Exercise bands, free choice of an activity, or frozen yogurt certificates make good incentives to help motivate students (see figure 3.4).

Be a Role Model

Provide your classes with a positive role model. Keep trim, exercise with your classes, eat healthy foods at lunch, keep nutritious snacks on your desk, and talk to your students about your after-school activities such as volleyball leagues, jogging, hiking trips, and so on. Looking good always counts, too! Dress professionally in sharp-looking warm-ups and T-shirts with a message—for example, *Physical education is the best health insurance.*

Accentuate the Positive

Of course, positive reinforcement strengthens existing habits as well as encourages student progress. Practice using the gestures and words of encouragement in table 3.1.

Organize a Health Club

To organize a health club, use the intramural sport model, but modify it for health-related fitness. Then, designate a club workout area. Students who join the club can work on their individual goals or participate in a group physical activity of their choice, exercising before school, during recess, or after school. Your job is to plan group activities and help participants plan their individual programs. T-shirts with the club name may motivate more students to participate.

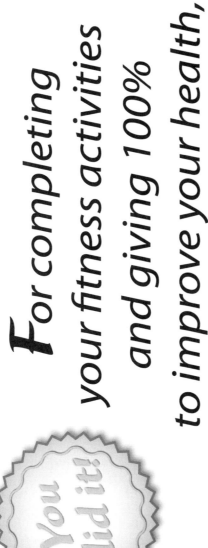

Fitness Reward

*F*or completing
your fitness activities
and giving 100%
to improve your health,
you are entitled to

_____
Student

_____
School

_____
Physical educator

Figure 3.4 Physical activity incentives like this customizable reward certificate can help motivate students.

From S.J. Virgilio, 2012, *Fitness education for children: A team approach* (Champaign, IL: Human Kinetics).

Table 3.1 Ways to Encourage Students

Words	Gestures
Wow!	Laugh with student
Great job!	Smile
Nice going!	Hug
Yes!	Raise eyebrows in delight
I'm proud of you for your effort!	Nod head
Good for you!	Give thumbs-up
Way to go!	Give high five
All right!	Shake hands
Terrific!	Pat back
Thank you for cooperating!	Wave
Much better!	Put hand on shoulder
Looking good!	Raise both arms (touchdown signal)
Beautiful!	Stare with smile and nod head
Keep up the good work!	Silent cheer with fists raised
Wonderful!	Jump up
I'm impressed!	Point with a nod
Very creative!	Stand with arms wide open

Encourage Self-Direction

Giving fourth-, fifth-, and sixth-grade students the opportunity to manage their own personal active lifestyle portfolios motivates them as well. Portfolios should include personal fitness scores, daily logs, individual programs, contracts, graphs, and other learning activities (see appendix A).

Use Authentic Assessments

Use authentic assessments throughout the year to give students ongoing information about their progress. This way, they can see what they need to improve before you do final evaluations at the end of the school year. After all, everyone appreciates having a chance to improve. Moreover, seeing incremental improvement is motivating in itself. It also helps students set realistic, yet challenging, SMART goals.

Involve Parents

Students feel additional support and reinforcement when they know their parents are interested and involved in physical activity. Create a parent newsletter that suggests home-based activities the family can do together to become more physically active (see also chapter 10).

Hold Special Events

Remember, special schoolwide or community events can bring needed attention to your program goals. For example, in the Geography Run, students calculate the walking and jogging miles they have done both in and out of school and report them to you. You, in turn, plot the school's total mileage on a large map, updating your school's run from, say, New York to California each week. Encourage the school lunch personnel and classroom teachers to help integrate learning experiences around this event. (See also chapter 15.)

Form Cooperative Learning Groups

Cooperative learning can enhance self-confidence and security in physical activity. For example, Group Hoops is an activity in which six students hold hands to form a circle, with a hoop threaded through one pair of grasped hands. The students pass the hoop around the circle counterclockwise without releasing their hands. You can vary the hoop size based on the developmental level and size of the students. Encourage them to cooperate to complete the task—not to race against other groups.

Invite Guest Speakers

Schedule guest speakers from the community who may have expertise to share with the class (e.g., a marathon runner, Zumba instructor, physical education professor, or health care professional). Include speakers from a variety of ethnic and racial backgrounds so that students can identify with these role models.

Organize Big Buddies

Arrange for each first-grader to have a fifth- or sixth-grade big buddy by scheduling classes in which students can occasionally be together.

Make the older students responsible for teaching the younger students certain concepts and exercises. Big buddies can also be pen pals, e-mail friends, and academic tutors to first-graders.

Vary Your Teaching Strategies

Because children learn in many different ways, use a variety of teaching strategies, such as small groups, independent activities, and partner workouts to meet the needs and interests of your students. Try to use the spectrum of teaching styles (Mosston and Ashworth 2002) throughout the school year (see chapter 6).

SUMMARY

Fitness education involves much more than providing highly active games and exercises. The contemporary approach to a high-quality physical education program includes a plan for long-term behavioral change and motivational strategies to encourage children to be physically active throughout their lives. Work with your colleagues, students' parents, administrators, and the community to create a supportive, healthy school environment. Plan learning experiences that feed into children's innate motivation to move, help them develop SMART goals, and emphasize the intrinsic value of physical activity as you guide children to follow the rainbow to an active, healthy lifestyle!

Principles of Health-Related Physical Fitness

> We are underexercised as a nation.
> We look instead of play. We ride
> instead of walk. Our existence deprives us
> of the minimum of physical activity
> essential for healthy living.
> —*John F. Kennedy*

Let's briefly review basic exercise principles so that you can properly plan health-related physical fitness instruction for your physical education program. As you reshape your physical education curriculum to educate children and develop positive values and behaviors relative to an active lifestyle, follow the guidelines in this chapter to help you teach safe, efficient, and developmentally appropriate physical activities. Tailor specific exercises to meet the individual needs and interests of children; however, keep in mind that children do not require a specific exercise prescription as adults do. Instead, children respond better to short periods of vigorous activity throughout the day than they do to one 30-minute intense workout. In fact, activity that is too intense may have an adverse effect on children's motivation to continue physical activity.

CORE PRINCIPLES OF HEALTH-RELATED PHYSICAL FITNESS

Although the core principles are the basis for planning health-related fitness activities, the exercise principles of frequency, intensity, time, and type (FITT) must also be considered when planning class physical activity and fitness routines.

This section provides the necessary information to help students derive the health benefits of an active lifestyle. Keep in mind that you should always consider students' motivational levels, personal goals, past behaviors (e.g., highly sedentary), and stages of maturation rather than simply their chronological age when recommending a program of physical activity and exercise.

To make it easy for both you and your students to remember the exercise principles and guidelines, use the acronym SPORT-FITT.

SPORT stands for

Specificity

Progression

Overload

Regularity

Train and maintain

FITT stands for

Frequency

Intensity

Time

Type

SPORT

The acronym SPORT includes the essential principles of exercise science and can help you and your students plan a sound physical activity program. Children find acronyms fun, and it will help them to remember the principles throughout the school year.

Specificity

The principle of specificity simply means that only the muscles or body systems being worked benefit from the exercise. In other words, you need to exercise the specific muscles you want to improve. For example, to improve cardiorespiratory endurance, children at level III should jog three or four days per week. This activity specifically develops muscular endurance in the legs and the cardiorespiratory system but does little for the arms, chest, and shoulders. Also, if a child wants to improve his baseball swing, it's not enough to work only on arm and shoulder exercises. The student should specifically work all the muscles used in the swing motion.

Progression

The principle of progression means that to improve, children should *gradually* increase their physical activity in a certain fitness component, by increasing the frequency, intensity, time, and type. The rate of progression depends on the person; however, you can generally apply the 10 percent rule, increasing duration by no more than 10 percent per week. For example, if a child can comfortably jog 10 minutes per day, five days

per week, she may jog for 11 minutes, five days the next week. The gradual increase is necessary for the body to adapt. However, children will not adapt or progress at the same rate as adults. For children who have been sedentary, a 5 percent increase will be enough at the early stages of the program.

Overload

To improve any component of fitness, the body must work above the normal level. This is the principle of overload. You may overload any activity by increasing the frequency, intensity, time, and type of the exercise or physical activity. Remember, though, that activity sessions need not be exhaustive or stressful to achieve health-related physical fitness. Fitness levels may be improved by slowly adding to the workload in a safe, comfortable manner. Use progression and overload hand in hand, but remember—there are limits to the physical changes that will occur in children, so use this information as a guideline to help children progress and stay motivated.

Regularity

Regularity simply means, Use it or lose it. Unfortunately, no one can store the benefits of fitness. Physical activity, therefore, must be a lifetime commitment. Fitness levels are lost when they are not maintained through continual activity. The levels of health-related fitness respond differently to discontinuation of activity. Cardiorespiratory endurance is significantly affected because your body's ability to transport and use oxygen diminishes quickly in the absence of cardiorespiratory activity.

Train and Maintain

Children who apply the exercise principles progress well and reach their physical bests. Once your students have acquired a comfortable level of physical activity and fitness, however, you must encourage them to maintain adequate activity levels and establish appropriate long- and short-term goals based on their individual needs. Keep in mind that more and more exercise is not always better. Encourage children to participate in a wide variety of physical activities that might include different levels of intensity as well as varied muscle groups and bodily movements. Excess amounts of physical activity can be counterproductive (Corbin, Welk, Corbin, and Welk 2011). For example, children heavily involved in only one activity for extended periods of time tend to develop joint problems, tendinitis, and soft tissue injuries more frequently.

FITT Guidelines

Using the FITT acronym helps both you and your students remember the health-related physical activity guidelines:

F—frequency

I—intensity

T—time

T—type

Remember, because this book is for teachers of school-aged children, these guidelines are included to help you regulate and monitor your students' physical activity levels—not to recommend a training regimen as normally described in the adult exercise prescription model. Keep in mind that the major purpose of a quality physical education program at the elementary school level is to emphasize the process and value of participating in physical activity. Don't lose sight of this by emphasizing the product—fitness test scores and exercising to achieve awards.

Frequency

Frequency refers to how often a child is physically active. Children should be physically active most days of the week, preferably every day when performing large-muscle activities such as walking, jogging, biking, playing games, dancing, and raking leaves. In the area of muscle fitness, children should participate on just two or three nonconsecutive days per week to allow their bodies to adapt.

Intensity

Intensity is how hard a child is exercising or playing during a physical activity. Checking heart rate is a way to monitor the body's stress levels during a large-muscle activity. By fourth grade, children should be able to take their resting heart rates to monitor their activity levels.

The two easiest places to locate the heart rate are at the radial artery and the carotid artery. To find the radial pulse, bend the wrist slightly downward and place the index and middle finger on the thumb side of the wrist (see figure 4.1). To find the carotid pulse, slide the index and middle fingers into the groove along the throat (see figure 4.2). Count the number of beats for 10 seconds and multiply by 6 to calculate the number of beats

Figure 4.1 Location of the radial pulse.

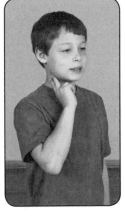

Figure 4.2 Location of the carotid pulse.

in one minute, or count for six seconds and add a zero to the number.

Ask children in grades K-3 to gauge their levels by feeling their hearts beat in their chests at rest, then after walking for three minutes, and then in the middle of a highly active game. They will begin to understand the concept of intensity related to physical activity. It is not recommended for school-aged children to calculate target heart rate zones (THRZ) during physical activity. This approach is more associated with training and not necessary at the elementary level. Calculating target heart rate zones is more appropriate for the 9th through 12th grades in high school. You may, however, teach children to calculate THRZ at the sixth-grade level to help them understand intensity and to integrate math into your physical education curriculum. Teach children about the various levels of physical activity, as follows:

- Low-intensity activity—stretching, picking up toys, playing baseball, playing horseshoes
- Moderate-intensity activity—playing four square, walking briskly, playing volleyball
- High-intensity activity—playing soccer or basketball, playing tag games, jogging, Zumba dancing

Two other ways to gauge intensity are to count the number of repetitions when performing a certain exercise and to count the number of seconds or determine the degree of difficulty of a muscle fitness activity. Students might increase intensity by moving from the level 1 yellow exercise bands (very light resistance) to the level 2 green exercise bands for the arm curl exercise. They might also increase the time spent in the push-up position from 10 seconds to 15 seconds.

Still another way to teach intensity is with pedometers. Students might log their steps throughout the day, and then set a goal for the week or over a six-week time frame, increasing the number of steps a little each day. A moderate level of physical activity for children is about 11,000 to 13,000 steps per day, five days per week.

Time

Time indicates how long the activity should be performed. At developmental levels I and II, limit the duration of high-intensity activity to shorter bouts of just a few minutes with intermittent rest periods of one to two minutes. At level III, you can safely prolong the physical activity to 10- to 15-minute bouts. You should vary the time depending on the health-related physical fitness component you are addressing and the objective of your lesson. The time will also depend on the intensity of the activity (low, moderate, high). Physical activity time may be extended at the low to moderate levels and shortened at the high level. All children should be physically active for a total of 60 minutes per day to derive general health benefits.

Type

Type refers to the mode, or the kind of physical activity performed within a particular health-related physical fitness component or general physical activity. To address this component, provide students with choices to enhance their cardiorespiratory endurance during class (e.g., jogging, in-line skating, rope jumping, or aerobic dance). For general physical activities to do outside of school, suggest raking leaves, washing the car, climbing stairs, or walking the dog.

STAGES OF A PHYSICAL ACTIVITY SESSION

Whether students are jogging, developing muscular endurance, playing basketball, or practicing kicking skills, you should teach them to follow the appropriate stages of a physical activity session: the warm-up, the main event, and the cool-down.

Warm-Up

The major objective of the warm-up is to prepare the heart, muscles, and joints for the main event.

You may think stretching should come first, but it's important to warm the muscles before stretching because stretching cold muscles can increase the risk of injury. Therefore, the first step is to raise the body temperature and increase blood circulation to the muscles. For example, begin class with three minutes of moderate to brisk walking, marching steps with arm movements, slow galloping, or light aerobics performed to music.

Once the muscles are warm, it would be optional to have your class perform a few static stretches for the major muscle groups. Research has shown that stretching as a warm-up may carry very little, if any, benefit. Keep in mind, however, that stretching for a warm-up is quite different from performing flexibility exercises. Concentrate on a few basic large-muscle static stretches, such as the calf stretch, the sit-and-reach (hamstrings), and the quadriceps stretch. Have them hold the stretch for only 10 seconds to avoid overstretching cold muscle groups. If necessary, add other stretches that fit the specific activity. If you are doing extensive leg activity, gently stretch out the calves, hamstrings, and quadriceps. But don't allow the muscles to cool off again before starting the main event; follow the warm-up period immediately by slowly getting into the main event with a low-level large-muscle activity.

Many researchers now believe that stretching might not be necessary at all before activity. The general recommendation for your classes, then, may be a series of low-level large-muscle activities for a few minutes followed by a gradual increase in intensity leading up to the main event.

Main Event

Have students spend the first two or three minutes of the main activity session at a moderate level of activity. This is what I call the bridge between the warm-up and the most vigorous stage of the class. For example, if students will be undertaking a jogging workout, have them move at a moderate pace for a few minutes before they accelerate to their normal running paces. Students about to play soccer or full-court basketball should begin the main event with a lead-up game or active skill activities.

When possible, tailor the main event itself to each student's personal preference and physical needs. For the main event itself, concentrate on a specific health-related fitness component or simply include a high percentage of moderate to vigorous physical activity. Students at developmental level III working to improve cardiorespiratory endurance should be working on their personal goals and activity levels and using personal judgment to decide when to rest, drink water, and slow down. At developmental levels I and II, the main event should be active with intermittent rest periods spaced appropriately throughout the class period.

Cool-Down

Begin the cool-down immediately after the main event by gradually slowing things down. Keep in mind that the large muscles of the body (legs and arms) return the blood back to the heart. If students stop suddenly after vigorous exercise, the blood will pool in their muscles, possibly resulting in dizziness or nausea. Continued light physical activity allows the body to recover by milking blood gradually back toward the heart.

After vigorous activity, have students do approximately two minutes of brisk walking, slow jogging, or any other large-muscle activity at a low intensity level. Because the muscles are warm from the main event, this is a good time to have your class perform several static stretches as well. This may prevent stiffness or muscle spasms later. In fact, this might be the best time to develop flexibility because the body temperature and blood circulation are at optimum levels to maximize muscle stretching.

COMPONENTS OF HEALTH-RELATED PHYSICAL FITNESS

For your students to experience the optimal benefits of physical activity, you must balance the health-related physical fitness components. Each component is equally important. Cardiorespiratory endurance strengthens the heart and lungs. Muscle fitness maintains body support, helping students perform daily tasks and participate in recreational games and activities. Flexibility helps the muscles and joints move freely. Finally, proper nutrition and daily physical activity help maintain healthy body composition.

Keeping in mind that you should emphasize process over product, let's take a more in-depth look at the components of health-related physical fitness so that you can plan a balanced physical activity program within your physical education curriculum.

Cardiorespiratory Endurance

Cardiorespiratory endurance is the capacity of your heart, blood vessels, and lungs to deliver nutrients and oxygen to your tissues and remove waste products (e.g., carbon dioxide), thereby providing the energy necessary for endurance exercises for prolonged periods. Jogging, biking, swimming, and skating all build cardiorespiratory endurance. Regardless of the type of physical activity your students use to enhance cardiorespiratory endurance, however, the main goal is always the same: to increase the amount of oxygen the heart pumps to the working muscles. Without enough oxygen, the body will not be able to work for an extended period of time.

Fortunately, continuous physical activity has significant positive effects on the heart. As the body begins to exercise, the muscles use the oxygen at a much higher rate, making the heart pump more oxygenated blood to meet this increased demand (Powers and Dodd 2011). As the blood continues to flow during exercise, it helps increase circulation because veins, arteries, and blood vessels (which transport blood, oxygen, and nutrients) are kept elastic, free from any obstructions, and working in concert with the rest of the body.

You can help your students improve their cardiorespiratory endurance with the following:

- Continuous activity
- Interval activity
- Fartlek training
- Circuit course

Continuous Activity

Continuous activity may include both aerobic and anaerobic exercise. *Aerobic* means "in the presence of oxygen." Activities that are continuous, longer in duration, and sustained are aerobic activities. *Anaerobic* means "in the absence of oxygen." During anaerobic activities, the body's demand for oxygen exceeds its ability to supply it. Anaerobic movements are explosive and short in duration, such as the 50-yard dash, playing basketball, running to first base in softball, and playing soccer. Anaerobic activity, at a moderate pace with brief rest periods, is highly appropriate for children because they are more able to handle short segments of activity. Good choices for continuous activity are any activities that continuously use large-muscle and whole body movements, such as jogging, walking, in-line skating, rope jumping, biking, swimming, hiking, aerobic dancing, step aerobics, and active games.

Interval Activity

Interval activity includes physical movements that alternate the intensity and active recovery time. In other words, periods of rest or lower-intensity training alternate with periods of higher intensity. Because of the lower-intensity periods, interval activity may actually allow for a higher total of intense activity over a longer period of time than continuous activity, although research is not conclusive about this. Vary intervals by varying the distance, intensity, number of repetitions, number of sets, and recovery time. (See chapter 11 for sample interval routines.)

Fartlek Training

Fartlek is Swedish for "speed play," meaning variation of speed. The fartlek training technique is similar to interval activity; however, the terrain controls the intensity and speed, not the clock. Most fartlek courses include uphill and downhill running. Some courses also include jumping or stepping obstacles, such as logs, rocks, and stumps. It's also beneficial to challenge and develop different muscle groups through the fartlek workout. Incorporate fartlek training into your physical education classes to add variety, thereby increasing motivation. (See chapter 11 for an example of a fartlek course.)

Circuit Course

A circuit course combines continuous activity with flexibility, strength, and muscular endurance activities as students jog from station to station. Choose station activities that use large-muscle movements continuously, arranging stations at least 30 yards (27 m) apart. Set up your circuit course outside where there is room to enhance physical activity levels (elementary gymnasiums are often small with limited space). Task cards are helpful to instruct students at each station. (See chapter 11 for a sample circuit course.)

Muscle Fitness

In this book, I have combined the components of muscular strength and muscular endurance into muscle fitness to better describe the use of resistance exercising with children. Muscular strength is the capacity of a muscle or muscle group to exert maximum force against a resistance in one movement or repetition. Muscular endurance is the capacity of a muscle or muscle group to exert force over a period of time against a resistance that is less than the maximum you can move. Muscular strength and endurance are related—to a point. For example, increasing muscular strength will enhance muscle endurance, but exercising for muscular endurance will produce only small gains in muscular strength (Powers and Dodd 2011).

Children in grades K through 6 should never perform maximum lifts. However, children as young as two years old can perform resistance exercises and activities to enhance muscle fitness (Virgilio 2006). Previous concerns that early resistance exercising adversely affected bone growth plates or produced hypertension have been discredited (Faigenbaum and Westcott 2009). The opposite may be true—resistance exercise may enhance musculoskeletal development in children. Research has shown that enhancing bone density in children through resistance activities and proper nutrition can prevent skeletal fragility as children age well into advanced adulthood (Faigenbaum and Westcott 2009).

We can classify muscle contractions into two major categories. The first is dynamic, or isotonic, contraction, which is the force exerted by a muscle group as a body part moves (e.g., most sport skills, weightlifting, push-ups, pull-ups, and curl-ups). The second category is static, or isometric, contraction, which is the force exerted against an immovable object in which movement does not take place (e.g., pushing against a wall, or placing your palms together and pushing as hard as you can for 8 to 10 seconds). An injured or disabled person may use isometric exercises to rehabilitate a body part when an adequate range of motion is not possible. In addition, isometric resistance exercises require little space and no equipment and are easy to do. Encourage the classroom teacher to have students perform isometric exercises at their desks in five-minute fitness breaks several times during the week.

The general benefits of muscle fitness include the following:

- Daily tasks such as opening a bottle, putting out the garbage, and cleaning out the garage are easier and place less undue stress on the joints.

- Muscular strength and endurance are increased.

- Posture is improved because the neck and back get the support they need from strong, flexible muscles.
- Stronger muscles reduce the stress on major joints, especially the knees, shoulders, and hips.
- Strong abdominal muscles keep the digestive organs intact.
- Well-developed shoulder, chest, and back muscles may help with general cardiorespiratory efficiency.
- Bone density is increased, and bone growth and development are enhanced.
- Metabolism is increased.
- Blood pressure levels are controlled.
- Sport tasks that require leg and arm strength and endurance such as running, jumping, striking, and demonstrating sudden bursts of speed are enhanced (e.g., in basketball, softball, soccer) because muscles are stronger and can work longer. Muscle fitness may also protect the joints from the overuse injuries often seen in youth athletes.

Two common ways to develop muscle fitness are resistance exercises and calisthenics. Resistance exercises usually involve performing movement with added weight, such as dumbbells or resistance bands, to vary intensity.

Set and *repetition* are common terms used in recommending exercises. *Repetition* refers to the number of times a movement is repeated; *set* refers to a number of repetitions to complete before resting. For example, if you did two sets of eight repetitions for arm curls, you would do eight arm curls, rest briefly for one to two minutes, and then do eight more repetitions. Allow children to choose the number of repetitions they feel comfortable with, and always check for proper form and technique.

Calisthenics are a form of resistance exercise for which your own body weight and gravity provide the resistance. Examples are the push-up, pull-up, and seal crawl.

Follow these key guidelines when developing resistance exercises and activities for children. Remember: Children should not use the adult model of a structured workout with specific routines and specific sets and repetitions (or reps) according to a scheduled timetable.

- Make sure children are supervised by a certified professional at all times.

- Ensure that children have had a proper warm-up before any resistance exercising.
- Increase resistance levels gradually by 5 to 10 percent as children's strength and form improve.
- Make sure resistance is light; children should never overexert or strain themselves to perform an exercise.
- Never allow children to try maximum lifts (i.e., lift the greatest weight they can in one repetition).
- Focus on proper form and technique.
- Make sure machines and equipment are appropriately sized for children. If not, the exercise may be harmful.
- Many experts agree that one or two sets of five to eight repetitions are sufficient for children (Faigenbaum and Westcott 2009). If children want to perform only one or two repetitions, allow them to do so and go on to another exercise.
- Select resistance exercises that target the major muscle groups: arms, back, chest, legs, and trunk.
- Incorporate resistance exercises on nonconsecutive days during the week.
- Have children perform the exercises slowly—one complete repetition every three or four seconds.
- Use various exercises and equipment to make exercise fun and exciting, such as animal movements, playground equipment, resistance bands, medicine balls, stability balls, and parachute play.

Flexibility

As you know, flexibility is the ability to move the joints in an unrestricted fashion through a full range of motion. Generally, young children have flexible muscles, ligaments, and tendons, but they still should be encouraged to stretch on a daily basis. To maintain flexibility, students should be physically active in a broad range of movement experiences (e.g., soccer, softball, swimming, biking, jogging). It is also important to include specific flexibility exercises in your program throughout the school year to do the following:

- Increase range of motion
- Prevent muscle-related injuries

- Reduce muscle soreness
- Maintain good posture
- Reduce stress on the joints
- Improve movement performance

As you can see, normal flexibility levels confer many health-related fitness benefits that are well worth the time and effort they take!

Keep in mind, however, that the degree of flexibility is specific to each joint. For example, a student who scored in the 90th percentile on the back-saver sit-and-reach test, demonstrating flexible hamstrings and hip flexors, may not be flexible in other body parts, such as the shoulders or quadriceps. So include a wide variety of flexibility exercises for various muscle groups in your physical education program.

The two most common techniques used to improve flexibility in children are static and ballistic stretching. As always, have children warm up their muscles with a few minutes of large-muscle activity before stretching.

Static Stretching

Static stretching stretches a specific muscle group slowly and steadily to a maximum position. Teach children to find their own limits by stretching until they feel slight tightness, *not pain*, and then holding for 10 to 30 seconds.

Ballistic Stretching

Ballistic stretching incorporates bouncing, jerking movements to stretch the muscles. Unfortunately, this force may cause a stretch reflex in which the muscle actually tightens instead of relaxes as a result of being stretched beyond its normal length. The bouncing may also place undue stress on the joints or cause muscle injury. For these reasons, I don't recommend that you add ballistic stretching to your flexibility program, with one exception: performing the movements around the joint slowly and with control, ballistic exercises may be helpful as a warm-up before a sport activity. But clearly, the controlled nature of static stretching places less stress on the joints and muscles than ballistic stretching, so therefore, static stretching is safer.

Body Composition

Body composition is the ratio of body fat to lean body mass (e.g., muscle, bones, and internal organs). Pay special attention to this health-related physical fitness component because increased levels of body fat are closely associated not only with obesity but also with other health problems, such as elevated cholesterol levels, high blood pressure, heart disease, diabetes, and cancer. Many of the early stages of these medical problems appear in childhood. The earlier the child has your help addressing a high percentage of body fat, the better! Remind children that genetics has a good deal to do with body composition and that we don't all look the same. However, we can all be healthier with physical activity and proper eating habits.

Increasing the levels of physical activity, cardiorespiratory fitness, and muscle fitness is a critical factor in controlling body fat; however, a high-quality fitness education program should also include nutrition instruction to assist children in maintaining a healthy body weight. There are a number of issues associated with body fat assessments such as privacy, embarrassment, logistics, testing, and children's perceptions of body fat. Many physical educators have gotten away from body fat assessments and have moved to teaching about weight control, addressing calories in/calories out ratios and the relationship of physical activity to body fat.

The U.S. Department of Agriculture (USDA) has developed a symbol called MyPlate, which is part of a larger initiative based on the *2010 Dietary Guidelines for Americans,* to help people make better food choices (figure 4.3). The symbol, which resembles a food plate, is sliced into four colorful wedges to illustrate the different food groups (fruits, grains, protein, and vegetables) that the USDA recommends for our daily diet. A small circle to the right of the plate resembles a glass of milk for our dairy intake. The website, www.ChooseMyPlate.gov, encourages Americans to avoid oversized portions and balance their calories. The most important foods to increase are fruits and vegetables, which should account for half of your food intake, and grains, half of which should be whole grains. The USDA suggests switching to fat-free milk and reducing sodium and sugar intake. The website includes recommendations for specific audiences, including the general population, expectant mothers, preschoolers, and kids. The website offers seven tips for eating more healthfully:

- Make half your grains whole grains
- Vary your veggies
- Focus on fruit
- Eat calcium-rich foods

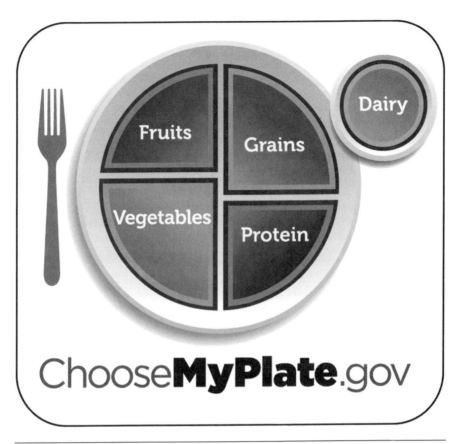

Figure 4.3 The MyPlate icon is a visual reminder of the dietary guidelines that helps people make better food choices.
From USDA

- Go lean with protein
- Balance food and physical activity
- Keep food safe to eat

Visit www.ChooseMyPlate.gov for more information.

SUMMARY

Use the basic principles, guidelines, and components of health-related physical fitness as a foundation for planning a high-quality fitness education program. As you plan your specific program content, refer often to the SPORT-FITT acronym and the descriptions of its components as well as the guidelines for any activity session (warm-up, main event, and cool-down). Most important, however, remember that children need not adhere to a specific exercise prescription. Try to tailor your activities to children's individual needs. In fact, a regimented approach to fitness will usually turn them off to physical activity. Simply encourage and facilitate physical activity 60 minutes per day, and help them address the health-related physical fitness components most days of the week, while teaching them the value of an active lifestyle.

Fitness Education for Children With Disabilities

> No one can make you feel inferior without your consent.
>
> —*Eleanor Roosevelt*

Meeting the physical, mental, and social needs of each student is the most difficult challenge facing physical educators today. At the elementary school level, children's developmental levels vary widely in the areas of physical development, mental and social readiness, motor skill abilities, physical activity behaviors, and fitness levels. This makes planning the typical physical education class lesson quite a challenge, often requiring instructional adjustments to ensure total participation.

Some children cannot meet the demands of traditional physical activity lessons because they have a developmental disability. In this chapter, we'll discuss how to plan activities for children with special needs. We'll cover specific disabilities and health limitations, including obesity, asthma, autism, spinal cord disabilities, and intellectual disabilities. For more information, I recommend that you read *Adapted Physical Education and Sport* (Winnick 2011) and *Adapted Physical Activity, Recreation and Sport* (Sherrill 2004).

The Education for All Handicapped Children Act (Public Law 94-142), which the U.S. Congress passed in 1975, was reauthorized as Public Law 108-446 as the Individuals With Disabilities Education Improvement Act of 2004. It requires that all disabled children ages 5 to 21 receive an appropriate education in the least restrictive environment possible. *Least restrictive* simply means that the child can participate successfully and safely in a setting as near to normal as possible. This law led to the educational practice of mainstreaming, which provides children with disabilities the opportunity to interact with and develop alongside nondisabled children in the same classes.

INDIVIDUALIZED EDUCATION PLAN

To comply with federal mandates, each U.S. school district must locate, identify, and evaluate all students with disabilities. A team of specialists must work with the classroom teacher to develop an individualized education plan (IEP) to carry out this mandate before placing the child. More recently, physical educators have been included in the IEP process to help develop, assess, and review each student's IEP. Formats vary from district to district; according to Winnick (2011), however, each IEP must contain these seven components:

1. **Present level of performance:** This section usually includes basic fitness and

motor skill test results. The assessment may be a mixture of standardized and teacher-designed tests. Standardized tests should be included to determine special needs and justify a stronger case for educational placement. See *Strategies for Inclusion* (Lieberman and Wilson 2009).

2. **Annual goals:** The annual goals are general statements that focus on the student's weaknesses as determined by the present level of performance (PLP) assessment. If, for example, the PLP reports that the student's level of flexibility is limited, it would be inappropriate to develop annual goals related to throwing skills.

3. **Short-term objectives (STO):** The short-term objectives are specific statements that describe the intended outcome: for example, "Bobby will perform a total of three curl-ups, demonstrating good form and technique, by the end of the unit."

4. **Statement of services:** At this stage, the IEP team places the student in the least restrictive environment. It also recommends specialized instructional materials, equipment, and media at this point. Finally, it documents the need for special services such as physical therapy, psychological services, and speech and hearing therapy.

5. **Schedule of services:** The IEP specifies when services will begin and end as well as a schedule that includes specified days, frequency, and time.

6. **Extent of mainstreaming:** The IEP team calculates the percentage of time the child with a disability will spend in regular classes. This section should state whether the IEP team recommends regular physical education classes.

7. **Criteria, procedures, and schedule for evaluation:** The IEP must specify how and when teachers will assess the student's progress. Monitoring should be ongoing, and the IEP team must review each child's plan.

GUIDELINES FOR INCLUSION

For many years, opportunities for physical activity have not been available to children with disabilities. As a physical educator, you have a legal and moral responsibility to change this situation by providing the necessary health and fitness instruction to children with special needs. Adopt this simple philosophy of inclusion: All children have the right to good health through physical activity at school, at home, and in the community.

The following guidelines will help you develop physical activity programs that include students with disabilities.

Review Permanent or Cumulative Records

Check the student's school records carefully. Look for any medical problems or medication taken. Then study the student's IEP. If the IEP format does not include a fitness and skill component, meet with the IEP committee to establish an assessment standard.

Involve Parents

Parents will provide you with the history of their child's disability and helpful insights as to how to help their child. So establish lines of communication between school and home, informing the parents of your efforts in the area of health-related fitness development. If possible, schedule a conference with the parents at the beginning of the school year to discuss the IEP and how to help the student progress throughout the school year. (See also chapter 10.)

Employ Teamwork

Lobby to be on the IEP committee if you're not already. Discuss the student's progress with the classroom teacher, special education consultant, and special services professionals on a regular basis. Communication with others will help you plan and develop a quality experience for the student.

Put Safety First

Children with disabilities may need specific considerations to ensure their safety and well-being. Be certain that all students have specialized equipment as needed, such as helmets, gloves, knee pads, mats, and safety glasses. Make sure that your facilities allow for everyone to participate freely.

Modify Fitness Routines, Skills, and Games

To include everyone in your class activities, you may have to modify certain fitness routines, skills, and games. For example, enlarge a target or goal, make equipment lighter (e.g., plastic rackets, foam balls), reduce the distance the student must kick or throw a ball, or reduce the tempo of the game by allowing the student to walk instead of run. See Kasser and Lytle's *Inclusive Physical Activity* (2005) for specific ideas.

Modify Teaching Behaviors

Plan to include more visual and demonstration techniques to explain skills and give directions, especially when intellectually challenged and hearing impaired students are enrolled in your classes. Physically walk through an activity or station rather than merely explaining the directions. Give step-by-step verbal cues that are direct and concise. Your special care in clearly communicating content will help all your students learn.

Be Sensitive

Provide disabled students with plenty of positive reinforcement. Speak to them about their friends, interests, hobbies, or favorite subjects in school. Children with disabilities will develop skills and increase physical activity levels when they feel a sense of belonging and warmth in your physical education classes.

Establish a Positive and Supportive Classroom Environment

Establish a class environment in which everyone helps and supports each other in the spirit of teamwork. Try not to pay special attention to or be overly cautious with the disabled child: this can be dehumanizing. Treat all students as equal members of your class. Concentrate on the physical needs, not the disability. Plan activities the student can do; don't get hung up on what she can't do.

Use Class Tutors

Draw class tutors from many sources. Students within each class can tutor each other. These peer tutors can provide the disabled student with individual attention and one-on-one feedback. Big buddies are older students you have trained to work with younger students. Give special instructions as necessary to those students who will be working with the disabled child.

If the student needs more than what a peer or a big buddy can provide, find the student an adult helper. The school district may hire a teaching assistant, or you may be able to find a volunteer. Choose someone who possesses a caring, patient demeanor, and make sure the assistant receives special training in special education. If you can't find anyone suitable, invite parents to help gather and program data, manage equipment, or supervise students, freeing you to focus on students with specific needs.

OBESITY

Childhood obesity is one of the most serious health problems today. In fact, obesity is addressed first in this chapter because it is the most common disability in elementary schools.

As noted in chapter 1, obesity is defined as a body mass index (BMI) over 30 or body fat levels over 30 percent. According to current statistics, almost 17 percent of American children can be classified as obese, and over 15 percent are overweight. This estimate is on the rise! It may not be necessary to assess an obese child with skinfold calipers or other body measurements. However, you can also use a visual screening. If a child looks obese, he is. Embarrassing tests and measurements may add more humiliation, creating a negative impression of physical education in the eyes of an obese child.

Children who are obese may seem relatively healthy in their youth; however, they usually face serious medical complications later in life. For example, these children are at higher risk for coronary heart disease, respiratory impairments, diabetes, orthopedic problems, gall bladder disease, and certain types of cancer.

Serious psychological complications may develop through adolescence as well. Other children often taunt, tease, and humiliate the overweight child. This has a significant impact on a child's self-concept and feelings about the need for physical activity.

Taking Action

Identifying obese students in your school is the easy part. But how can you help them? Follow these important steps as you begin to take action.

Intervene Early

The earlier you begin intervening, the better. Take a very close look at children in preschool through grade 3. Once you have identified the obese students in your school, design a plan of action. Intervening early can also help prevent serious psychological problems.

Develop a Team Approach

Organize a committee to help design a plan of action. This committee should consist of the school nurse, a dietitian, a psychologist, and you, the physical educator. Try to involve the child's family physician; it will give your committee credibility as well as an additional clinical perspective.

Enlist the Parents' Support

Ask the committee to meet with the parents of each student. This meeting is critical for the proper implementation of your program. State your concerns about the student's emotional and physical health. Ask the parents if they are willing to help; if they are, you're on your way! Provide the parents with a handout describing your program goals as well as a list emphasizing their responsibilities. Establish follow-up conferences at least every three months. If the parents are unable to come to the meetings, set up phone conferences and send home progress reports and literature through the mail. Organize a family health promotion night specifically for this group, and include teachers and service professionals. Children may participate with their parents to learn how to eat and exercise together as a family. If the parents will not work with you, continue to work with the student at school and send literature home. Parents might need time to realize the severity of the problem.

Design a Plan

The plan should address three major areas of intervention: eating behavior, physical activity patterns, and behavioral strategies. Each professional should be responsible for developing specific strategies and activities in his or her area of expertise.

Develop a Portfolio

A portfolio will help organize the student's progress and make your efforts more credible. The portfolio may include a profile, contracts, log sheets to record eating and activity patterns, a plan with short- and long-term goals, schedules, and specific activities (see appendix A). Other committee members may add pertinent documents and instructional materials. This portfolio is the property of the student, but keep it in the classroom unless the student uses it for home-based assignments.

Schedule Additional Time

You will need additional time to interact with students who are obese to help increase physical activity levels. Request to meet with students individually, or arrange to meet with small groups of three or four students during the school week. Find time for a special physical activity class during recess, free periods, your planning time, early bird sessions before school, after-school activities, or regular homeroom class time. Communicate closely with the principal and classroom teachers to help arrange special time for the obese student.

Schedule Discussion Sessions

Besides additional physical activity time, schedule individual or small-group discussion sessions with obese students. Each meeting should have a theme that is accompanied by a learning activity. Possible themes include responsibility, making new friends, assertiveness, making healthy decisions, and self-concept development. For example, to enhance self-concept, ask children to complete the Me Tree activity (pages 122-123).

Provide Feedback

Once the student has started working with the committee, be sure to provide feedback to maintain motivation and progress. Use charts and graphs to indicate improvement in such areas as weight, activity patterns, and eating habits. Give the student buttons, stickers, caps, or yogurt certificates as incentives for completing certain aspects of the program. As the school year continues, begin to phase out the incentives and accentuate the intrinsic value of weight loss, such as good health, self-confidence, added energy, and greater success in games and sports.

Guidelines for Activity

Guidelines will help you design useful activities for obese students. Large-muscle activities are the most beneficial because they expend the most calories. Activities such as walking, jogging, hiking, swimming, jumping rope, and tag games are just a few examples. Start with low-intensity activities, however, such as walking at a moderate pace. Do not demand or expect a certain level of performance during the initial stages. Instead, for example, design a minitrack around your outdoor facility and ask the students to walk and jog around the track until they feel uncomfortable. Have them record the number of laps they do and calculate any improvement.

Find out what types of physical activity they enjoy. Once you know their likes and dislikes, you'll be able to plan more exciting, interesting lessons. For example, try to individualize aerobic dancing by using music with slower beats per minute to sustain moderate activity levels. Students seem to enjoy this activity as long as it is not too demanding, the music is up-to-date, and the activity environment is positive. When it comes to obese students, it's especially important to emphasize variety and fun in physical education. Introduce activities such as in-line skating, games of low organization, dance and rhythmic activities, lead-up sports, and recreational activities such as nature hikes to demonstrate a variety of ways to stay active. Never use performance expectations and competition to motivate obese (or any other) students.

Self-monitoring is a good way to reinforce increases in student activity levels. Have the students keep track of their physical activity times every day for a few weeks in their portfolios. Suggest a total of 20 to 30 minutes of continuous large-muscle activity, which students may break into segments (e.g., three 8- to 10-minute segments completed anytime during the day).

Include resistance exercises for muscle fitness, using a low-weight and high-repetition format. Rubberized resistance equipment and light dumbbells (2 to 3 lb, or 1 to 1.5 kg) are ideal. Students should perform five different exercises, one set of 10 repetitions each, creating a total body workout two or three times per week. After three weeks, gradually increase to two sets of 10 repetitions each. (See chapter 11 for specific exercises.)

Too many physical educators neglect to include flexibility exercises for obese students' physical activity programs because they are concerned about increasing large-muscle exercise. You should include flexibility exercises, though, because range of motion in obese students is usually restricted by excess fat around the joints. Encourage students to perform a series of stretching exercises each day for at least 7 to 10 minutes. (See also chapter 11.)

Assess each student's progress every two or three weeks. Arrange brief private meetings with the student and occasionally the parents to review the portfolio. Reinforce the positive successes, talk about home-based activities, and encourage the student to evaluate and monitor his own progress.

ASTHMA

Over six million American children have some form of asthma, and this figure is rising. Asthma constricts the airways, reducing the flow of air into and out of the lungs, causing panting, wheezing, or coughing.

Many years ago, educators did not encourage children suffering from asthma to exercise or engage in normal physical education activities. Research over the last 15 years has proven this approach to be wrong. Today, children with asthma who exercise on a regular basis can increase the duration of physical activity they can tolerate and reduce the severity of asthma attacks (Rimmer 1994).

Yet, you should be aware of a condition known as exercise-induced asthma (EIA). In this condition, exercise of high intensity or duration may make the bronchial tubes contract, causing an asthma attack. Students with asthma who follow certain guidelines, however, may participate in physical activity.

Taking Action

To begin helping the student with asthma, consult with the school nurse and carefully review the student's medical records. Note special medications the student is currently taking and any physical activity limitations. Be aware of the student who uses an aerosol medication. She should use this medication 30 to 60 minutes before exercising and keep it with her throughout the physical education class.

Guidelines for Activity

Students prone to EIA need to warm up before exercise. Sudden, high-intensity activity will place them at high risk for an attack. Allow them more time to warm up than the rest of the class—at least 10 to 15 minutes of low-intensity activity such as walking, calisthenics, and performing moderate-intensity large-muscle movements. The intensity of the activity should progress gradually to a level of no more than 50 percent of the target heart rate, progressing to 60 percent only when they are physically ready. You may want them to use a heart rate monitor to determine a level suitable for physical activity.

Interval activity, discussed in chapter 4, is ideal for the asthmatic student because the intensity level varies throughout the exercise session. Break the main event or bout into five-minute intervals with three- to five-minute rest periods between sets. In more serious cases, decrease the amount of time in activity and increase the amount of rest. It is also important to end with a 10-minute cool-down period using exercises similar to those performed in the warm-up. This will enable the student to gradually and comfortably bring the heart rate back to a normal range, preventing any sudden changes that could cause undue stress on the body. Experts recommend that students with asthma engage in the typical length of a physical education class and that they be physically active for 60 minutes most days of the week—on the low end of normal frequency, intensity, and duration.

Certain types of strength-related activities can benefit the asthmatic child. For example, development of the abdominal, chest, back, and shoulder muscles may help the student breathe more efficiently. Other activities that should not give the asthmatic child major difficulties include activity circuits or stations, tumbling and gymnastics, resistance exercising, and softball and volleyball games.

Finally, as an extra precaution, establish an emergency procedure for dealing with an asthma attack. You may ask the family to provide you with an extra inhaler, along with the instructions that come with it. Be prepared to call for an ambulance if the inhaler doesn't provide immediate relief.

Despite the potential problems, asthmatic children should participate in a well-balanced physical education program. As they learn to pace themselves, they will become aware of the many benefits of enjoying physical activity. Your professional guidance and support are critical to developing in them a positive attitude about their physical capabilities.

AUTISM SPECTRUM DISORDER

Physical education classes can offer the autistic child a number of opportunities to develop social, cognitive, and physical skills. The interaction with peers in an open environment will enhance an autistic child's socialization process, which is normally delayed. Experts believe that peer interaction can be more powerful than adult guidance in developing the social skills of an autistic child. As a teacher, try to be patient, allow the other children in class to take the lead, and facilitate the social process through the class games and activities.

Although some children with autism might have normal intelligence, most have a number of cognitive deficits that may be accompanied by language deficiencies. Provide the child with a number of short, simple steps in a slow, orderly fashion, and give positive feedback during each step. Furthermore, autistic children often have motoric delays. With practice and the appropriate instruction, these delays may be corrected giving them needed confidence and support to further develop their social and language skills.

Taking Action

Work closely with the team of professionals that are servicing the autistic child in your school. Be aware of a number of potential difficulties or red flags that might upset other children in your class or cause physical harm to the autistic child. For example, an autistic student who is sensitive to noise or touch may become excited and display abnormal behaviors such as rocking or spinning erratically when overly stimulated by noise or physical contact. In more extreme cases, an autistic child may become so excited or stressed that he displays self-injurious, erratic physical behaviors such as kicking, biting, head banging, and scratching. In this case, the student should be removed from the class by the paraeducator.

Guidelines for Activity

The following strategies for inclusion were recommended by Rouse (2009). Keep in mind that all the strategies might not work; you may have to adjust and modify your techniques to meet the needs of a student on a day-to-day basis.

Emphasize Social Interaction

Create as many opportunities as possible for the autistic child to interact with peers. One technique that works well is to have a peer facilitator assigned to the child. Be sure to educate the facilitator about the condition and the characteristics of the autistic child. Also, provide a list of simple safety precautions or steps to take if the autistic child's level of stress appears to be rising.

Adapt Communication

Because autistic children can have problems with pronoun reversals, it may help to speak to them in the third person. For example, you might say "Susan can kick the ball" rather than "Susan, kick the ball." Use consistent language for directions and class procedures. Try to use very short verbal expressions, because too much language may upset the child and cause undue stress. Finally, use simple sign language when communicating basic commands such as stop, go, yes, or no. The entire class might learn these cues to communicate with the autistic student.

Allow Extra Response Time

After giving an autistic child either verbal or visual directions, allow several seconds for a response. Also, only one person at a time should be interacting with the autistic child. If no response is given, repeat the process. If there still is no response, show the student what you want her to do.

Use Positive Reinforcers

Autistic children often get fixed on, or locked in to, an object or toy such as a small figurine or a key chain. Use this as a motivator to get them to complete a task. Once the task is completed and they have followed directions, allow them to sit with their object and play with it for several minutes. Use a number of positive reinforcement expressions to keep them motivated (e.g., "Nice job," "You did great today," "You had a super physical education day," or "I like the way you kicked the ball").

Use Written Language Strategies

Written language is an excellent way to communicate with the autistic child. To reduce the stress levels of a child in physical education, have her read a simple list of your lesson activities on a task card just prior to the beginning of class. Here is an example:

Fifth Grade

1. Free play warm-ups to music
2. Fitness stations
3. Ball-handling skills
4. End of class

In fact, task cards would be helpful for all students. Also, you can use pictures or graphics for directions and tasks as well as activity choices. Students who need more specific directions may respond well to social stories. Social stories are basic stories dealing with a number of social situations that are difficult for the autistic child to grasp. Each story has a general theme and includes implied responses to various situations. This technique was developed by Gray (2000) to help students understand social situations and help correct inappropriate behavior or provide additional instruction. The following is a social story for behavior management:

> My name is Tom. I must stop pushing my friends in physical education class. If I continue, people might get hurt. They will also stop being my friends.

Autistic children need the support and understanding of a physical educator. When properly planned for, they will be able to participate in a high-quality physical education program and derive all of the benefits it has to offer.

SPINAL CORD DISABILITIES

Spinal cord disabilities are a result of a traumatic injury to or a disease of the vertebrae or the nerves of the spinal column (Kelly 2011). For example, children suffering from serious injuries caused by car accidents, diving into shallow water, or falls may experience permanent nerve damage resulting in a form of paralysis. Diseases such as spina bifida, in which one or more vertebrae fail to completely fuse during fetal development, may also cause similar paralysis. The vertebrae become very unstable and cause severe nerve and tissue damage resulting in a loss of movement capabilities (Rimmer 1994). Whether the disability is due to a birth defect or an injury, the student with spinal cord disabilities has limited upper-body movement and usually uses a wheelchair.

Taking Action

The following guidelines will help you design appropriate physical activity programs for children with spinal cord disabilities. Keep in mind that you should tailor your exercise recommendations to the student's level of fitness, medical history, physical ability, and personality. You should also take into account certain safety precautions and equipment limitations.

Guidelines for Activity

First, children with spinal cord disabilities may not have control of their bladders. If they do not have a catheter, you may suggest to the classroom teacher that the student use the restroom before each physical education class. To aid in kidney function and temperature regulation during exercise, the student with a spinal cord disability must have intermittent water breaks. As a precaution, the student should carry a sport bottle of chilled water on the wheelchair.

Normally, students with spinal cord disabilities lack muscular endurance. So in the beginning stages of exercise, reduce the number of repetitions in resistance exercises as well as the number of arm movements in an aerobic dance routine to ensure success and continued physical activity. Through careful observation, assess what muscles the student can use, the strength and endurance of those muscles, and how they can be used in a physical education class. Oftentimes, the student with a spinal cord disability develops muscle imbalances from the overuse of the muscles needed for manipulating the wheelchair. Provide such a student with a number of flexibility exercises for the shoulders, back, and hip flexors. (*Caution:* Do not encourage extensive flexion of the back because overstretched, nonfunctional muscles may not keep the back well supported, resulting in additional physical problems.)

Be especially aware of restrictions placed on a student who has a spinal rod or spinal fusion. Flexion and rotation may have an adverse effect on such a student's physical condition, creating a more dangerous situation during physical activity. It helps to closely monitor trunk balance and control during movement. If the student in the wheelchair needs additional support because of the physical activity, secure a 2- to 3-inch (5 to 7.6 cm) padded belt across the waist to keep the child stable in the wheelchair.

Students with spinal cord disabilities should follow the same basic principles of exercising and stages of physical activity (warm-up, main event, cool-down) as children without disabilities (see chapter 4). Some children with disabilities, however, must maintain a moderate intensity to keep exercise safe and to prevent overexertion from causing a decline in normal functioning (Miller 1995). The following exercises may be appropriate for students with spinal cord disabilities.

Flexibility Exercises

Flexibility is just as critical for the student with a spinal cord disability as it is for anyone else. Unfortunately, this component of fitness is often overlooked. For students who use wheelchairs, stretching may help to maintain muscle balance and improve certain functional abilities.

LATERAL TORSO STRETCHER

Slowly reach upward with one arm, fingers extended. Keep the opposite arm bent at the elbow. Bend the torso slightly to the side, reaching slightly across with the raised arm (see figure 5.1).

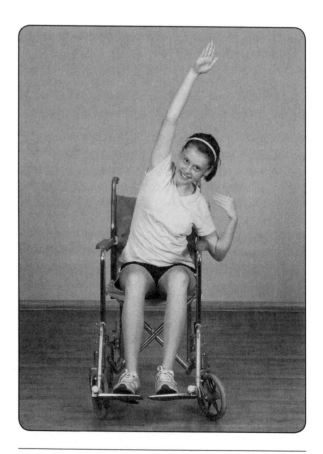

Figure 5.1 Lateral torso stretcher.

BACK STRETCHER

Keep the chin tucked to the upper chest and the back flat and stable. Bend forward from the hips. Support the upper body with the hands gripping the ankles (figure 5.2). Take care to maintain balance to avoid a fall. (*Caution:* Postural changes may affect blood pressure and cause lightheadedness.)

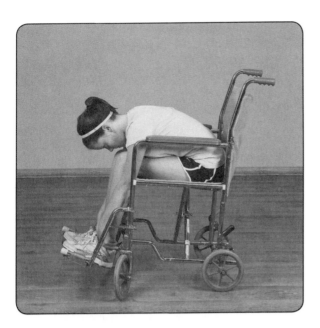

Figure 5.2   Back stretcher.

FOREARM AND SHOULDER STRETCHER

Clasp the hands in front of the body about shoulder height with the palms facing away. Extend the arms forward and slightly upward (figure 5.3).

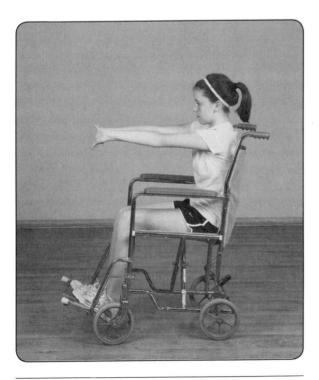

Figure 5.3   Forearm and shoulder stretcher.

SHOULDER AND CHEST STRETCHER

Reach back and extend both arms behind the midback area, palms facing upward. Gently lift the arms, stretching the shoulders and the chest (figure 5.4).

Figure 5.4   Shoulder and chest stretcher.

HAMSTRING STRETCHER

Sit toward the edge of the chair, placing one leg straight out with toes up. Keep the knee slightly bent. Lean forward slightly, keeping the back stable (figure 5.5).

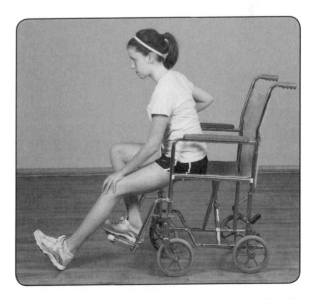

Figure 5.5   Hamstring stretcher.

CALF STRETCHER

Place a towel or strap around the ball of one foot and extend the leg, pulling the strap toward the chest (figure 5.6).

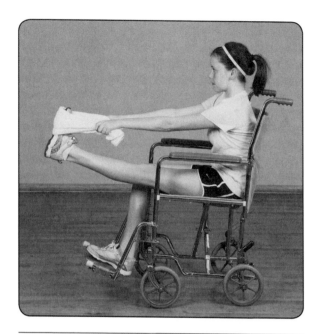

Figure 5.6 Calf stretcher.

Muscle Fitness

The following set of exercises develops the major muscle groups of the body. I have not listed specific resistance levels, sets, or repetitions, however, because these depend on individual abilities. Remember, students should perform the exercise slowly and with control, and should never lock or hyperextend a joint. Keep the number of repetitions even on both sides of the body, and remind students to maintain proper sitting alignment. The photos feature rubberized resistance bands and the toner from the SPRI Quik-Fit for Kids program (see the website in appendix B). You may substitute other resistance equipment.

BOW AND ARROW
STRETCHER FOR SHOULDERS

Grasp the toner with one arm straight out to the side as if holding a bow. Draw the toner across the chest to the opposite shoulder (see figure 5.7). Hold for three seconds. Change sides and repeat.

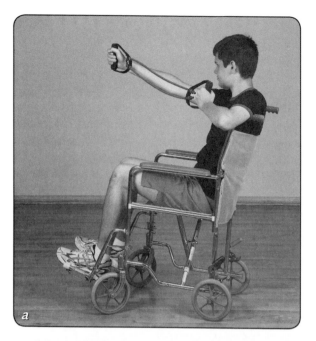

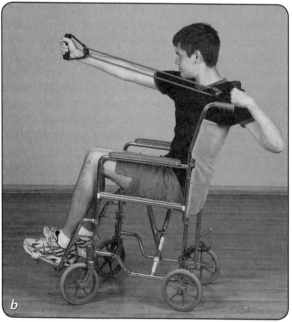

Figure 5.7 Sequence for bow and arrow stretcher for shoulders.

FRONT BUTTERFLY
FOR CHEST AND BACK

Grasp the toner with both hands in front of the body with palms facing inward and elbows slightly bent. Pull the toner out to each side (figure 5.8). Hold for three seconds and return slowly.

making the toner go behind the back (figure 5.9). Hold for three seconds. Return slowly to the starting position.

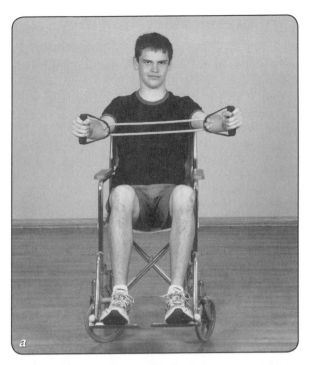

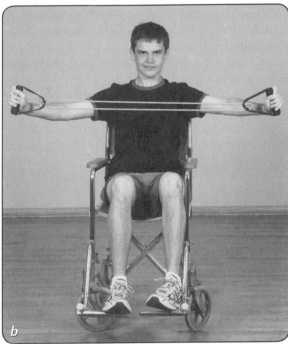

Figure 5.8 Sequence for front butterfly for chest and back.

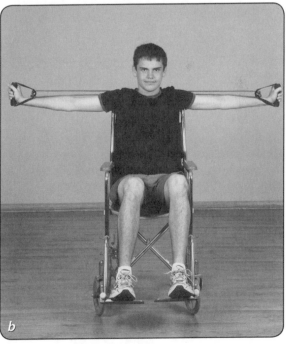

Figure 5.9 Sequence for overhead butterfly for back and back of arms.

OVERHEAD BUTTERFLY FOR BACK AND BACK OF ARMS

Grasp the handles overhead with palms facing outward. Extend the arms down to the side,

CHEST PRESS FOR CHEST AND BACK OF ARMS

Place the toner directly behind the back with the center pad just below the shoulder blades. Grasp the handles with the palms facing inward. Extend both arms straight out, keeping elbows slightly bent (figure 5.10). Return slowly to the starting position.

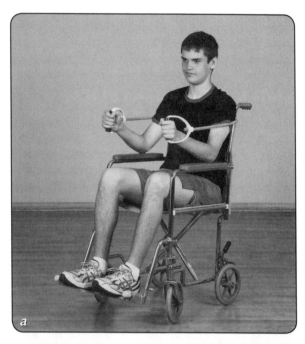

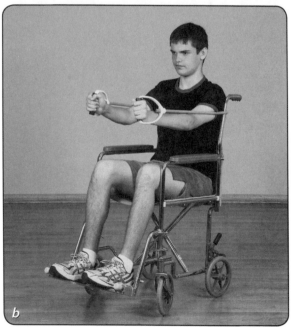

Figure 5.10 Sequence for chest press for chest and back of arms.

Cardiorespiratory Activities

Physical disabilities often limit large-muscle movements in the lower body, making it difficult to develop cardiorespiratory endurance. The following activities use smaller movements to gain the benefits of cardiorespiratory endurance: wheelchair aerobic dance; wheelchair basketball; upper body ergometry, which is arm pedaling; and wheelchair ergometry, which is moving the wheelchair on stationary wheels.

INTELLECTUAL DISABILITY

According to the American Association on Intellectual and Developmental Disability (AAIDD), intellectual disability is a disability characterized by significant limitations both in intellectual functioning and in adaptive behavior, which covers many everyday social and practical skills. For many years, the criterion to measure intellectual functioning has been an IQ test. Scores between 70 and 75 indicate a limitation in intellectual functioning. Standardized tests can also determine limitations in adaptive behaviors in three skill categories: conceptual skills, social skills, and practical skills.

In schools, children diagnosed as educable, with IQ scores between 50 and 75, are usually mainstreamed and scheduled for regular physical education classes. In terms of motor performance and physical fitness, children with mild disabilities are usually three and a half to four years behind their peers. Many children with intellectual disabilities also have problems with obesity, poor posture, gross motor coordination, and other physical disabilities.

Taking Action

The following guidelines will help you plan developmentally appropriate activities for children with intellectual disabilities. These children might find exercise quite rewarding because they may achieve a certain degree of success and accomplishment.

Guidelines for Activity

When teaching children with intellectual disabilities, make sure they are aware of your verbal instructions and feedback cues. For example, most children with intellectual disabilities do not understand such basic directions as "Pace yourself during the one-mile run" or "Do as many push-ups as you can." Give slowly spoken, concise instructions. Repeat your directions if necessary.

Demonstrating instead of explaining a skill or concept may facilitate the child's understanding of the activity. Help the student walk through the game, skill drill, or fitness activity to get a feel for the movements before participating in the activity.

Give children with intellectual disabilities praise and positive reinforcement at every reasonable opportunity for effort and participation as well as for accomplishments. Reward them with stickers, tokens, or similar incentives when they have successfully completed a task or a goal of their IEP. Use extrinsic rewards more liberally throughout the school year with these children to keep them on task and motivated.

It is especially important for children with intellectual disabilities to have consistent class procedures in a controlled learning environment. A certain amount of repetition may develop a sense of security and confidence. The following are a few examples of set procedures you can use to help children with intellectual disabilities:

- Have the student walk on a line to enter the gym and take his place for the beginning of class.
- Always use the same attendance and warm-up procedures.
- Use the whistle for only one general command, "Stop, look, and listen."
- Always hold the closure segment of the lesson in the same physical location.
- Have children hold hands to form partnerships, small groups, or large circles.
- Use hula hoops to indicate personal space or a set spot on the field or court.

Finally, establish small weekly goals in the area of health-related fitness for children with intellectual disabilities. Monitor the progress each student makes, reinforcing it to motivate them to participate in physical activity. Whenever you see a student improve, reward the positive behavior and design a plan to continue moving forward. Here's an example: week one, 10 minutes of physical activity, five times; week two, 15 minutes of physical activity, five times; weeks three and four, 30 minutes of physical activity, five times per week. If students have lower skill and fitness levels, give them short bouts of activity with longer rest periods. The rest periods are a great opportunity to provide immediate feedback.

To monitor student progress, collaborate with the special education team to develop appropriate lesson plans and ensure that students have physical education four or five days each week.

Community-Based Opportunities

Children with moderate levels of intellectual disabilities should have all the opportunities that other children have. Camps, playgrounds, YMCAs and YWCAs, CYO leagues, Jewish community centers, health clubs, and other programs should have trained personnel able to serve the special needs of these youngsters.

For many years the Special Olympics program and Special Olympics International, sponsored by the Kennedy Foundation, have been a tremendous success story throughout the world. Each year, more than one million people, eight-year-olds to adults with IQs of less than 75, participate in this program. The Special Olympics organization sponsors 14 events, including swimming, bowling, skiing, skating, hockey, and wheelchair events. Recently, the Special Olympics developed sport and fitness programs that occur throughout the year. Contact your local Special Olympics chapter for more information.

SUMMARY

Increasing the physical activity levels of, and encouraging healthy lifestyles for, all children remains a major goal of schools regardless of race, color, gender, or ability. Studies have indicated that children with disabilities are at higher risk for disease because they have lower levels of health-related physical fitness and are more likely to be obese. Therefore, you should give specific attention to children with disabilities by designing a physical activity plan to meet their individual needs.

Use the guidelines, safety precautions, and activity recommendations in this chapter for students with obesity, asthma, autism spectrum disorder, spinal cord disabilities, and intellectual disabilities to personalize and adapt your physical education program for these students. Remember to always let this simple philosophy guide you in the instructional and moral decisions you make as a teacher throughout your career: All children have the right to good health through physical activity and should be afforded opportunities to be physically active at school, at home, and throughout the community.

Planning and Teaching Fitness Education

Teaching Strategies

> Education is what survives
> when what has been learned
> has been forgotten.
>
> —B.F. Skinner

Over the last decade our society has been quite concerned about the childhood obesity issue. To solve this problem, physical educators have included more physical activity time in their classes and emphasized updated fitness testing approaches. As physical educators, we have debated major issues such as the award system, measuring body composition, and which specific test items to use to get the best data on our students' fitness levels. For many years we have been teaching children about physical activity through national fitness testing programs, which may be the very reason past generations have become discouraged and unmotivated about physical activity.

Enough is enough! It's time to change our teaching methods and generate intrinsic interest in physical activity with updated approaches.

TRADITIONAL TEACHING MODELS

Traditional models of teaching fitness education have proven unsuccessful. Do you recognize the models outlined in the following sections? Unfortunately, they may still be alive and well in your district.

Military Model

The military model uses direct commands to get children to exercise. The military-style physical

educator organizes children in squad formation to perform exercises in unison and uses physical activity as punishment for not conforming to class procedures. This model is unsuccessful because it does not allow for individual differences. Moreover, it forces children to exercise on command without a true understanding of the value of physical activity. Indeed, many children feel threatened by this approach. Certainly, it fails to lead to long-term positive physical activity behaviors.

Pretest and Posttest Model

Some physical educators begin the school year with a fitness pretest and end the year with a posttest. To prepare children for the pretests, these teachers usually give a few lessons about proper techniques for the exercises on the tests. Otherwise, they rarely teach health-related physical fitness or incorporate it into their traditional unit plans. This model has proven unsuccessful because it makes children view fitness as something that is evaluated simply to separate the fit from the unfit. Improving fitness scores and receiving awards are the only motivators in this model.

Five-Minute Warm-Up Model

In the five-minute warm-up model, class starts with five minutes of calisthenics and a short run, usually while the teacher is taking attendance. This model leads to repetitious and inappropriate exercises. Students exercise like robots, usually

This chapter is dedicated to the memory of a friend and colleague, Muska Mosston.

resulting in boredom and poor exercise techniques. Rarely do teachers who use this model present fitness concepts; therefore, students never learn why they are exercising. Also, because teachers usually give very little attention to this stage of the class, students eventually see exercise as unimportant.

Fitness Unit Model

Some physical educators design a four- to six-week fitness unit as a separate component of the yearly curriculum. As a result, children tend to view fitness as an isolated subject rather than as an ongoing activity that is important in their daily lives. That said, a good strategy for kicking off your fitness program for the school year is to present a fitness education unit in September and continue to infuse the concepts and activities throughout the school year.

Games and Sports Model

The games and sports model uses games and team sports to teach the value of exercise and increase physical activity levels. Because of large class sizes, time constraints, and limited player responsibilities, games are often short, producing only moderate levels of physical activity for a minimal number of children. In game situations the most active participants are usually the most skilled and conditioned children, leaving a large percentage of children inactive—usually the children who have the greatest need to develop their skills and increase physical activity levels. This model presents games and team sports as an end in themselves. A better approach is to teach students how certain activities such as games and team sports are agents of health-related fitness and active lifestyles.

Fitness Concepts Model

Some physical educators believe that if children know how their bodies work and understand basic exercise principles, they will become active because they understand the value of and need for exercise. Yet, by itself, a strong academic approach is not enough; it is only one component of a high-quality fitness education program. Children need to experience fitness, interact with their peers through activity, and learn by doing. Thus, I advocate the more comprehensive model of fitness education described throughout this book.

HUMANISTIC APPROACH TO TEACHING FITNESS

Humanism is not so much a theory as it is a teaching approach. The humanistic physical educator values children rather than the activity, values physical activity rather than fitness scores, and values student choice and responsibility rather than class control. Using this mind-set, humanistic physical educators help develop a positive long-term attitude in children concerning the role of physical activity in their lives.

The Teacher's Role

According to Rodgers (1994), significant learning takes place when you adopt three basic attitudes toward students and their learning: be genuine, value individuals, and offer empathy.

First, be genuine. Share your thoughts and feelings with students as openly and honestly as possible. When students are misbehaving, share your frustration and disappointment with them while also showing warmth, caring, and encouragement. If you make a mistake, admit it, apologize, and move on. If you can't answer a fitness question, say so and work together as a class to find the answer.

Second, value individuals. Learn to value students for who they are—whatever their skills, thoughts, or feelings. Rodgers calls this an attitude of "unconditional positive regard," meaning an open, nonjudgmental, nondefensive approach to others. If, for example, a student is clowning around in your aerobic movement class, she has a real need for attention and respect. The student may feel a genuine fear of being rejected if she acts normally. Recognize the needs behind the behavior.

Third, offer empathy. Place yourself in your students' shoes as much as you can. Seek to understand their feelings, and work to express this knowledge to them in a concrete manner. Don't merely say, "I know how you're feeling"; describe the feelings clearly and offer suggestions. This opens the way for a trusting student–teacher relationship. For example, if an overweight student is having trouble jogging in your class, speak to him privately about the frustration and anxiety he may be feeling, and share a similar experience you may have had in math class when you were in school. Reaffirm that you accept him as a person, and offer your support. With your assistance, it won't be long before the student will accept responsibility for planning his own fitness goals. Empathy has great power to set the stage for genuine learning and development.

Instructional Applications

Several ways exist to make fitness education more humanistic, or student centered. Start with what students consider important. Students relate better to educational goals that are associated with things that are relevant to their personal development. For example, teach first-graders aerobic dance through cartoon characters, animation, and playacting. Use exciting DVDs that feature popular Disney characters or other current media sources.

Provide a variety of resources to meet the various needs of your students, thereby enhancing the learning environment. For example, use books, handouts, exercise videos, charts, guest speakers, and special equipment (e.g., medicine balls, exercise bands), and digitally record students doing activities.

Furthermore, don't always use class time for traditional instruction. Infuse your program with variety by letting students decide how they will achieve their personal goals and program goals. For example, have Open Gym now and then. Set up 8 to 10 fitness stations in the playing area. Let students choose any station in any sequence. If you plan enough variety and emphasize individual choice, students will avoid clustering at certain stations. And have Practice Time classes, giving students time to practice dance fitness routines or work on whatever aspects of fitness or movement skills they believe need extra attention.

Variety must not only come from using a variety of resources and changing the way you use class time; you can also vary your teaching strategies. But where do you start? Let's examine a number of practical, easy-to-use teaching methods based on Mosston and Ashworth's spectrum of teaching styles (2002).

SPECTRUM OF TEACHING STYLES

Because your preferred teaching style may not be reaching every student, you need to use a variety of styles. Stretch yourself and match your approach to different learning styles at different times. Your classes will be more interesting and accessible to all of your students, and learning will increase accordingly.

Before selecting a particular teaching style for a particular lesson, however, you must decide what the learning objective is for the lesson, clearly identifying what students will learn. Regardless of the teaching style, children learn more when you clearly state the purpose for the activities. The learning objective should be something concrete that you can observe and assess to determine whether learning has taken place. Furthermore, develop class objectives that speak to the three major aspects of learning: cognitive (knows), affective (values), and psychomotor (does). The following is an example of learning objectives for level III:

- **Cognitive:** Students will be able to locate their biceps and identify one exercise to develop these muscles.
- **Affective:** Students will be physically active for at least 60 minutes per day independently after school, on weekends, or during recess and report their activities in a personal active lifestyle portfolio (see appendix A).
- **Psychomotor:** Students will walk or jog 1 mile (1.6 km) at their own pace to the best of their abilities.

Keep in mind when selecting a teaching style that one method is not better than another. Indeed, each style has its advantages and disadvantages. Choose a style based on your objective. With experience, you'll be able to choose an appropriate style or mix of styles to elicit the outcome you desire. Certainly, effective teachers possess a wide repertoire of styles and techniques. Be innovative and use a variety of techniques to add excitement to the learning experience (Mosston and Ashworth 2002).

Command Style

The command style is highly teacher centered. Students learn to do tasks accurately within a short period of time, directly under your control. You instruct students *en masse*, using the demonstration and explanation technique. In this style, use command signals for each movement learners perform. The advantages of this approach are that it uses time efficiently, develops listening skills, increases safety, and streamlines class management. The command style is useful when you are introducing a new activity or teaching certain types of lessons, such as swimming, mass exercises, or aerobic dance.

Practice Style

The practice style allows students to accept more personal responsibility for learning. As with the command style, you decide the learning objectives and class content. In contrast to the command style, however, you allow the learners to perform the task at their own pace. Add variety by having students complete tasks individually, in pairs, or in small groups. Have everyone work on the same task at once, or have several different activities going on at the same time.

One easy way to organize several activities at once is to incorporate the station approach with task cards to help with instruction. Task cards give students practice learning independently, making the practice style more student centered than the command style. Each task card lists directions, giving you more freedom to give feedback (see figure 6.1). Write tasks on large index cards or on posters placed around the gym. Use pictures, graphics, and color to make the task card more visually appealing. The major advantage of this style is that it frees you to give individual attention to students.

Reciprocal Style

In the reciprocal style, you establish the learning objectives and class content, but the students take responsibility for teaching each other.

The first step when using the reciprocal style is to develop a criteria checklist for students to use to provide feedback to their partners (see figure 6.2). Include a simple breakdown of the important skill components. Pictures may also be helpful. You may want to attach each checklist to a clipboard. Laminate the sheets and have students write on them with erasable overhead projector marking pens so you can wash the cards off and reuse them for years to come. Criteria checklists are especially effective when teaching the specific movements of certain exercises. You could also post large task cards on the gym wall to help supplement and reinforce appropriate techniques.

In the reciprocal style, students work in pairs in a teaching–learning partnership, so the next step is to pair the students in your class at random. Talk to them about how important it is to be a teacher and how you need their help. Ask each pair to decide who will be the doer performing the activity first and who will be the observer, or teacher, first. The doer performs the physical activity according to your directions, and the observer gives feedback, using the checklist as an instructional resource. After several trials, have the students switch roles. Try not to interfere with the doer–observer relationship, thereby reducing the impact of this style. Your role as the teacher is to stay neutral and act as a facilitator. Therefore, the reciprocal teaching style is highly student centered.

Self-Check Style

In the self-check style, more decisions are shifted to the learner to promote greater responsibility. The purpose of this style is to encourage self-reliance and self-improvement and show students how to honestly and objectively assess their performance.

The self-check style allows a great deal of freedom for you and for the students. You can design the learning objectives and content activities yourself. Have all students work on the same task, or include a variety of activities. The criteria checklist used in the reciprocal style may also be used here (see figure 6.3 for another example).

Ensure that you have already given several related lessons on the chosen skill or activity before attempting the self-check style. This lays the foundation for safe and high-quality independent work. (Remember that exercises performed incorrectly may result in injury.) Then have students move throughout the play area performing the assigned tasks and stopping periodically to review the checklists to evaluate their performances. Students may either move on to another task or repeat the task to correct their performances. Circulate through the play area, allowing students to develop independently; provide feedback only when students are acting unsafely or need disciplinary action.

The self-check style allows students to set their own pace better than they can with a partner. Show respect for individual differences by giving students ample time to complete tasks to their own satisfaction. With the self-check style, you can learn many interesting things about your students' affective, cognitive, and psychomotor development from observing their independent behavior.

An extension of self-checking is the personalized learning contract. Once you get to know your

Name _____ Date _____

Class _____

Level III

Upper-Body Strength

Practice each exercise as described in the chart. Place a checkmark (✓) next to each completed task. Turn in your card when you are finished.

Exercise	Task	Completed	Comments
A. Regular or bent-knee modified push-up	Maximum completed _____		
B. Bent-arm hang	Maximum hang time _____		
C. Horizontal ladder	One crossing or number of rungs _____		
D. Cargo net climb	One round (up and down)		
E. Medicine ball catch	10 individual catch and throws		

Figure 6.1 Individual task card for upper-body strength.

From S.J. Virgilio, 2012, *Fitness education for children: A team approach* (Champaign, IL: Human Kinetics).

Doer 1 _____   Date _____

Doer 2 _____   Class _____

Level III

Jogging Criteria

Observer: Give the doer some pointers about jogging form. Use the tips in the chart to help you. Try to be friendly.

Doer: Jog at a moderate pace. When the teacher signals, slow down; then change roles.

	DOER 1		DOER 2	
	Yes	No	Yes	No
1. Runs tall, leans slightly forward.				
2. Swings legs from hip, knees bent.				
3. Lands on heels with weight rolling along the outside portion of foot to toes.				
4. Points toes straight ahead, lands heel directly under knee.				
5. Swings arms straight forward and backward, hands relaxed.				
6. Breathes in an even, controlled rhythm—in through the nose, out through the mouth, if possible.				

Figure 6.2   Reciprocal style: criteria checklist for jogging technique.

From S.J. Virgilio, 2012, *Fitness education for children: A team approach* (Champaign, IL: Human Kinetics).

Name _____   Date _____

Class _____

Level III

Self-Check: Flexibility

Directions: Follow the steps in the following chart. Practice each exercise five times on each leg. Check (✓) the box to the right after completion.

Hamstring stretch	OK	Feels uncomfortable
1. Sit with your left leg extended; bend your right leg at the knee and place the sole of your foot on the floor near the knee of your extended leg.		
2. Flex the foot of your extended leg, toes up, against a wall, box, or other support.		
3. Bend forward from your hips, keeping your low back straight. Your bent knee may rotate slightly outward.		
4. Relax and breathe normally. You should not feel pain!		
5. Hold the stretch for 10 seconds. Repeat with the opposite leg.		

Figure 6.3   Self-check style: criteria checklist for flexibility.

From S.J. Virgilio, 2012, *Fitness education for children: A team approach* (Champaign, IL: Human Kinetics).

students, you may want to use learning contracts to give them more independence and accelerate their individualized fitness development. You design the contracts ahead of time, basing the number of options you include on each learner's needs (see figure 6.4).

Inclusion Style

The inclusion style is based on the premise that everyone has the right to participate and be successful in class activities. For this style, you establish various levels of performance for each fitness activity. Then the learners select their entry levels based on their own preferences and physical abilities. Your role is to encourage them to evaluate their own performances. Encourage students who are having trouble to stay at the same level of difficulty. The hard part—if you naturally lean toward the command style of teaching—is to allow students to choose their own levels of activity. Keep in mind that this style gives students the right to choose to enjoy mastery of a particular level before moving on. Task cards at various stations can also help (see figure 6.5). (See chapter 5 for ways to include students with disabilities.)

Guided Discovery and Problem Solving

Guided discovery and problem solving represent a significant change from the techniques discussed thus far. When using guided discovery and problem solving, you ask students to think differently about the subject matter. The process, or the learning itself, becomes more important than the final product or achievement levels.

Guided Discovery

In guided discovery, you establish a predetermined answer to a problem. Then you plan a series of questions (Q) and anticipated responses (AR) that will lead the learner to the final answer. Your response (YR) is listed after the anticipated response.

> **Q:** What are the largest muscles in your body?
> **AR:** Legs.
> **YR:** Right!

> **Q:** What are the muscles in the back of the legs?
> **AR:** Hamstrings.
> **YR:** Excellent!

> **Q:** Suppose your dad asked you to move a few boxes from the garage. How would you approach the box to pick it up?
> **AR:** Bend the knees, keeping the back straight.
> **YR:** OK!

> **Q:** What body part should be used to get to a low position to reach down and pick up the box?
> **AR:** Legs.
> **YR:** Yes!

> **Q:** So what muscles are used to do most of the work when we pick up anything?
> **AR:** Leg muscles.
> **YR:** Very good. Now let's practice.

Problem Solving

In the problem-solving style, the answers are unlimited. You still select the general subject matter content, posing a specific movement problem for the small group or individual students to solve, which may have hundreds of potentially correct answers. You must be careful to establish class procedures and closely supervise the class for safety and organization. But once the students are involved in the problem, don't interfere, or you will detract from the learning process. An example of small-group problem solving for level II may simply be to ask children to design a highly active game using four hoops, two jump ropes, and two 8.5-inch (22 cm) playground balls. Possible interpretations are endless, and all are correct.

Add a problem-solving aspect to the basic personalized learning contract by using an open-ended contract that allows students to develop their own goals and to design activities to reach those goals (figure 6.6). (See also the family fitness contract in figure 10.5.)

INSTRUCTIONAL TECHNOLOGY

In light of the rapid changes in technology, NASPE (2009b) developed a position statement to guide teachers in the use of technology in physical education. The advent of wireless technology, computer projection systems, interactive whiteboards, and physical activity–monitoring devices has made it possible for physical educators to bring more up-to-date instructional technology techniques into the gym.

Name _____ Date _____

Class _____ Level _____

I, _____, desire to improve my physical activity or fitness level by agreeing to perform the following activities designed by _____, my physical education teacher.

I realize I must stay on task and complete the program to the best of my ability.

This contract will begin on _____ and will end on _____.

I will perform the following activities each class period.

Warm-up: Jog for two minutes

Muscle fitness: One-minute of curl-ups, minimum

                 Jump rope for one minute

                 Push-ups—one set, as many as I can do

                 Obstacle course—twice around

Sport activity (select one):

                 Basketball: 2v2 game or individual practice

                 Soccer: Goal kick practice

                 Softball: Running bases or throwing against a wall

                 Cool-down: Walk two minutes; do three minutes of static stretching.

If I successfully complete this program I will be rewarded with a frozen yogurt certificate and a free physical education period.

Student signature _____

Teacher signature _____

Figure 6.4 Personalized learning contract.

From S.J. Virgilio, 2012, *Fitness education for children: A team approach* (Champaign, IL: Human Kinetics).

Name _____ Date _____

Class _____

Level III

Push-Ups: Upper-Body Strength

Directions: Select any color push-up. Perform as many as you can. Record your score in the space provided to the right. When you master one color, try selecting another.

	Repetitions
A. Blue: 90-degree arm push-up	
B. Green: Bent knees	
C. Red: Wide hands	
D. Tan: Push up and hold (seconds)	
E. Yellow: Chair push-up	
F. Brown: Wall push-up	

Figure 6.5 Inclusion style task card for push-ups.

From S.J. Virgilio, 2012, *Fitness education for children: A team approach* (Champaign, IL: Human Kinetics).

Name _____ Date _____

Class _____ Level _____

Physical Activity/Physical Fitness Contract

I, _____, would like to improve my physical activity levels or health-related

fitness performance. I understand that I need additional work in the area of _____

_____. My long-term goal is _____

_____ .

   I understand that I will be given class time to achieve this goal. I also promise to work on my

goal outside of school at least three days per week. (Select three days: M Tu W Th F Sat Sun)

   This contract will begin on _____ and will end on _____. I

agree to inform my teacher each week about my progress and the specific activities I used

to achieve my goal. I will report this information on my Physical Activity Log on a daily basis.

   If I achieve my goal, I will reward myself by _____ .

Student signature _____

Teacher signature _____

Parent or guardian signature_____

Figure 6.6 Open-ended student choice contract.

From S.J. Virgilio, 2012, *Fitness education for children: A team approach* (Champaign, IL: Human Kinetics).

The development of exergaming (i.e., video games turned into physically active contests) has added still another possibility for gym use. The Dance, Dance Revolution (DDR) activities and dance steps and Wii Fit software can now be used on a large projection screen set up in the gymnasium. Pedometers and heart rate monitors (wristwatch or finger style) have become more accurate and affordable tools for monitoring physical activity and heart rate levels during various activities. Fitnessgram/Activitygram (Cooper Institute 2010) software offers another technique for monitoring students' fitness and physical activity levels. You can also help students record their physical activity by developing a template and placing it on a flash drive so that they can track their levels throughout the week (see appendix A for an example).

NASPE's position is that technology can enhance teaching and learning in physical education. The guidelines outline four key principles to ensure proper use in relation to the national standards and developmentally appropriate practices.

- **Guideline 1:** The use of instructional technology in physical education is designed to provide a tool for increasing instructional effectiveness.
- **Guideline 2:** The use of instructional technology in physical education is designed to supplement, not substitute, effective instruction.
- **Guideline 3:** The use of instructional technology in physical education should provide opportunities for all students, versus opportunities for few.
- **Guideline 4:** The use of instructional technology in physical education can prove to be an effective tool for maintaining student data related to standards-based curriculum objectives.

Reprinted from NASPE 2009.

CLASS STRUCTURE

Once you determine which style of teaching is right for a particular lesson, you are ready to organize the lesson. Structure your lesson plans into three parts: set induction, lesson focus, and closure.

Set Induction

Children feel more secure if they know what is going to happen before it happens. So explicitly set up each lesson. Review what the class accomplished in the last activity, and then introduce what you've planned for this lesson. Orient the learners to what they'll be doing, how they'll be doing it, and why it is important. Here is an example for level II: "Last week we learned how important exercise is for our hearts. Today we are going to learn how to take our heart rate, which we'll call HR, and count how many times our heart beats before and after our basketball skills lesson. At the end of class, I'll give you a learning activity to do at home with your parents. Remember, you really have to take good care of your heart. It is the most important muscle in your body. Even LeBron James needs a strong heart to play basketball every day!"

Lesson Focus

Be sure to organize your class so that you give the primary focus of the lesson top priority. In other words, don't try to do everything in one class. If the focus of the lesson is teaching children to take their heart rates, then direct most of your time to this end. Add other related learning objectives to help facilitate and extend the primary focus of the lesson as time allows.

Closure

To close a lesson effectively, give a brief review of what the lesson attempted and accomplished. If appropriate, compliment the students' efforts, but don't criticize. Review what will be coming up in physical education, making them eager to attend the next lesson. If the lesson was very strenuous, use this time to have students cool down and relax before leaving.

Here is an example of closure for level II: "OK, let's finish class. Please come over and sit by this tree. I thought we had a great class today. Everyone seemed interested in finding their HR and counting the number of heartbeats in one minute. Next week we are going to play a game called Circle Circulation and learn how the heart pumps blood throughout our bodies. Tonight, when you are at home, show your parents how to take their HRs and have them calculate their one-minute resting HRs. Have a great day, and remember to stay heart smart!"

SUMMARY

Traditional fitness education models and teaching strategies have proven unsuccessful in developing fitness levels and patterns of physical activity in children because they emphasized results (i.e., fitness levels) over the process of developing long-term positive physical activity behaviors. But there are alternatives to traditional approaches to fitness education! Let's emphasize *how* we teach children physical activity, making sure we vary our teaching styles to meet our educational objectives. Adopt a humanistic philosophy, which places each student's personal needs and abilities first, before planning a quality program of physical education. The spectrum of teaching styles introduced by Mosston and Ashworth (2002) offers a number of creative choices from which to select an appropriate teaching style for each set of objectives.

Planning
for Fitness

> Our plans miscarry
> because they have no aim.
> When a man does not know
> what harbor he is making for,
> no wind is the right wind.
>
> —*Seneca*

Curriculum planning is one of the most difficult responsibilities facing physical educators today. In the past, physical educators usually assumed that movement skills, games, dance, gymnastics, and sports developed health-related physical fitness levels and maintained physical activity patterns in children. A more contemporary approach supported throughout this book is that health-related physical fitness and motor skills should be taught in concert throughout the school year.

This chapter provides model curricula, including an example of a yearly plan for developmental level III that integrates health-related physical fitness concepts with the various skill themes. We'll also take a look at sample fitness education and fitness integration lesson plans for developmental levels I, II, and III. Remember, children in each grade will vary widely in their developmental levels. However, I have divided the levels as follows:

Developmental level I: Kindergarten and first grade

Developmental level II: Second and third grade

Developmental level III: Fourth through sixth grades

The fitness education lesson plans focus solely on providing instruction in health-related physical fitness. The fitness integration lessons illustrate how to integrate health-related physical fitness and increase physical activity levels in a skill or sport theme lesson. In this chapter you will learn how you can integrate fitness, values, physical activity concepts, and skill themes to develop a high-quality program of physical education.

SAMPLE YEARLY PLAN FOR DEVELOPMENTAL LEVEL III

Block out segments of time for the major components of your curriculum on your school calendar. Consider overall body development, and strive for a well-balanced curriculum. Look for opportunities to combine a skill activity with a fitness activity if the skill-related lesson includes a high percentage of vigorous physical activity. For example, a rhythmic and dance unit may include an aerobic dance routine.

Table 7.1 shows a yearly plan for developmental level III, designed for classes meeting twice a week for 30 minutes. See chapter 8 for lesson plans that address health-related physical fitness concepts in detail (levels I, II, and III).

Later in this chapter are sample fitness education lesson plans for level I (Superpump), level II (Back to the Basics), and level III (Smart Heart). These are followed by a model fitness integration lesson plan that corresponds with weeks 12 through 14 of the same yearly plan. This structured approach to curriculum planning will ensure that your physical education program has appropriate fitness education content and continuity.

Table 7.1 Sample Yearly Curriculum Plan for Developmental Level III

Weeks	Curriculum focus	Fitness activities	Fitness concepts
1	Introductory activities, cooperative games	Flexibility stretches	Wellness concepts
2-3	Health-related physical fitness pretest	Sit-and-reach, push-ups, curl-ups, PACER, body composition	Physical activity and wellness exercise techniques
4-6	Physical activity, lifestyle activities, health-related physical fitness components and concepts	Fitness circuits, muscle fitness	Proper techniques of resistance and flexibility exercising, exercises to avoid
7-8	Health-related physical fitness activities and concepts, using the active lifestyle portfolio	Cardiorespiratory endurance (CRE)	Fitness principles (components, FITT, heart rate, interval activity)
9-11	Soccer skills	Active soccer skills and lead-up games	Fitness principles (resting HR, HR recovery, preventing injuries)
12-14	Basketball skills	Upper-body exercises, lower-body exercises	Exercise science: upper-body anatomy and lower-body anatomy; introduction to a personal active lifestyle portfolio
15-17	Volleyball skills	Medicine ball exercises, fitness games	Exercise science: specificity, progression, overload, reversibility, train and maintain (SPORT), and bone anatomy
18-20	Tumbling and gymnastics	Push-up routine, flexibility, fitness games	Foods for fitness
21-22	New games	Fitness circuits	Making healthy food choices (teach substitutes for unhealthy foods, snacks, and drinks)
23-27	Rhythms and dance	Aerobic dance, step aerobics	Family physical activity: parent and community involvement
28-31	Softball skills	Free choice fitness activities	Maintaining a personal active lifestyle portfolio
32-34	Physical activity for healthy lifestyles	Individual contracts for physical activity choices	Fitness forever: making choices, decision making
35-36	Health-related physical fitness posttest	(See pretest, weeks 2-3)	Review major fitness principles, summer physical activity, summer safety, recreational opportunities
36	Field day activities	Total body development	Maintaining physical activity levels (60 minutes per day)

SAMPLE LESSON PLANS

This section includes examples of fitness education lesson plans and fitness integration lesson plans. Each example includes a lesson from developmental levels I, II, and III. Keep in mind that these lessons are single-class-period lessons extracted from a unit plan.

Because the amount of class time varies, I suggest allotting the following percentages to the lesson segments:

Set induction	15 percent
Fitness education	30 percent
Developmental movement	45 percent
Closure	10 percent

Each teacher has his or her own approach to lesson plan formats, and content may be integrated within lesson segments. Certain guidelines, however, should remain consistent regardless of the level or content of the class.

- **Lesson focus:** This is the specific content to which you should direct class instruction.
- **Objectives:** The lesson plans illustrated in this chapter use student-centered objectives. These objectives describe what students will do as a result of the lesson activities in the cognitive (knowing), psychomotor (moving and physical development), and affective (valuing) areas.
- **Equipment and facilities:** This category lists all of the equipment, instructional materials, and facilities you will need to present the lesson, including equipment-to-student ratios.
- **Safety considerations:** Proper safety planning will help prevent accidents and keep your classes running smoothly.
- **Set induction:** Also called the anticipatory set, the purpose of the set induction is to motivate children, orienting them to what they will learn, why it is important, and how they will accomplish the learning objectives.
- **Procedures:** This section offers a detailed account of the activity, the instructional strategy, the time allotment breakdown, and class management tips.
- **Closure:** A closure is often difficult to include because of time limitations, but it is necessary for a number of reasons. First, it is a good time to review the lesson content. Second, it will help you evaluate whether students grasped the concept of the lesson. Third, it can be a time to show students how the lesson is relevant to their daily lives. Finally, the closure is an opportune time to prepare students for the next class activity by giving a brief preview of the exciting lessons to come.

As you read through the lessons, think about how you can update your own lesson plans to include each essential component. Remember, incorporate fitness into your lessons throughout the school year.

FITNESS EDUCATION LESSONS

Superpump (Level I)

Lesson Focus

Increasing physical activity levels through creative expressive movement and exercise and learning the role of heart rate in exercise

Objectives

- **Cognitive:** The student knows that physical activity increases the heart rate, which in turn exercises the heart.
- **Psychomotor:** The student participates in a wide variety of activities to increase physical activity levels.

♦ **Affective:** The student values physical activity as both a means to strengthen the heart and a form of creative expression.

Equipment and Facilities

Music, music player, and an open playing surface with line markings

Safety Considerations

Check the playing surface for any hazards. Make sure students are dressed properly for active movement.

Set Induction (3 minutes)

Say, "All muscles are important and should be exercised, but the heart is the most important muscle in the body." With students sitting in a circle, ask them to feel their hearts beating on the left side of their chests. Ask them to notice the rhythm of the beats. Reinforce that as the heart beats stronger, it sends fuel to the muscles. Say: "Have you ever felt your legs get really tired? It may be that you need to exercise to strengthen your heart muscle. Today we will actively move to strengthen the heart, and we'll make it fun by adding music."

Procedures

Warm-Up (5 minutes)

Students stand in a circle. Direct them to do the following:

Walk in a circle.	30 seconds
Walk briskly in a circle.	30 seconds
Skip in a circle.	30 seconds
Sidestep in a circle.	30 seconds
Gallop in a circle.	30 seconds
Walk briskly with forward punches.	30 seconds
Walk briskly with arm curls.	30 seconds
Perform march steps.	30 seconds

Activity 1: Creative Movement to Music (8 minutes)

Have students move throughout the playing area, staying in their personal spaces. When the music stops, students perform a seal crawl walk.

Do	*Instruct*
Begin music.	Walk.
	Walk with stiff legs.
	Walk with spaghetti legs.
	Walk on your heels.
	Walk on your toes.
	Walk in a straight line.
Stop music.	Seal crawl.
Begin music.	Jog lightly.
	Jog lightly and give a friend a high five.
	Jog and pretend you are a bird.
	Jog and pretend you are a car.

Stop music.	Seal crawl.
Begin music.	Hop like a kangaroo.
	Hop like a rabbit.
	Leap like a frog.
	Can you name another animal to imitate?
Stop music.	Seal crawl.
Begin music.	Walk as if you are very happy.
	Walk as if you are very sad.
	Walk as if you are very angry.
	Walk as if it is a sunny, warm day.
	Walk as if it is a cloudy, rainy day.

Activity 2: Heart to Heart (7 minutes)

Divide students into pairs and have them scatter throughout the playing area. Give students a series of movement problems. Say, "When I give the command 'Heart to heart,' find a new partner and stand left shoulder to left shoulder and place your right hand over your own heart to feel it beat." Try the following commands:

- Take three giant steps forward.
- Take two giant steps backward.
- Balance on one foot.
- Walk fast changing directions.
- Heart to heart!
- Skip around the gym.
- Gallop like a horse.
- March like a soldier.
- Heart to heart!
- Take five steps forward.
- Take five steps backward.
- Take five steps sideways.
- Heart to heart!
- Take two hops; then one leap.
- Walk on a line painted on the floor.
- Walk backward on the line.
- Find anyone in class and shake that person's hand.
- Heart to heart!

Cool-Down (2 minutes)

Say: "Everyone walk quietly and feel your heart beating. This faster beating means you are exercising your heart." (Play cool-down music.)

Closure (3 minutes)

Have students stand in a circle. Conduct the following discussion:

"What movements made your heart beat faster? What other types of activities make your heart beat faster? Everyone feel their heartbeat again (place your right hand on your chest). Feel how it has slowed. That is because we are resting. The heart needs rest, but we should all exercise our hearts every day! Next week we are going to use the parachute to exercise and play a fun fitness game."

Back to the Basics (Level II)

Lesson Focus

Increasing general physical activity levels and performing exercises correctly for neck and back care

Objectives

- **Cognitive:** The student knows how to perform certain exercises to prevent stress on the neck and back.
- **Psychomotor:** The student participates in cardiorespiratory endurance, muscle fitness, and general physical activities specific to each station.
- **Affective:** The student makes a personal choice of activities based on individual physical fitness level.

Equipment and Facilities

- Large playing area, one horizontal ladder, four task cards, music, music player, four to six tumbling mats
- For every four students: one hula hoop, one jump rope, one streamer, one soccer ball, one basketball
- For each student: one 8.5-inch (22 cm) playground ball, one foam soccer ball

Safety Considerations

Ensure that mats are clean. Check the playing area, all equipment, and the horizontal ladder.

Set Induction (3 minutes)

Explain to the class that this lesson will help develop the following components of fitness: cardiorespiratory endurance and muscle fitness. Each station will have a fitness objective. Say: "Does anyone know someone who got hurt from exercising? Sometimes exercise can hurt our bodies if it is not done properly." Demonstrate the curl-up with bent knees, not straight legs, and the neck exercises—drop head, look over, tilt neck (not the head straight back). Remind students to perform these exercises correctly to avoid placing stress on the back or neck. (See chapter 11 for additional unsafe exercises to avoid.)

Procedures

Warm-Up (5 minutes)

Have students form a single line around the basketball court. Each time they complete a lap, they change the activity. Direct students to do the following:

- Walk around the outside of the basketball court area.
- Dribble a ball around the basketball court area.
- Kick a foam soccer ball around the basketball court area.

Activity: Circuits (16 minutes)

Divide students into groups of four. In this small-group activity, color-code the choices at each station. Play music during activity. Tell students, "When the music stops, move to the next station." Move around the class, providing individual feedback to students. The selections should be posted at each station with a reminder to students to do their physical best.

Station 1: Upper-body muscle fitness

Yellow	Walk across the horizontal ladder, two turns.
Red	Bent-knee push-ups—perform two sets of maximum repetitions.
Green	Seal crawl, one or two times up and down tumbling mat.

Station 2: Cardiorespiratory endurance

Yellow	Jog around the court area three times.
Red	Jump rope, three sets of 15 turns with rests in between. (Use lines to jump if students have trouble jumping rope.)
Green	Dribble a soccer ball or basketball at a jogging pace around the designated area until it is time to change to the next station.

Station 3: Abdominal endurance

Yellow	Curl-ups—5, 10, or 15 repetitions (whatever is more comfortable for the student)
Red	Curl-up twists—5, 10, or 15 repetitions
Green	Diagonal crunch—5, 10, or 15 repetitions

Station 4: Free play for physical activity

Students select desired movements and create physical activities.

Yellow	Hula hoops
Red	Playground balls
Green	Streamers

Cool-Down (1 minute)

Have students walk around the play area in any direction.

Closure

Say: "Why is it important to perform exercises correctly? What were the two dangerous exercises we reviewed at the beginning of class? Why are they so dangerous? Remember, perform the exercises correctly so you won't put any additional stress on your neck or back. Next week we will be playing an active game to increase fitness."

Smart Heart (Level III)

Lesson Focus

Increasing cardiorespiratory endurance through interval activity

Objectives

◆ **Cognitive:** The student knows the technique of interval activity to enhance cardiorespiratory endurance.

> ◆ **Psychomotor:** The student participates in interval routines at his or her own ability level.
> ◆ **Affective:** The student values intervals as a means to enhance his or her personal best.

Equipment and Facilities

Stopwatch, music ("Twenty-Five Miles to Go" by Edwin Starr), music player, 10 cones, whistle, outdoor playing area (check facility availability)

Safety Considerations

Check the playing surface for glass, debris, potholes, and other hazards.

Set Induction (3 minutes)

Say: "Has anyone thought about how certain sports such as basketball, soccer, and floor hockey require a great deal of running with short rest periods? Basketball, for example, is active until the game flow changes or there is a violation. Then all the running stops for a short while. Well, this is a form of interval training. Today we will perform interval activities that will enhance your heart and lungs, maybe enabling you to play certain sports without tiring so quickly."

Procedures

Warm-Up (5 minutes)

Have students form a single line around the playing area. Then have them walk around the playing area to the song "Twenty-Five Miles to Go" by Edwin Starr.

Activity 1: Leader Change (3 minutes)

Divide students into groups of five and have groups stand in single file. The line leader begins jogging in any direction at a moderate pace. Say, "When I say 'Change,' the last student in line becomes the leader and the previous leader becomes the second person in line." Change leaders every 30 seconds. If you wish, have leaders vary their movements; for example, allow them to skip, hop, sidestep, seal crawl, or crab walk.

Activity 2: Walk-Jog Intervals (8 minutes)

Use cones to mark the perimeter of a large running track on your outdoor area. Spread students around the track so that they don't bunch up. Say: "We'll start by walking briskly around the track. When I whistle, start jogging at a pace that is comfortable for you. When I whistle again, you walk briskly again, and so on." Alternate walking and jogging in 45-second intervals. Continue for seven to eight minutes total.

Activity 3: Destination Choice (7 minutes)

Stand in the middle of the field and ask the students to walk briskly to you for further instructions about the next activity. Explain to them that in this next activity they have a choice of destination. Provide them with a number of possibilities from which to select their jogging destination. Be certain that all destinations are within your view so that you can properly supervise. Here are some examples:

- ◆ Large oak tree
- ◆ Basketball standard on court
- ◆ North edge of the school building
- ◆ Pull-up bars

◆ Soccer goal

◆ Softball field backstop

Say: "Jog to your destination at a moderate pace, and then run back to this spot at a faster pace. But this is not a race!" Then allow students to select their own destinations.

Cool-Down (3 minutes)

Ask the class to walk back to the court area from the field at a moderate pace.

Closure (2 minutes)

Ask students whether they enjoyed the interval activity. Then say: "What other activities do we participate in that are considered interval activities? What types of intervals do you do at home? [Possible responses: Biking, roller skating.] Next week we will learn another exercise principle: heart rate recovery. We will be taking our heart rate before, during, and after exercise and calculating what we'll call the recovery index."

FITNESS INTEGRATION LESSONS

Heart Jump (Level I)

Lesson Focus

Jumping, leaping, doing support movements, moving at various levels, identifying shapes and letters to develop the heart muscle through jump rope activities

Objectives

◆ **Cognitive:** The student knows the heart is a muscle that needs to be exercised and becomes aware of various movement forms, levels, and support.

◆ **Psychomotor:** The student participates in various movement skills using the jump rope as well as a highly active game to increase physical activity levels.

◆ **Affective:** The student values using the jump rope and game-related activities as a way to exercise the heart and stay active.

Equipment and Facilities

Music, music player, one jump rope per student, flat playing surface

Safety Considerations

Check jump ropes and the playing surface for hazards; make sure that no one is wearing jewelry.

Set Induction (3 minutes)

Introduce the use of jump ropes to develop movement skills and stay physically active. Review the muscles used for jumping. Ask students to tighten the thigh muscles and place a hand on the muscle as it tightens. Ask students to make a fist and place it on the left side of the chest. Say: "This is where your heart is and your fist is the size of your heart. The heart is also a muscle and is exercised when you jump and leap."

Procedures

Warm-Up (3 minutes)

Arrange students in one large circle. Use music and direct cues. Have students walk around the circle and then walk briskly, shake their arms and walk, skip, bunny hop, and jog at a moderate pace.

Activity 1: Rope Shapes (15 minutes)

Have students scatter throughout the playing area, staying in personal spaces. Use guided discovery with these individual jump rope activities:

- Shape your rope into a circle.
- Can you place one body part inside the circle? Two? Three? Four?
- Can you get inside your circle?
- How small can you get?
- How big can you get?
- Can you jog around your circle?
- Discover ways you can move around the outside of the circle.
- Shape your rope into a square.
- Can you take one giant leap over your square?
- Show me how you can hop in and out of the square.
- Lay your rope in a straight line.
- Can you walk on your rope as if you were a tightrope walker in the circus?
- Can you walk backward?
- Can you move down the rope at a low level?
- Can you move down the rope at a high level?
- Can you travel down your rope from side to side?
- Shape your rope into the letter V.
- Can you leap over the letter V at the widest part?

Divide students into groups of three:

- Can you place three letters together? Try to make a word.
- Step through your letters without touching the rope.
- Can you jog around your letters?
- Can you walk in and out of your letters?

Activity 2: Lifeline (7 minutes)

Divide students into small groups of four or five with one standard jump rope per group. Explain the game: "One student in each group holds the end of a jump rope, which is the lifeline. At the signal 'Go!' that student runs throughout the play area dragging the rope along the ground and shaking it. The other students in the group try to pick up the end of the jump rope. The student who picks up the lifeline then gets to run with the rope." Make sure each student in the group has a turn running with the lifeline. Remind the class: "The reason the rope is called a lifeline is that jumping rope is a good exercise for the heart, and exercise will improve your life and keep you healthy." Remind the students to keep the rope on the floor.

Cool-Down (2 minutes)

Have students find a line on the court area and walk on it as if it were a tightrope. Have them walk sideways, backward, on their toes, on their heels, and while dipping.

Closure (2 minutes)

Reinforce the value of jump ropes for fitness development. Ask, "What muscle besides the leg muscles is exercised when you jump rope or run? [Heart.] Next week in class, we will try long rope jumping. This is when two students turn the rope and another student jumps through."

Chute the Works! (Level II)

Lesson Focus

Ball handling, tossing and catching skills, increasing muscle fitness

Objectives

- ◆ **Cognitive:** The student knows that muscle fitness is important to accomplishing a variety of activities in life.
- ◆ **Psychomotor:** The student participates in a variety of ball-handling skills and develops upper-body muscle fitness through parachute activities.
- ◆ **Affective:** The student gains confidence in ball-handling skills and understands the need for arm and shoulder development.

Equipment and Facilities

One large parachute, two medium parachutes, one 8.5-inch (22 cm) playground ball for each student, a large playing surface or grassy field

Safety Considerations

Check parachutes for small rips or holes. Show the children how to hold the handles with an overhand grip.

Set Induction (5 minutes)

Say: "Today we're going to develop our ball-handling skills and our upper-body strength and endurance, using the playground balls and the parachutes. To enjoy this lesson, we need to cooperate as a group."

Ask: "What kinds of chores around the house require you to use your arms and shoulders? [Washing the car, vacuuming, cleaning windows.] What sport activities require strong arms and shoulders? [Throwing a softball, hitting a softball, bumping a volleyball, shooting a basketball.] What other types of things do you do that require strong arms and shoulders? [Climbing trees, hanging on the playground equipment, digging, swimming.] To do all those things without getting tired, you need to exercise your arms and shoulders. Today we will be using the parachute in class to help strengthen our upper bodies."

Procedures

Warm-Up (3 to 5 minutes)

Arrange students around the large parachute. Ask them to walk, skip, or jog around the parachute. Then, have all students grasp the parachute with both hands, raise it overhead, and lower it back to waist level two times. Next, have all students grasp with their left hands and jog counterclockwise in a circle while holding the chute—skipping, hopping, galloping.

Activity 1: Have a Ball (12 minutes)

Have students scatter throughout the playing area, staying in personal spaces, each with an 8.5-inch (22 cm) playground ball. Present the following problem-solving situations:

1. Holding the ball in two hands at waist level, walk in general space without dropping the ball.
2. Repeat 1, jogging with the ball.
3. Place the ball on the floor or ground in front of you. Find a way to go over the ball without touching it.
4. Hold the ball and roll it on different body parts.
5. Toss the ball in the air, let it bounce once, and then catch it.
6. Toss the ball in the air and catch it before it bounces.
7. Throw the ball in the air and count how many times you can clap your hands before catching it.
8. Can you toss the ball in the air and catch it while you are running?
9. Throw the ball in the air and catch it at a high level, medium level, and low level.
10. Throw the ball up while sitting; then stand and catch it.
11. Find ways of keeping the ball in the air without using your hands.

Activity 2: Group Chute Catch (5 to 7 minutes)

Divide the class into two equal groups. Have each group grasp a medium-sized parachute. Have the two groups stand about 10 feet (3 m) apart. Place a playground ball in one chute to begin the game.

The objective is for the group with the ball to pop the ball over to the other group's parachute. Emphasize teamwork and cooperation. Say: "See how many times our two groups can catch without dropping the ball. See if you can beat your own record!"

Activity 3: Popcorn (5 to 7 minutes)

Arrange students around the large parachute. Place several types of balls in the parachute. Have the students grasp the parachute with overhand grips. Explain: "When I say 'Simmer,' you shake the chute, creating small ripples. When I say 'Cook,' make the balls move more rapidly by adding a slight chop in the ripples. When I say 'Popcorn,' make large, fast ripples by waving your arms and jumping up and down to pop the balls straight up, trying to keep the popcorn in the pan. When I say 'Pop Out,' pop the balls outside the chute."

Cool-Down (2 minutes)

Have students place the chute down and walk around it performing arm crosses and overhead arm stretches.

Closure (1 to 2 minutes)

Say: "Do your arms feel a little tired and sore? Good, that means you were exercising your arm and shoulder muscles. But you also need rest. Whenever you are feeling bad or experience pain, you should stop and tell an adult. Who can name games and sports that use round balls and require arm and shoulder strength and endurance?" [Basketball, volleyball, baseball, softball, four square, tetherball, parachute play.]

Basketball Cats (Level III)

Lesson Focus

Practicing basketball skills (layups and dribbling), working on upper-body muscle fitness, and increasing physical activity levels through basketball play

Objectives

- **Cognitive:** The student knows the proper techniques for a right- and left-sided layup and can identify the biceps and triceps as well as the exercises that strengthen each.
- **Psychomotor:** The student practices the layup and dribbling skills, using proper form and technique.
- **Affective:** The student cooperates with classmates in small-group activities.

Equipment and Facilities

- 18 cones, 6 hula hoops, 15 plastic bowling pins, 4 task cards, 1 roll of gym tape, whistle, basketball court and goals
- For every four students: one yellow tube, one green tube, one red tube
- For every two students: one 2-pound (1 kg) medicine ball, one 3-pound (1.4 kg) medicine ball, one 5-pound (2.3 kg) medicine ball
- For each student: one junior-size basketball, one 3-by-5-inch (8 by 13 cm) index card, one jump rope, two 2-pound (1 kg) and two 3-pound (1.4 kg) dumbbells

Safety Considerations

Check all equipment and facility surfaces for hazards. Create a sufficient buffer zone between the station activity and the gym wall. Ensure that students maintain proper spacing as they move through the obstacle course.

Set Induction (1 to 2 minutes)

Say: "Does anyone have a basketball goal at home or nearby at a local playground? This is a great way to stay active and practice the basketball skills you learn in physical education. The purpose of today's class is to practice skills that will help you play the game better so that you may enjoy basketball in school as well as at home with friends and family."

Procedures

Warm-Up (3 minutes)

Have students line up around the gym, each with a junior-size basketball. Have them jog twice around the gym floor, dribbling the basketball. When they have completed their second trip around the gym, have them enter the basketball dribble obstacle course (figure 7.1). Have students jog and dribble to each activity within the obstacle course. Remind them to move slowly and not to race.

Activity 1: Basketball Dribble Obstacle Course (7 minutes)

Area 1—Weave through cones: Have students dribble around the cones.

Area 2—Hoop dribble: Place hoops at least 3 feet (1 m) apart. Have students dribble the ball once in each hoop and alternate dribbling hands as they change sides.

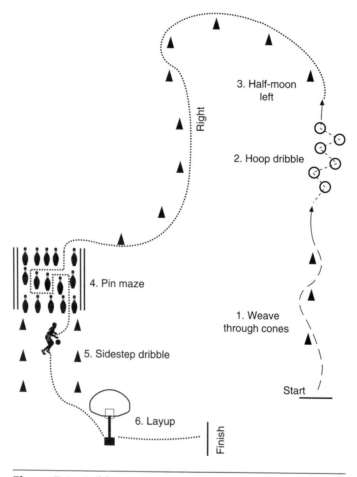

Figure 7.1 Dribbling obstacle course.

Area 3—Half-moon left then right; half-circle left, half-circle right: Have students dribble around the cones placed in a left curve and then around the right curve, using the hand farther from the cone.

Area 4—Pin maze: Set up 15 plastic bowling pins in a maze configuration. Make lines with tape on both sides to set the boundaries. Have students try to dribble through without knocking the pins over.

Area 5—Sidestep dribble: Set up large cones in a narrow pathway, approximately 15 yards (13.7 m) long and 2 yards (1.8 m) wide. Have students attempt to sidestep through the area while dribbling with the dominant hand.

Area 6—Layup: Have students attempt one right-handed layup.

Activity 2: Stations (16 minutes)

Divide students into four equal groups. Create task cards for each station that give skill and fitness instructions. Ask students to perform the exercises and skills with proper form for as long as they would like. Have them record the number of sets and repetitions, the weight, and the type of exercise they performed at each muscle fitness station on an index card.

Station 1—Layups (right side and left side): Have students form two even lines 20 feet (6 m) from the goal. One is a layup line, and one is a rebounding line. Have students practice dribbling while waiting for their turns.

Station 2—Quick-shot layup challenge: Give each student 30 seconds to make as many layups as possible. Have two students shooting at once. Allow them to position themselves on any side at any angle. Have students waiting for a turn participate in an individual rope jumping activity.

Station 3—Center layups with students in two lines: Have students in one line perform center layups from the line at the top of the key. Have those in the other line form a rebound line on the left side, angled to the basket. Remind students that they should shoot center layups just over the front of the rim. Using the backboard is optional.

Station 4—Muscle up: Have students select a cat group and the number of repetitions and sets they wish to perform. Give each cat group a task card that illustrates the biceps and triceps. Label and shade the two muscles to highlight them.

Jaguars: Use resistance tubes with color codes to denote various resistance levels (yellow = easy; green = medium; red = hard). Have students do arm curls (biceps) and arm extensions (triceps).

Cougars: Have students select from three weighted medicine balls (2, 3, or 5 lb, or 1, 1.4, or 2.3 kg) and choose a friend to toss the ball with. (See chapter 11 for specific activities.)

Mountain lions: Have students do push-ups, either bent-knee or straight-leg.

Bobcats: Have students do dumbbell arm curls (biceps) and arm extensions (triceps), using 1-, 2-, or 3-pound (0.5, 1, or 1.4 kg) weights.

Cool-Down (2 minutes)

Have students jog twice around the court and perform hamstring, quadriceps, calf, and arm-cross stretches.

Closure (2 minutes)

Emphasize the importance of basic skills to the game of basketball. Say: "Basketball is a game you can play for many years ahead, especially if you have a goal at home or at a nearby playground. If you would like to join a local basketball league (park district or community center team), I have the phone numbers and sign-up sheets. This would be a nice way to develop your basketball skills. Who can tell me what muscle the arm curls exercise? [Biceps.] How about the arm extensions? [Triceps.] It may not appear to be important, but arm strength *is* an important factor in the game of basketball. Who knows the professional basketball player LeBron James? Next time you see him play, look at the size of his biceps and triceps! Next week we'll learn the muscles of the legs."

SUMMARY

You can reform your physical education program by changing your approach to physical education curriculum planning. Use the level III sample yearly plan in this chapter as a model as you plan how you'll include health-related physical fitness in harmony with skill and sport activities throughout the year. Next, use the traditional fitness education lesson plan models as you plan fitness units. Remember, a fitness unit is a great way to kick off the school year, making it easier to integrate fitness throughout the year. Then you'll be all set to follow the fitness integration lesson plans as you strive to integrate physical activity, fitness activities, and concepts throughout your skill- and sport-related units. Adopt this new perspective on including physical activity and fitness concepts in your physical education curriculum, and your overall program is sure to reap great benefits. Keep in mind that for change to take place in our physical education programs, careful planning must be a major priority.

Teaching Health-Related Physical Fitness Concepts

> If you are planning for a year,
> sow rice; if you are planning
> for a decade, plant trees;
> if you are planning for a lifetime,
> educate people.
>
> —*Chinese proverb*

Now let's discuss a plan for teaching health-related fitness concepts and active lifestyles within your physical education classes. To help get you started, I'll give you models of practical learning activities for each developmental level. Then, in chapter 9 we'll extend our discussion of teaching health-related fitness concepts with a discussion of ways to collaborate with your partner, the classroom teacher.

As we discussed in chapter 3, knowledge is the foundation for teaching children the necessary skills and behaviors for an active lifestyle. Each major learning domain (cognitive, affective, and psychomotor) is important to a well-balanced, high-quality program of physical education. Try not to fall into the trap of neglecting the cognitive component of your curriculum to ensure ample physical activity. Instead, take the time to help children get the most out of new activities by teaching them the relevance of the exercises. Indeed, students need a strong background in health-related fitness concepts to understand the value and importance of physical activity. This understanding, in turn, will help them pursue active lifestyles long after they leave your program.

Just as you plan the physical activity components of your curriculum so that they occur in an appropriate sequence, you must plan the knowledge components. Use the Rainbow to Youth Fitness and Active Lifestyles (see chapter 3) to guide your selection of developmentally appropriate health-related fitness concepts. Begin with simple learning experiences that are associated with active fun and creativity found in developmental level I. Progress to level II, the level of concrete facts, with relevant examples and activities that apply to a concept. Finally, move your students to independence by giving them the opportunity to solve problems and make decisions, as characterized by developmental level III. Remember to teach health-related physical fitness concepts and active lifestyles throughout the school year, incorporating them into each unit of your curriculum.

STRATEGIES FOR TEACHING FITNESS CONCEPTS AND ACTIVE LIFESTYLES

You can incorporate concepts into a physical education class through five basic strategies:

- Set induction
- Teachable moments
- Class activities
- Closure
- Classroom sessions

Set Induction

The set induction involves introducing a health-related fitness concept and giving a concrete example to create interest in the lesson's objective. In other words, don't just tell students what they'll be learning; tell them why, relating the concept to the unit you are teaching.

Let's look at a set induction for level II. First, have students find their heart rates at rest. Then conduct a two- to three-minute soccer activity and have students take their heart rates once again. Explain why they are elevated. Say, "Soccer requires a lot of running." Then make the concept connection for the students. Say: "Soccer is a great exercise for your heart. To play any sport well, you must keep active and exercise on a regular basis. Today in class we will be practicing several skill drills that will call for a great deal of running. This will prepare you for soccer games and also keep your heart healthy."

You can also use set induction as a lecture to introduce a concept. Visual aids and props will help you make your point and add interest to the lesson. Be brief and succinct, limiting your mini-lecture to no more than three minutes at level I, four minutes at level II, and five minutes at level III.

Teachable Moments

A great way to incorporate fitness concepts is through teachable moments. With experience, you can pinpoint opportunities in class when students are ready to truly learn. This can be an exciting way to teach fitness concepts because most children find it difficult to sit and listen for more than a few minutes in physical education class!

For example, at level I, you may find a quiet, shy child laughing and having fun during a game activity. Reinforce this behavior by letting the student know how great it is to see him enjoying your physical education class. Then, ask him how he feels when he plays and moves with his friends. This type of interaction will begin to create a positive feeling within the student about physical activity. At level III during a basketball activity, you may notice a student who is constantly losing possession of the ball by having it taken from her hands. Through private instruction, show the student specific skill techniques to protect the ball. Then, help the student increase wrist and forearm strength (see chapter 11 for specific exercises). Explain that she needs muscle fitness to control the ball, rebound, and even shoot baskets. The student will appreciate your concern and feel supported.

Class Activities

Incorporate fitness concepts into the class activities themselves. Task cards can help introduce or reinforce a concept, such as muscle identification at a fitness station (see chapter 6). A game-related activity such as Jogging Through the Circulatory System will help children understand the cardiovascular benefits of exercise (see the description later in this chapter). Games can reinforce fitness concepts, such as learning food groups and healthy snacking, through active participation in games. Incorporate fitness education content in every class you teach throughout the school year.

Closure

During your lesson closure, don't simply summarize the activity: use this vital lesson component to teach or reinforce a fitness concept. You can briefly review the concept that you introduced during the set induction portion of the class. Or you can integrate a health-related fitness concept example with the specific sport or game activity the class just completed. At level III, you might remark: "OK, class, it seems everyone is making progress developing dribbling skills. Just remember to keep your head up so you can see the entire court. Also, remember to keep exercising because basketball does require a great deal of cardiorespiratory endurance. What types of cardiorespiratory endurance exercises would be helpful for the sport of basketball? Who can identify other types of exercise that may help basketball players?" In this example, you refer to the class objective—developing dribbling skills—as well as a fitness concept, cardiorespiratory endurance. Another technique is to have a varsity basketball player visit your classes to discuss her exercise routine and preseason and in-season workouts, and how the exercises helped her become an effective player.

Classroom Sessions

Sometimes, a few minutes during regular lessons in the gym are not enough for teaching fitness concepts. So occasionally hold a classroom session to prepare and motivate students for upcoming class activities. Take the opportunity to present a concept with added depth through a variety of classroom techniques and visual aids. DVDs, PowerPoint slides, interactive whiteboards, books, handouts, guest speakers, and cooperative learning groups can all help you expand on a concept. But avoid scheduling classroom sessions only when there is inclement weather or a facility problem. If you use fitness concept education as a replacement lesson, it will give students the message that concepts are only a filler when something goes wrong—rather than valuable instruction. Instead, schedule and plan these class periods at least one day per month—as another way to routinely incorporate fitness concepts into each unit of your physical education curriculum. (See also chapters 9 and 10 for ways to gain parent and classroom teacher collaboration to integrate concepts into other subjects and daily life.)

SCOPE AND SEQUENCE

Tables 8.1, 8.2, and 8.3 represent scope and sequence models for developmental levels I, II, and III. The tables include a sampling of titles and potential related concepts. The rest of this chapter describes many (but not all) of these examples. Each month focuses on a different health-related fitness concept. When you have a fitness concept theme planned, you can easily organize several relevant learning activities throughout the month to facilitate the primary concept. As children move through the developmental levels, you can repeat the primary concepts, adding appropriate information to advance student understanding of the concepts.

Study the following learning activity examples to get more ideas for incorporating fitness concepts into your physical education classes throughout the year. Think about how you can best include these concepts in your program.

Table 8.1 Developmental Level I Fitness Concepts: Physical Activity Is Fun

Title	Concepts	Month
Fit Is Fun	Promotion of an active lifestyle. Send the message: Physical activity is fun with friends and family.	September
Body Part Identification	Body part identification. Body awareness. Exercise is important for growth and development.	October
I'm Important—Inside and Out	Children learn to feel good about themselves and their bodies.	November
Physical Activity Is for Everybody	All children must be included in physical activity. Developing sensitivity to others.	December and January
Superpump	How the heart works, listen to the beat, the value of physical activity, types of exercise.	February
Safety First	Rest, exercise, safety precautions (e.g., heat, water breaks, appropriate footwear, traffic safety).	March
Fuel for Fitness	Eating healthy snacks, making good food choices, weight control.	April
Summer Physical Activity Fun	Swimming, summer fitness ideas, biking, swimming, hiking. Review of major concepts.	May and June

Table 8.2 Developmental Level II Fitness Concepts: The Best I Can Be

Title	Concepts	Month
Superstretch	Static stretching techniques, flexibility exercises.	September
Muscle Mania	Muscle identification and accompanying exercises.	October
The Heart Facts	Basic anatomy of the heart, circulation, effects of exercise, safety (e.g., exercising in heat).	November
Back to the Basics	Neck and back care, anatomy, posture, lifting techniques, dangerous exercises.	December and January
Heart-Healthy Habits	Eating and exercising for heart health.	February
Exercise Techniques	Critical components of exercise movements, proper body alignment, and positioning.	March
Body Systems	How physical activity affects various body systems: skeletal, muscular, nervous, circulatory, digestive, respiratory.	April
My Choice	Promoting student choice, decision making, and responsibility for physical activity.	May
Recreational Time	Selecting recreational activities to promote an active lifestyle (e.g., hiking, swimming, biking, individual and team sports, in-line skating).	June

Table 8.3 Developmental Level III Fitness Concepts: Let's Get Heart Smart

Title	Concepts	Month
Wellness	Wellness concepts: physical, mental, social, emotional, spiritual. Exercise techniques. Establishing a personal active lifestyle portfolio.	September
Heart Smart	Risk factors of heart disease, anatomy, good and bad cholesterol, heart-healthy foods, snacks. Effects of exercise on the heart.	October
Health-Related Physical Fitness Principles	Why fitness? Components of health-related fitness: FITT (frequency, intensity, time, type of exercise). Interval techniques, heart rate, training heart rate, recovery stages of a workout. Identifying, preventing, and treating injuries.	November and December
Exercise Science	Basic anatomy and physiology. Exercise foundations, specificity, progression, overload, regularity, train and maintain.	January and February
Food for Fitness	Heart-healthy nutrition for an active lifestyle. MyPlate guidelines, snacking ideas, food for fuel.	March
Family Physical Activity and Community Involvement	Parent and student homework assignments, family activities, parent and child learning experiences.	April
Personal Active Lifestyle Portfolio Review	Review of goal setting, designing an individualized program, logging eating and exercise patterns. Monitoring fitness levels. Reviewing main exercise concepts.	May
Fitness Forever	Understanding healthy fitness zones, techniques to improve scores, designing independent activity plans, making responsible lifestyle choices, planning for summer fitness.	June

DEVELOPMENTAL LEVEL I FITNESS CONCEPTS: PHYSICAL ACTIVITY IS FUN

Fit Is Fun

Concept

Students express why they like the physical activity in physical education class.

Equipment

Large colored banner paper, digital camera, tape, markers, magazines, and one pair of scissors per student

Activities

Select one grade level for this project. Take individual pictures of each student moving. Attach the pictures to a large piece of colored banner paper for each class. Label the banner Fit Is Fun. Ask your students to cut out pictures from magazines of active people to add to the collage. Then have students write a word or draw a picture under their photos about physical activity. Finally, have students write what they enjoy most about physical education. (You may have to write what younger students dictate or have older buddies do so.)

This is a great activity to do just before an open house at the beginning of the school year. Place the banners for each grade you select around the gym or in the hallway.

Body Part Identification

Concepts

Students practice body part identification and develop body awareness.

Equipment

Chalk, outdoor playground surface, large roll of colored banner paper, markers

Activities

Before class, draw a large figure of a child about 15 feet (4.6 m) long on the outdoor playground surface with colored chalk. Divide the class in half, making one group the Hearts and the second group the Smarts. Call out specific directions, such as, "Hearts walk to the knee; Smarts skip to the ears. Hearts gallop to the elbow; Smarts hop to the ankle." Remind students to stay in their own personal spaces.

Divide students into pairs. Give each pair a section of banner paper and a marker. Have each student trace the other lying on the paper. When they are finished, have them draw in the body parts they have learned. Then ask them to verbally identify various body parts.

I'm Important—Inside and Out

Concept

Students learn that as they become older, they grow and become stronger, enabling them to do advanced physical activities.

Equipment

5 to 6 feet (1.5 to 1.8 m) of cord, five clothespins, five socks of different sizes (infant to adult), five clothespins, five index cards, markers

Activities

Attach the cord along a wall or fasten it between two standards to resemble a clothesline. Hang five socks on the cord of various sizes from infant to adult. Attach an index card to each sock identifying the appropriate age. Have students identify the differences between the socks. They will notice the socks get bigger as the wearer gets older. Ask them to describe the changes people go through as they get older: physically, mentally, and socially. Ask: "What kind of physical activities can an infant, 6-year-old, 10-year-old, 16-year-old, and adult do? Why can't a 6-year-old run as fast or climb as well as a 10-year-old?" They will probably remark, "Because the 10-year-old is bigger." Reinforce that physical activity promotes growth and makes bones and muscles stronger. Ask, "What other body parts change in size as a person gets older?"

Physical Activity Is for Everybody

Concept

Students learn about the physical differences among people.

Equipment

Mats, playground equipment, playground balls

Activities

Ask students to think about the people in their neighborhood. Ask them to describe them: short, tall, dark, light, blonde hair, black hair, thin, heavy. Remind the class that people are different and that is a wonderful, natural part of life. Say: "Just as people are different looking—they also have different physical abilities. Just think about our class; some are strong, fast, or quick, and some are graceful and very coordinated. Over the next few minutes, think about what you do best and practice that activity or exercise." After a few minutes, ask the students one by one to demonstrate and explain what they do best.

Each student should be guided to a certain physical ability. For example, a student with a weight problem may be able to exercise with the heavy resistance bands or may be powerful enough to pick up a tumbling mat. The student who may be unskilled may be very flexible. A student confined to a wheelchair may perform arm exercises. At the end of the activity, emphasize that exercise, games, and sports are for everybody. Some students have certain abilities, but all students have their own personal strengths.

Safety First

Concepts

Students learn about exercise breaks, the use of water during exercise, and traffic safety.

Equipment

15 to 20 cones, one medium-sized hoop for each student, paper stop signs

Activities

Plot a simple roadway course on your gym floor or outdoor facility. Use cones to create driving lanes, and place stop signs at some intersections. Provide each driver with a medium-sized hoop to use as a steering wheel. Have students tell you what type of car they are driving (give them hints: truck, jeep, van, and so on).

Send students through the course four at a time. Students may only jog, not sprint, to pass other students or to go in reverse. When they come to a stop sign, they must make a full stop and then look left-right-left.

Set up a water station to allow the automobiles to cool off and rest. Remind students: "Everyone needs water and rest periods when they exercise to be safe, especially in hot weather." Teach and reinforce personal safety: allow several students to be pedestrians crossing at an intersection. Students must look left-right-left for oncoming automobiles.

DEVELOPMENTAL LEVEL II FITNESS CONCEPTS: THE BEST I CAN BE

Superstretch

Concepts

Students recognize that flexibility is the range of motion of a joint. Stretching prevents muscle and connective tissue injuries, improves the range of motion to fully benefit from the activity, and prevents muscle soreness that overextension can cause.

Equipment

1 pound (0.5 kg) of uncooked spaghetti, 1 pound (0.5 kg) of cooked spaghetti, one tennis ball (kept warm), one tennis ball (from freezer)

Activities

Explain the need for warming up before physical activity. Say: "We need to raise the temperature of our muscles before stretching through a couple of minutes of large-muscle activity such as jogging or brisk walking. A warmed muscle is less likely to become injured because it takes more force and stretching to tear the muscle. Experts now believe that to improve flexibility, we may be better off stretching directly after an exercise or activity session because the muscles are warm and circulation is increased." Give examples of typical activities such as Little League games, physical education class, housework, and gardening. Then, demonstrate the difference between warm and cold muscles. Hold up 1 pound (0.5 kg) of uncooked spaghetti, which represents a group of cold muscle fibers. Remark that the muscle fibers are cool, stiff, and brittle, limiting any movement. Now hold up 1 pound (0.5 kg) of cooked spaghetti. Show the class how warm and flexible muscles can move and bend more freely.

Demonstrate the same concept with two tennis balls. First, bounce the warm ball. Ask the class to notice how high it bounces. Next, bounce the frozen ball. Reinforce the difference in performance between the two tennis balls.

Have students practice a typical warm-up:

- ◆ Walking in a large circle (30 seconds)
- ◆ Walking with long strides (30 seconds)
- ◆ Walking briskly (30 seconds)
- ◆ Skipping (30 seconds)
- ◆ Sidestepping (30 seconds)
- ◆ Jogging slowly (30 seconds)

Muscle Mania

Concepts

Students practice muscle identification, learn the difference between muscle contraction and relaxation, and learn specific exercises for arm muscles.

Equipment

One long balloon, poster board for task card, markers, several exercise toners (rubberized resistance equipment)

Activities

Ask students to extend their arms with their palms facing the ceiling. Show the class where the biceps is located. Have students place the opposite hand across the muscle. Remark that the muscle appears flat. Now ask them to "make a muscle," keeping the hand on the biceps muscle. As the muscle pops up, explain that the muscle is contracting.

Blow up the long balloon. Grab both ends and stretch it. Show the class that the balloon becomes *elongated* (stretched out) just like a muscle when it is relaxed. Then explain the concept that a muscle in a *contracted* state will shorten and become wider. Tell students that the balloon is now going to contract. Push gently from both ends to make the balloon come back slightly. Have students describe why the balloon becomes wider (Meeks and Heit 2010).

Design a fitness station with muscle fitness for the arms as its primary focus. Develop a task card with the picture of the entire arm illustrating the biceps. Color the biceps red and label it. Describe the arm curl movement using the exercise toner (see chapter 11) and illustrate it on the task card. Ask students to perform the arm curl three to five times with the resistance toner of their choice.

The Heart Facts I

Concept

Students learn the benefits of good circulation: exercise increases blood flow throughout the body and helps keep the veins and arteries from clogging.

Equipment

Two rubber tubes about 2 feet (0.6 m) long, small pieces of modeling clay, 2 cups (480 ml) of cranberry juice, gym tape, hula hoops, posters, markers, cones, two boxes, tennis balls, paper balls

Activities

Hold up two pieces of rubber tubing approximately 2 feet (0.6 m) long. Tell students, "The tubes represent arteries, which carry blood from the heart." Fill one tube with a few pieces of modeling clay and keep the other clear. Pour a cup of cranberry juice through the clear tube. Ask, "See how easily the juice passes through?" Now, pour a cup of juice through the tube with modeling clay. The juice will trickle. Explain: "Exercise may help keep your arteries clear so that blood can get to various parts of your body. Eating fatty foods (e.g., cheeseburgers, ice cream) and not getting enough exercise can clog your arteries. What other fatty foods might clog your arteries?"

Jogging Through the Circulatory System: Have students act as the blood traveling through the heart, arteries, and veins (see figure 8.1). Explain: "The arteries and veins are the one-way highways that the blood travels through." Remind students of the following concepts: "Arteries carry blood away from the heart; veins carry blood to the heart. The blood carries oxygen to the working parts of the body. As you jog through the lungs, pick up oxygen (tennis balls) and deposit (leave) carbon dioxide (paper balls). As you enter the working parts of the body, deposit the oxygen and pick up the carbon dioxide. Jog throughout the system following the red arrows on the gym floor. Read the signs that tell you the various areas of the circulatory system. Bright red signs mark the parts of the system with oxygen. Light brown signs mark the parts without oxygen" (Kern 1987; Ratliffe and Ratliffe 1994). Figure 8.2 shows the anatomy of the heart.

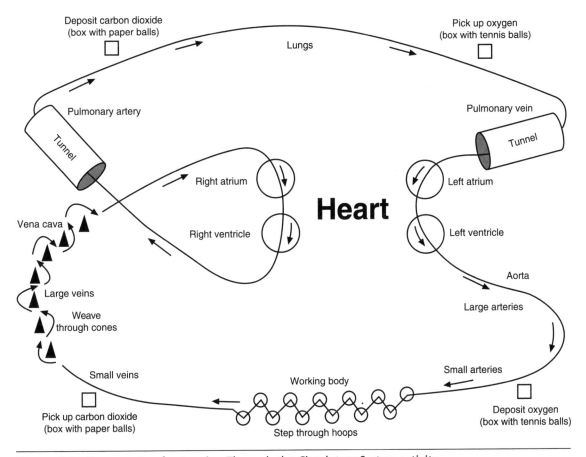

Figure 8.1 Course setup for Jogging Through the Circulatory System activity.

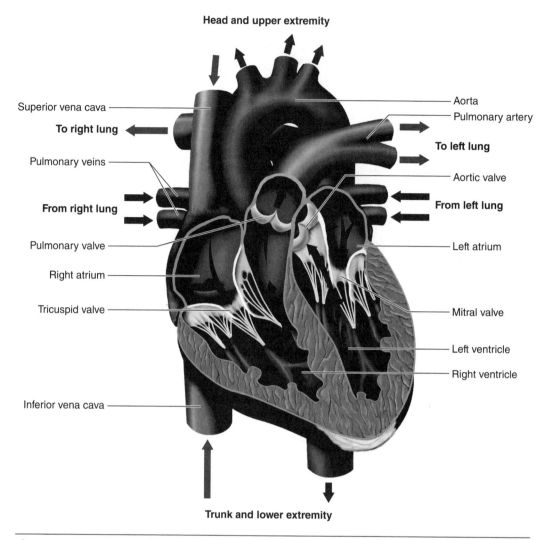

Head and upper extremity

Superior vena cava

Aorta

Pulmonary artery

To right lung

To left lung

Pulmonary veins

Aortic valve

From right lung

From left lung

Pulmonary valve

Left atrium

Right atrium

Tricuspid valve

Mitral valve

Left ventricle

Right ventricle

Inferior vena cava

Trunk and lower extremity

Figure 8.2 Anatomy of the heart.

Reprinted, by permission, from National Strength and Conditioning Association, 2008, Structure and function of the muscular, cardiovascular, and respiratory systems, by G.R. Hunter and R.T. Harris. In *Essentials of strength training and conditioning*, edited by T.R. Baechle and R.W. Earle (Champaign, IL: Human Kinetics), 14.

The Heart Facts II

Concepts

Students explore safety at home, especially the warning signs of a heart attack, and learn that exercise may prevent heart disease.

Equipment

Six cones

Activities

Discuss with students that when there is an emergency at home, they should call 911, stay on the phone, and give the operator specific information, such as their name and address and the situation.

Review the warning signs that tell us someone is having a heart attack or is very ill:

- Shortness of breath
- Clutching the left side of the chest
- Pain down the left arm
- Dizziness
- Passed out

Heart Alert: Reinforce your discussions with this active game. Mark boundaries in the gym with cones. Select two "its" who will be taggers. Explain: "At the signal 'Go!' the its try to tag the rest of you. The first time a student gets tagged, he grabs his chest. The second time, he grabs his left arm. The third time, he grabs his throat and yells 'Heart alert! Heart alert!' Then another student runs over to him, and they both perform 10 power jumps (jumping straight up as high as possible). After doing the power jumps, the student who had the heart alert is symptom-free. But the other student keeps any symptoms he already had from being tagged earlier. While the two students are exercising, they are safe from being tagged." Rotate the its every two minutes using a random selection process such as picking names from a hat.

Back to the Basics

Concepts

Students learn about back anatomy and proper posture, specifically that the vertebral bones and disks are the supportive columns and cushions for the entire upper body, and that correct posture is important for a healthy back.

Equipment

Four hockey pucks, table, three jelly donuts, 5.5-foot (1.7 m) piece of white string per small group, one small 3- to 5-pound (1.4 to 2.3 kg) dumbbell

Activities

Ask the students in class to reach back and feel the bones in their backs. Then, show them a stack of four hockey pucks on a table. Explain: "When you run or jump, the pucks (bones) come together. To prevent the bones from compressing (pushing) into each other, a soft jelly-like substance called a disk is located between each pair of bones." Now place the jelly donuts between the hockey pucks. Say: "The jelly donuts represent disks. One way to prevent injury to the disks (so that they don't get stressed by the bones) is to have good posture. If there is too much stress on the disks, they might become weak and leak fluid (jelly) or become displaced, placing undue stress on the nerves." Press on the vertebrae (hockey pucks) and show students how the disks (jelly) could leak and move out of alignment. Explain that this is why we learn how to do the exercises correctly—so we don't place too much stress on our necks or backs.

Poor posture can lead to backaches. Flexibility and strong neck and back muscles are very important to good posture. (See chapter 11 for specific exercises.) Tie a weight to a piece of white string that is as long as the students are tall. In pairs or small groups of three or four, have one student hold the string just above the head of another student who is standing sideways. Or, you may want to assess each student individually. Either way, with the string hanging straight along the side of the student, check the following posture points:

- Is the head straight up or does it lean forward or backward?
- Are the upper back and shoulders even like the string or curved forward or backward?
- Are the hips even with the string, or are they tilting forward or backward?

Report any significant imbalances to the school nurse and parents. You may want to assess each student individually to avoid any embarrassment.

Body Systems

Concept

Students explore the effects of exercise on the digestive system.

Equipment

One 26-foot (8 m) piece of white yarn

Activities

Crumble the yarn against your body where the intestines are located. Explain: "The yarn represents the intestines. A section of the intestines called the small intestines is the part through which food is absorbed into the bloodstream. The other section is called the large intestines, where food is released from the body." Have two children hold the yarn in a straight line. Ask students to guess the length of the small and large intestines (large intestines = 5 feet [1.5 m] long, small intestines = 21 feet [6.4 m] long).

Explain that active play and vigorous exercise help us digest our food properly by allowing the blood to flow evenly so that the intestines can work better. Remind students that after a complete meal, they should wait at least one hour before participating in vigorous physical activity. The digestive system needs the blood flow for a period of time to process the food; exercise would interrupt this and may cause nausea. Ask, "What exercises would help improve digestion?" [Walking, jogging, biking, swimming, hiking, active games, any continuous large muscle activity.] Explain to students that one of the reasons you ask them to do curl-ups is to strengthen the abdominal muscles, the supportive area of the intestines. Strong abdominal muscles protect the digestive system and help keep the intestines in the right place so that they can digest properly. Say: "If the abdominal muscles are flabby and weak, the intestines will move lower and not work as well. Also, too much fat between the organs of the body causes digestion problems. This is why some adults have stomachaches."

DEVELOPMENTAL LEVEL III FITNESS CONCEPTS: LET'S GET HEART SMART

Wellness

Concepts

Students consider accepting friends for who they are, not what they look like, and recognize that games and sports are a good way to enjoy old friends and an opportunity to make new friends.

Equipment

One roll of yarn, one book with a plain cover, one book with a colorful cover and blank pages, one large parachute

Activities

Show the class two books, a plain book and a colorful, fancy book. Ask, "Which book do you like the best? Why?" (Most students will prefer the colorful book.) Now show them what is inside the fancy book: nothing but blank sheets of paper. Now explain to them that the plain book is an important work of a famous author. Explain: "Just because someone is a little heavy or wears glasses does not make them less of a person. That's just the outside. What really counts is what's on the inside." Ask: "Have you heard the expressions 'Beauty is only skin deep' or 'You can't judge a book by its cover'? These old expressions hold true even today!"

Friendship Knots

Have students sit in a large circle. Take a roll of yarn, tie it around your index finger, and state a characteristic that you like in friends—for example, honesty. Now pass the yarn around the circle and have each student tie a knot around his or her index finger and state a positive characteristic he or she values. When everyone has had a chance, ask the class what the yarn has done. [It connects us.] Explain to the group that classes in school should work together as teams, help each other, and develop close friendships.

Parachute Jog

Have each student grasp the parachute with the inside hand. Explain that they will be going on a class jog up to the large tree and back. Say, "Some in class are faster runners, but in this activity, everyone has to stay together as a class." Jog with the class the first time you introduce this activity, reinforcing working as a team and some of the positive characteristics mentioned earlier in the class.

Team Concept

Hold up a poster with the word TEAM written on it. On the back of the poster show the class what TEAM stands for: Together Everyone Achieves More. Ask students to describe the benefits of teamwork when they play a game or team sport. Ask them to name a popular professional team that plays well together and is a good example of good sporting behavior. Another example of teamwork is a family working together to help with routine chores and responsibilities around the house.

Components of Health-Related Physical Fitness Principles

Concepts

Students learn that the components of health-related physical fitness are cardiorespiratory endurance, muscle fitness, flexibility, and body composition, and that they can develop each component by incorporating certain exercises into a balanced physical activity plan.

Equipment

Four boxes, each labeled as a fitness component (cardiorespiratory endurance, muscle fitness, flexibility, and body composition) and colorfully decorated; 20 index cards, each labeled with an activity or food (e.g., 1-5 push-ups, 1-5 curl-ups, jog in place, frozen yogurt, sit-and-reach)

Activities

Organize a learning station for a small group of students. Set up the four fitness component boxes. Offer task cards face down to students so that they can each select one. Have them turn their cards over, perform the activities on the cards, and then place them in the appropriate fitness component boxes. Have at least two cards for each member of the group so that students can repeat the process. When the students are finished, go over to the boxes and check the cards. If you find mistakes, don't ask who placed them incorrectly. Simply reinforce the correct answers.

Health-Related Physical Fitness Principles: Exercise Intensity

Concepts

Students learn that exercise intensity refers to how vigorous an activity must be to develop the specific area of fitness; that they might, at times, exercise at a level that is too high for their individual needs; and that higher levels can become dangerous and often result in muscle injury.

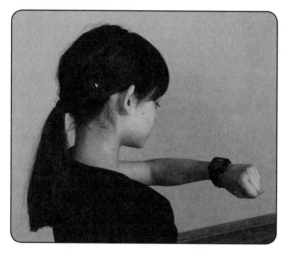

Figure 8.3 A wristwatch monitor can measure heart rate.

Equipment

Paper and pencil for each student; heart rate monitor for each student if possible (if not, students can share and take turns over the next few class meetings)

Activities

Say: "To have a safe, productive physical activity session, you should monitor your intensity level. Knowing how your body responds to activity can also help you plan your individual fitness program. One way to monitor cardiorespiratory endurance is by checking your heart rate." (See the description of taking a pulse in chapter 4.)

Have students calculate their own heart rates during exercise. Have them work in pairs to check and record heart rates. Also, have a few students wear heart rate monitors or wristwatch monitors (figure 8.3) and download their heart rates during the three activity segments.

Provide students with three levels of physical activity during your class, each lasting about five minutes. Start off with a low-level activity such as moderate walking, having a catch with a partner, or basic calisthenics. Then have them check their heart rates and record them.

Next, provide the class with a moderate-level activity such as skipping, jogging at a moderate pace, or a soccer dribbling skill drill. Then have them check their heart rates and record them.

Finally, have students perform a high-level activity such as running, playing three-on-three basketball, or playing a highly active tag game. Then have them check their heart rates and record them.

Have students graph the results and show how different physical activities represent different levels of intensity as indicated by their three levels of heart rate.

Health-Related Physical Fitness Principles: Heart Rate Recovery

Concept

Students learn that their heart rates will increase less during exercise and will return to a normal level faster after exercise if they lead active lives.

Equipment

Stopwatch, one bench (or box) 8 inches (20.3 cm) from ground level for each student, one chair (or bench) for each student (optional: metronome)

Activities

(*Caution:* Students who have experienced knee problems should not participate in this assessment.) This is a baseline assessment to teach students the concept of heart rate recovery. Begin with three to five minutes of warm-up. Then say: "At the signal 'Begin!' start with your left foot and step up on the box (or bench); then step down again (four count: left-right-up, left-right-down). Continue stepping up and down, alternating feet for three consecutive minutes at a rate of 24 steps per minute (two steps every five seconds)." A metronome can help maintain the rhythm, or students can count in unison. Stop at the three-minute mark, and have the students sit on their chairs (or on benches). At exactly one minute after completing the test, have the students take their pulses for 30 seconds, and then multiply by two to obtain a one-minute heart rate recovery score.

Average heart rate recovery scores for boys ages 10 to 19 should be 72 to 88 beats per minute. Girls the same age should range from 82 to 96 beats per minute. Heart rates above these levels could mean that a student needs to increase physical activity to enhance cardiorespiratory endurance. Scores closer to the lower end may indicate higher levels of cardiorespiratory endurance and heart rate recovery. Use these data to help students, not to grade or categorize them.

If you decide to retest periodically, remember to assess under the same conditions, equipment, time of day, exact warm-up routine, and test procedures. Heart rates vary in most people, so use this assessment as a way to teach the concept of heart rate recovery. *Never* use the results to label children or use this as a training activity.

Exercise Science: Overload Principle

Concepts

Students learn about the overload principle—that to improve cardiorespiratory and muscle fitness, they must exercise at higher-than-normal levels. This involves working against increased resistance to progressively make advances in physical development.

Equipment

1 pound (0.5 kg) of regular spaghetti, 1 pound (0.5 kg) of angel hair pasta, one exercise tube with handles for every two students (rubberized tubing), one resistance band for each student

Activities

Divide the students into pairs and have one partner stand behind the other. Have the front partner place an exercise tube around his waist and the back partner hold the rubber tubing by the handles, applying light resistance (see figure 8.4). Tell both partners to walk briskly in the same direction. Point out that the front partner should experience how much more difficult it is to walk against the resistance of the band. Reverse roles and repeat. The resistance provides an overload to the normal walking movement.

Hold up 1 pound (0.5 kg) of regular spaghetti. Explain: "Each piece of spaghetti represents a muscle fiber, and many fibers make up the muscle. When you increase the resistance on a muscle, the muscle fibers grow thicker." Hold up the pound of angel hair spaghetti. Remark, "This is how the muscle fibers look before you begin a resistance program for muscular fitness." Now hold up the regular spaghetti. Say, "The fibers (just like the spaghetti) become larger when you progressively increase the resistance in your muscle fitness strength exercises." This will begin to become more evident at the onset of puberty—and more so in boys as a result of increased testosterone levels.

Explain to the class that lifting weights or using the exercise machines may be dangerous without the supervision of a trained instructor. Give examples of how students may safely practice this principle by slightly increasing their jogging distance, doing two more push-ups with open hands, or using the next color level of the rubberized resistance exercise toners or bands.

Have students do several leg kicks from a standing position in front, back, and to the side; do marching steps; and do cross-kicking. Now have them use a resistance band suited for their levels. Do the same leg movement exercises. (See chapter 11 for instructions.) Ask, "How does the added resistance feel on your leg muscles?" [Harder, heavier.] Explain: "This resistance will build muscle fitness in the particular muscle group you exercise."

Figure 8.4 Resistance walking.

Food for Fitness

Concepts

Students learn that eating according to the MyPlate model can limit the fat, sodium, and sugar in their diets and create a balance of vegetables, fruits, grains, protein, and dairy. Eating properly will increase physical performance and energy levels and will help control weight.

Equipment

One MyPlate image for each student, four cones, four paper grocery bags, pictures of various food groups on a different color paper for each bag, chalk or gym tape, one large MyPlate image drawn on the gym floor or outdoor surface as shown in figure 4.3 on p. 43 (You can print the MyPlate image at www.ChooseMyPlate.gov.)

Activities

Hand out copies of the MyPlate image to each student. Explain the importance of balance in their diet. Discuss how we can increase energy levels by eating more calories from bread, pasta, fruits, and vegetables than we can with foods with empty calories and high sugar content, such as chocolate cake, ice cream, and candy bars. Remind students to use their nutrition log (in their personal active lifestyle portfolios) to keep track of their daily eating (see appendix A).

Plate Power: Before class, paste pictures of various foods on colored paper. Have the students help cut out pictures from magazines in previous classes, reinforcing a nutritional concept while saving you time. Use four different colors of paper so that each team will have its own color. Fill a paper grocery bag with pictures of food for each team. Position a large MyPlate image on the gym floor and label the sections.

Divide the class into four groups. Give each team one grocery bag. Place the four teams in lines 25 yards (23 m) from the MyPlate image. Use a cone to mark where each team should line up. Say: "At the signal 'Go!' the first student from each team reaches down and grabs a food picture; then runs to the place on the plate where it belongs. Students then run back, give high fives to the next students in line, who go next." The first team to finish is not the winner. (Remind students of this before they do the activity.)

Go over to the plate and check the food pictures placed on the image sections by matching the color to the team. Have the entire class walk to the plate and give corrective feedback. Competition is not the purpose of this game. On occasion, you may see what groups are getting the most correct responses. Say, "And you thought this was another typical relay race!"

SUMMARY

We must teach more health-related physical fitness content in our physical education programs so that our students will have the knowledge they need to lead healthy, active lives. But how do you find the time without reducing physical activity time? A well-designed curriculum plan is the answer, one that includes important concepts planned in sequence each year throughout the elementary school experience. Use the examples of a yearly plan for each developmental level and the sample learning activities as models of how to incorporate fitness education into your program without sacrificing precious physical activity time.

Encouraging children to achieve their personal fitness goals and to increase their physical activity levels are very important objectives in a fitness education program. I cannot stress enough, however, that knowing why they are doing certain activities is just as valuable as doing the activities themselves. Most important, however, is the fact that knowledge builds a foundation for understanding and valuing health-related fitness. This, in turn, increases the probability that your students will develop healthy and active long-term behaviors. So integrate fitness education into your program throughout the year, as you hope your students will integrate fitness and physical activity into their lives for many years ahead.

Collaborating With the Classroom Teacher

> Reading furnishes our minds
> only with materials of knowledge;
> it is thinking that makes
> what we read ours.
>
> —*John Locke*

Most of us simply do not have enough time to accomplish the cognitive, affective, and psychomotor objectives of a yearly physical education curriculum. Classroom teachers at the elementary school level can be important allies in helping you reach your program goals. Certainly, if you intend to develop positive long-term attitudes toward physical activity in your students, then the classroom teacher should become a member of your team (Virgilio 1996).

This chapter provides practical strategies for developing a cooperative relationship with the classroom teacher and a sample of a cardiovascular health thematic unit with instructional activities for developmental level II to help you begin your collaborative relationship. This interdisciplinary unit incorporates content around a major theme into several subject areas. The chapter also offers examples of how to integrate health-related physical fitness concepts into the subject matter content areas of the classroom at other levels as well.

INTERACTING WITH THE CLASSROOM TEACHER

Classroom teachers serve as excellent role models for young children and have extraordinary potential as change agents. With the exception of family members, few people have more influence on the health of children than elementary teachers. As a former elementary physical educator, I have worked with hundreds of elementary classroom teachers at many public schools, and as a teacher educator, I have interacted with thousands more through professional conferences, seminars, and workshops. In general, I have found elementary classroom teachers to be caring people, sensitive to the needs of their students, and receptive to new ideas. Classroom teachers become especially interested in physical education objectives when they can clearly see the educational as well as the health benefits for the students in their classrooms.

The responsibility for establishing a close relationship with the classroom teacher is yours; you must initiate the interaction. Classroom teachers are often not familiar with the subject of health-related physical fitness. As the authority, they would expect you to provide the leadership in this area, educating both the students and the faculty about the benefits of an active, healthy lifestyle.

Administrative Support

To ensure success, gain the administrative support of the principal and school health or wellness committee. Arrange a private meeting with the principal to discuss your plans to include classroom teachers in your endeavors to meet your curriculum goals. Reinforce the belief that the health and well-being of the students should be a schoolwide goal shared by the entire school and community. Once you have gained the principal's support, request to meet with the school's health or wellness committee.

Identifying Your Role

Physical education specialists are often isolated from the school curriculum and classroom teachers simply because theirs is considered a special subject. Physical educators also perceive their roles in the school as separate or different because the medium for student learning is through the physical, not through the intellectual. This traditional stereotype can inhibit collaboration. Thus, as a physical educator, you must see yourself as a true professional and a valuable member of the school community. When you perceive yourself in this manner, others will too!

COMMUNICATION STRATEGIES

As with parents and the community, communication is the key to establishing a good relationship with classroom teachers. Follow the strategies in the following sections to open the channels of communication.

Schoolwide Health Committee

Establish a schoolwide health committee consisting of several representatives from the school and community. The ideal committee consists of two classroom teachers (one each from the primary and intermediate grade levels), the lunch director, the guidance counselor or school psychologist, a parent, and a member of the community (perhaps a senior citizen). Have the committee meet every month or so to discuss any health issues, assessment plans, or special projects, such as a health fair. Good communication through committee meetings helps promote a multidisciplinary team approach.

Newsletter

The schoolwide health newsletter (discussed in chapter 10) shouldn't be only for parents and students. Classroom teachers can also benefit from the health and fitness information. In addition, they'll enjoy your reports of special fitness events as much as everyone else. Insert an extra page directed solely at them that describes specific activities to help integrate health-related concepts into the classroom and announces activities that students in various grades are participating in during physical education (Virgilio and Berenson 1988).

Meeting With Grade Level Leaders

Ask to attend a grade level leader meeting. At this meeting, discuss your desire to work closely with the faculty. Provide each grade level with a copy of the scope and sequence of health-related fitness concepts that you intend to cover during the year (see tables 8.1 through 8.3 for examples). Then simply ask for their help. Allow teachers to brainstorm. They will feel more enthusiastic about your plans when they know you value their input.

Faculty Meetings

Establish a physical education report as a segment for each general faculty meeting. Report upcoming events and special projects, and announce updates of the curriculum integration approach using specific examples. This is a sure-fire technique to keep everyone informed as you take advantage of this opportunity to motivate teachers who have yet to participate in your new curriculum strategy.

E-Mail

Send updates, announcements, and any other pertinent news by e-mail to the faculty on a regular basis. E-mails can be sent to parent groups as well, to inform the school community of upcoming physical education events. Create your own stationery by developing a letterhead with graphics on your computer.

School Website

Develop a web page on your school's website. You can include updates about the curriculum for each grade level and dates of schoolwide events, and even upload photos of students participating in a variety of your physical education classes. (Parents should grant permission to publish photos of their children—last names are rarely used. Check with the principal before posting any photos.) Photo galleries are easy to insert onto web pages and help to create excitement about your program.

Education

Focus your efforts to educate the faculty on two specific areas: health-related fitness content and school curriculum materials. Teachers need to understand what health-related physical fitness is all about. Remember the wellness room we discussed in chapter 2? Use this as a fun way to reach and educate your colleagues. In addition, provide the instructional materials and learning activities you want them to use in the classroom curriculum.

Health-Related Fitness Content

You need to educate the faculty and staff about the benefits of exercise, basic fitness principles, cardiovascular health, wellness concepts, and the like. Also helpful is establishing an exercise class for the teachers and staff in addition to increasing their knowledge of physical fitness. The following are strategies for educating the elementary classroom teachers, staff, and administrators:

- **Fitness class for teachers:** Teach a fitness class after school. Include aerobics, resistance training, and flexibility. For each class, include a health concept, such as lowering your cholesterol or how to have a healthy back, as well as at least 20 minutes of physical activity. This is a great opportunity to show teachers how they can learn through the physical—as their students do. It is also a superb way to get to know your faculty better and establish deeper professional relationships.
- **In-service workshops:** Give in-service workshops to the faculty and staff. The county or school district or a teacher center may sponsor this workshop and award in-service credit as an incentive for all teachers to attend and become better informed. Enlist the help of physical education professors at a nearby university.
- **Guest speakers:** Schedule guest speakers in the areas of health and fitness to speak at a faculty meeting. Speakers may also be scheduled during early bird sessions before school, lunchtime seminars, or evening PTA meetings (see chapter 10).
- **Health fair:** Teachers can benefit alongside parents and students from information and activities presented at a schoolwide health fair (see chapter 10). Consider asking the students in each grade level to design a health station. Request assistance from a local university, the local chapter of the American Heart Association, or a local hospital.
- **Health and fitness reading area:** If you're not able to do so in a teacher–parent wellness room, designate an area in the school library, faculty cafeteria, or curriculum lab to give teachers an opportunity to read or check out various articles, brochures, and books related to general health.

Curriculum Materials

A hands-on in-service workshop or faculty meeting is the ideal setting to introduce curriculum materials to teachers. You may design your own classroom activities, use published material, or pull together a combination of materials that will best match your curriculum goals. This book would make an ideal resource for classroom teachers.

Remember, however, to always keep the classroom learning activities simple, concise, and easy to follow. If the content is too technical, teachers will not feel comfortable using this new curriculum approach. Moreover, to match the content and concepts being taught in physical education with classroom instruction, you will need to become aware of the curriculum guidelines on each grade level for other subject areas.

Once classroom teachers recognize the value of health in their own lives and the important role it plays in the overall development of children, they will become important allies in your efforts. So let's get down to business and study sample thematic units, health-related physical fitness classroom activities, and practical strategies you can use to help, support, and guide the classroom teacher. Remember: You are the key!

THEMATIC UNITS: AN APPROACH TO INTEGRATED LEARNING

The thematic unit has always been recognized as an exciting and challenging approach to learning at the elementary school level. The basic notion of thematic units is that learning should be integrated, multidimensional, and multidisciplinary. Simply put, a thematic approach provides students with a series of lessons on a particular topic that are interesting, meaningful, and an important part of the curriculum at any grade level (e.g., dinosaurs, ocean life, ecology, chemistry, nutrition, cardiovascular health). It also integrates a variety of subject areas, such as language arts, science, math, and art.

When designing thematic units, teachers take into consideration the needs, interests, and developmental levels of their students. Furthermore, they try to incorporate a selection of children's literature and a number of instructional resources to establish connections across the curriculum. Thematic units are planned to include a number of hands-on activities with many opportunities for decision making and critical thinking.

The use of thematic units also offers the classroom teacher a unique way of differentiating the instruction for students in the classroom. Teachers use thematic units to meet the individual needs of their students by providing a wide variety of learning activities on various instructional levels. By doing so, each student can achieve a degree of success while everyone is learning the new concept or idea. Well-designed thematic units can accomplish the following educational goals:

- Increase the effective use of technology
- Integrate word processing skills into creative activities
- Control safe Internet access for students
- Compact the curriculum
- Demonstrate the interdisciplinary nature of learning
- Enhance student interest in learning
- Consider alternative assessment strategies
- Increase collaborative and cooperative learning activities

Thematic units enable the classroom teacher to provide students with varying attitudes and skill and knowledge levels with a wide variety of resources both in and out of the classroom. According to Meinbach, Fredericks, and Rothlein (2000), using thematic units offers numerous advantages. They refer to these advantages as the seven Cs:

1. **Contact:** Thematic units break the boundaries of the clock and schedules. This approach creates an open feeling to learning. The blocked time periods of traditional education, which separate one subject from another, may limit learning opportunities and motivation.

2. **Coherence:** Thematic units send children the message that learning is not an isolated activity: it takes place continuously and throughout one's life.

3. **Context:** Learning must have a purpose. Many times children study or read merely because they are told to or because the content will be on a test. Thematic units help children identify the meaning and context of the content as they apply the experiences to the real world.

4. **Connections:** Thematic units help children understand the relationships among subject areas, such as between math and language arts or between science and physical education. This approach offers opportunities to make connections among the facts in various subject areas, thereby enhancing comprehension and opening the door for more meaningful learning in all subject areas.

5. **Choices:** Thematic units give students a sense of ownership of their educational time. Instead of telling students what they should learn, ask them what they would enjoy learning and how they would like to learn it. When students believe that they have made important choices, they will be more active and enthusiastic learners.

6. **Cognitive expansion:** Children inherently learn at the level at which they are taught. If you ask a majority of low-level or rote memory types of questions, students will approach learning in the same manner.

The purpose of thematic units is to have children investigate, discover, and explore with very few predetermined answers. In fact, you can even ask children to develop their own questions; then solve the problem or research the answers on their own.

7. **Cooperation:** Learning can be enhanced by interacting with peers. Children need experiences working as a team rather than as competitors for grades. Thematic units create a purpose for cooperative learning groups when they emphasize group, rather than individual, achievement.

CARDIOVASCULAR HEALTH: A THEMATIC UNIT

The following is an example of a thematic unit for developmental level II. Enlist classroom teachers' support by discussing with them how vital the study of cardiovascular health is to your program and how important it is to have students learn about health as a schoolwide goal. Explain to them that this thematic unit will help them integrate curriculum areas, providing the students with a wide range of activities and opportunities to enhance their learning across the curriculum.

When introducing the unit on cardiovascular health, suggest that the teacher begin by assessing what the students know about the topic and what they want to learn about the topic. Although the classroom teacher may have a clear direction of what content to plan for the unit, as illustrated in the cardiovascular health curriculum web (see figure 9.1), they must be flexible and willing to use student ideas and interests to enhance the learning experience.

Brainstorming, making lists of what students know and what questions they want to investigate, is a good method to use. At the end of the unit, ask the classroom teacher to have the students list what they have learned about the

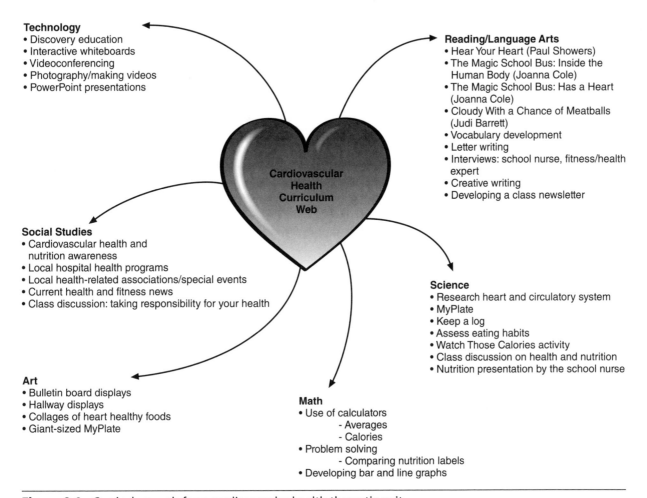

Figure 9.1 Curriculum web for a cardiovascular health thematic unit.

topic. Making and displaying these lists in the classroom are effective techniques for reinforcing the learning objectives, empowering children by allowing them to make decisions within the context of the theme.

The classroom teacher can plan learning activities for specific content areas or can integrate them throughout the day in the blocks of time set aside for the unit. Although I list the following activities under the broad categories of language arts, math and science, art, and technology, they can be easily integrated into several subject areas. Classroom teachers may use the activities as is, modify them to meet the needs of the students, or use them to supplement their own creative ideas on this topic.

Overall Introduction

Collaborate with the classroom teacher to collect a library of books to display and use in the classroom for this unit. When introducing a unit, explaining the book display can create excitement about the approaching topic. Ask students to bring in other books or resources that will help in their study of cardiovascular health. Check with the local chapter of the American Heart Association for more titles and materials. Suggest that the classroom teacher introduce the idea of the importance of the heart to the body by reading a book with the students, such as *The Magic School Bus: Inside the Human Body* by Joanna Cole (1991).

Language Arts

Suggest to the classroom teacher that the class integrate language arts skills with the content of cardiovascular health by writing and producing a Heart-Healthy Newsletter. The process of writing a newsletter automatically includes a variety of skills that are essential to children at this developmental level. Reading, writing, communication, computer applications, and math are all integrated to bring a certain confluence to the learning experience.

Let the students brainstorm many of the components of this newsletter, and then divide the class into appropriately sized groups to handle each task. Allow students to work on more than one area to make the newsletter as comprehensive as possible.

Sections may include the following:

- **Crossword puzzles:** Use exercise and fitness terms and healthy foods.

- **Word searches:** Include important terms relating to the heart, exercise, and nutrition (see figure 9.2).
- **Unscrambling activities:** Scramble key words relating to the heart, exercise, and nutrition.
- **Teacher highlights:** Have students interview a teacher in the school who exhibits healthy eating habits or who is often seen exercising to stay healthy (e.g., walking or jogging during lunchtime).
- **Family involvement:** Encourage students to brainstorm several family-oriented activities that would be fun to do on a weeknight or during the weekend (e.g., biking, a hiking trip at the local state park).
- **Heart-healthy recipes:** Have students find two or three heart-healthy recipes (perhaps one each for breakfast, lunch, and dinner). A list of healthy snacks for school would be also be helpful as a reminder to parents to avoid packing too many sweets!
- **The Lunch Bunch:** Have students interview the principal, cafeteria manager, teachers, and other students to gather information on ways to improve the school lunch program.
- **Cereal Alert:** Have students survey the students in the school for their favorite cereal and graph the results on a poster displayed in the hallway. Next to the graph, have students compare the labels on the five most popular cereals. Show them how to analyze the calories, fat from calories, and trans fat, sugar, and sodium content using the nutrition facts label (see figure 9.3). Include these results in the newsletter as well.
- **Fitness tips:** Have students interview a fitness expert (or you) and list tips for staying healthy through physical activity.
- **Nutrition tips:** Have students interview the school nurse or district dietitian to help make a list of nutrition tips to share in the newsletter (e.g., list of low-fat substitutes such as skim milk, frozen yogurt, and fat-free cookies).
- **School highlights:** Help students list special events that are scheduled at school such as the dates for Nutrition Week, Jump Rope for Heart, ACES, or the updated results of the Geography Run (see chapter 15).

Word Search

H	E	A	R	T	P	I	K	S	L
C	Y	O	G	J	O	G	E	R	W
A	O	S	Y	O	G	A	X	H	A
L	G	U	Y	A	L	P	E	E	L
O	U	G	I	E	S	G	R	A	K
R	R	A	C	V	O	N	C	L	I
I	T	R	M	I	D	I	I	T	N
E	X	I	R	T	I	K	S	H	G
S	W	O	U	C	U	I	E	Y	C
S	A	T	N	A	M	B	E	A	X

Find these words:

HEART	SWIM	SUGAR
BIKING	YOGURT	CALORIES
YOGA	SODIUM	WALKING
ACTIVE	EXERCISE	HEALTHY
RUN	PLAY	SKIP

Figure 9.2 A sample word search for a cardiovascular health newsletter. When students create items like this for the newsletter, it reinforces both language arts and cardiovascular health concepts.

- **Family survey:** Have students develop a survey to ask families about their favorite physical activities. Compile the results and list the top 10 family activities.
- **A message from the school nurse:** Have students interview the school nurse for a special section of the newsletter. The message may include general health and hygiene information.

- **Scanning the news:** Have students read their local newspapers for articles on how the local, state, or national government is dealing with important health issues such as lack of physical activity, obesity, or heart disease. Examples might include the planting of an organic garden at the White House or First Lady's Michelle Obama's initiative, Let's Move!

Nutrition Facts

Serving Size 1 cup (228g)
Servings Per Container 2

Start here

Amount Per Serving

Calories 250 **Calories from Fat** 110

Check calories

% Daily Value*

Quick guide to %DV

Total Fat 12g	**18%**
Saturated Fat 3g	**15%**

**5% or less is low
20% or more is high**

Trans Fat 3g

Cholesterol 30mg	**10%**
Sodium 470mg	**20%**

Limit these

Potassium 700mg	**20%**
Total Carbohydrate 31g	**10%**
Dietary Fiber 0g	**0%**

Get enough of these

Sugars 5g

Protein 5g

Vitamin A 4%	Calcium 20%
Vitamin C 2%	Iron 4%

Footnote

*Percent Daily Values are based on a 2,000 calorie
diet. Your daily values may be higher or lower
depending on your calorie needs:

		Calories	2,000	2,500
Total Fat	Less Than		65g	80g
Saturated Fat	Less Than		20g	25g
Cholesterol	Less Than		300mg	300mg
Sodium	Less Than		2,400mg	2,400mg
Total Carbohydrate			300g	375g
Dietary Fiber			25g	30g

Figure 9.3 How to interpret the nutrition facts label.
From FDA 2006.

Encourage the classroom teacher to work closely with the students as the editor of the newsletter. Ask that the classroom teacher provide time each day for students to use the computer, discuss progress on the various sections, and solve any concerns that arise. As the physical educator, you should come in once or twice during the week to consult with students, distribute materials, discuss their ideas, and offer support.

As a culminating activity, help the classroom teacher plan a publishing party. Invite parents, administrators, the school nurse, and other teachers to a special gathering in the classroom. Give each guest a copy of the published newsletter. Serve healthy snacks and refreshments to the guests. You might even consider using this classroom-generated newsletter as a schoolwide project during the school year. Be sure to acknowledge the hard work done by the classroom teacher and all of the students throughout

the process of planning and publishing the newsletter. Remember to emphasize the collaboration between the classroom teacher and yourself.

Math and Science

Math and science have their places in health-related physical fitness, too. In fact, integrating math and science into your curriculum can make these subjects more meaningful and interesting to children. Try these fun and relevant activities, but work with the classroom teacher to ensure that the students are capable of doing the activities you choose.

WATCH THOSE CALORIES!

Divide students into cooperative groups. Provide each student with a handout or make a large poster titled Watch Those Calories! that describes several meal choices (see figure 9.4). Ask the students to predict which meal would have the fewest calories. Then have them use a calorie chart to find the total number of calories for each meal (see figure 9.5). (Have them do calculations by hand or use calculators, depending on which skill the classroom teacher wishes them to practice.) Compare their predictions to the meal that was actually the lowest in calories. Discuss why the two meals are different.

PLACES ON THE PLATE

Ask students to keep track of their food intake for three days, using the MyPlate image as a point of reference (see figure 9.6). Use the data to determine whether students are eating nutritious, well-balanced meals. The MyPlate website (www.ChooseMyPlate.gov) is a great resource for students and teachers. The plate image and a variety of links, including nutrition tips, are available on the site and will add excitement to this activity. The links on the website offer various audiences nutritional tips that will help them plan well-balanced meals and stay healthy.

At the end of the week, plan an assessment activity (see figure 9.7). Discuss what types of foods the students eat more often, whether they're following the USDA Dietary Guidelines, and if they need to improve their eating habits. Then ask the groups to make five large charts listing the foods they ate in each of the food groups. Display these charts in the classroom or hallway.

Watch Those Calories!

Meal choices	Total calories
1. Hamburger patty, french fries, cola	_____
2. Pizza, cola	_____
3. Three pancakes, bacon, orange juice	_____
4. Turkey, whole wheat bread, salad, water	_____
5. Cornflakes, banana, low-fat milk	_____
6. Spaghetti and meatballs, salad, water	_____
7. Tuna salad, potato chips, apple juice	_____
8. Steak, broccoli, mashed potatoes, water	_____
9. Fried shrimp, green beans, rice, cola	_____
10. Macaroni and cheese, salad, skim milk	_____
11. Chicken cutlet, baked potato, spinach	_____
12. Hot dog, french fries, cola	_____

Figure 9.4 Which meal would have the fewest calories?

From S.J. Virgilio, 2012, *Fitness education for children: A team approach* (Champaign, IL: Human Kinetics).

Calorie Chart

Food Item	Calories	Food Item	Calories
Apple	25	Milk, skim (1 cup, or 240 ml)	85
Apple juice (1 cup, or 240 ml)	120	Milk, whole (1 cup, or 240 ml)	210
Bacon (2 strips)	97	Orange juice (1 cup, or 240 ml)	120
Banana	100	Pancakes (3)	177
Broccoli (1 cup)	55	Pizza, cheese (2 slices)	360
Carrots, cooked (1 cup)	44	Potato, baked	97
Chicken cutlet, fried (3 oz, or 90 g)	160	Potato chips (10 chips)	115
Cola (8 ounces)	107	Rice (1/2 cup)	100
Cornflakes (1 cup)	88	Salad (1 cup)	96
Egg, scrambled (1)	106	Spaghetti (1 cup with 1 oz, or 30 g, cheese)	331
French fries (8)	157		
Fried shrimp (3 oz, or 90 g)	190	Spaghetti and meatballs (1 cup)	260
Green beans (1 cup)	30	Spinach (1 cup)	92
Hamburger patty (6 oz, or 175 g)	632	Steak (3 oz, or 90 g)	330
Hot dog	124	Tuna salad (1 cup)	350
Macaroni and cheese (1 cup)	430	Turkey (2 slices)	150
Mashed potatoes (1/2 cup)	120	Water	0
Milk, low-fat 2 percent (1 cup, or 240 ml)	120	Whole wheat bread (2 slices)	130

Figure 9.5 Use this calorie chart to find the meal on the Watch Those Calories! worksheet with the fewest calories.

I CAN TAKE MY PULSE!

Distribute the handout I Can Take My Pulse! (figure 9.8). Have students record their heart rates after each of the four activities under the column labeled "Me." Make sure that students rest for a minute or two before they begin another activity. After completing and recording all four readings, have the students figure the class average for each one and record it under the column "Class average." Give a mini-lesson in finding averages; then let students use calculators.

Not enough room for the pulse-taking activities in the classroom? Use the hallway, too.

Modify or change the activities you use to meet your needs.

GRAPHING

Take the results of the I Can Take My Pulse! activity and ask the students to develop a bar graph. Make a giant-sized graph for the class to put on display. Ask students to compare their personal results and the classwide results by creating a line graph. Students may do this activity at home with at least one family member, recording results on a line graph using different colors to denote each family member. You can also incorporate graph-

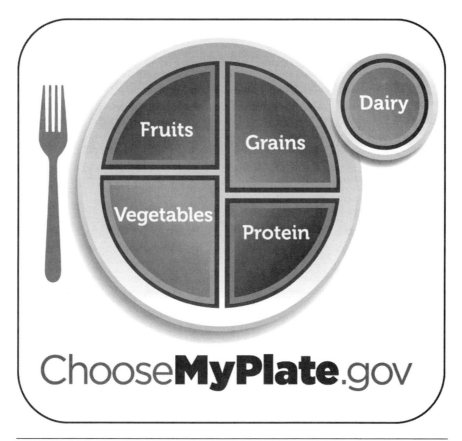

Figure 9.6   Students will use the MyPlate image as a guide when tracking their food intake.

From USDA

ing activities using the food group information that the students have gathered throughout the week. For example, cooperative groups could use their charts to make bar graphs or line graphs of favorite snacks or drinks and display them in the hallway.

A great tool for older students is the Create A Graph website (see appendix B). It allows students to input all of their information and create different types of graphs, by selecting all variables, color, style of presentation, and so on. Their graphs can then be printed and displayed.

CEREAL SEARCHING

Have students bring in empty boxes of their favorite cereals. Begin the activity as soon as there are enough boxes for each cooperative group of three to five students to do comparisons. Give a mini-lesson on the importance of reading labels for fat and sodium content. Discuss other items found on the labels and the importance of reading the ingredients on labels. Make copies

of the labels for each child or group so that all students can see them easily, or project them on an interactive whiteboard. Ask students to choose three different cereal labels and compare them for calories, fat from calories, and trans fat, sodium, and sugar content. Have students discuss their findings with group members and present one healthy cereal to the rest of the class, discussing why their group selected it. Prepare and share a healthy breakfast at the end of the week. Include the cereals that were found to be the healthiest. (You may wish to do this activity in conjunction with the Cereal Alert and newsletter activity already discussed.)

Art

You can develop and enhance a child's awareness of shape, form, texture, and color by connecting art in a classroom unit of study to the child's life. Curriculum specialists have historically suggested integrating art with other subject areas to meet the intellectual (problem solving), emotional

Places on MyPlate Assessment

Name _____ Date _____

Grade _____ Class_____

Use this assessment sheet to tally and record the total number of foods you ate in each food group over the three-day period.

Food group	Day 1	Day 2	Day 3	Total
Dairy				
Fruits				
Grains				
Protein				
Vegetables				

Figure 9.7 Do the numbers of foods you ate from each food group match MyPlate's recommendations?

From S.J. Virgilio, 2012, *Fitness education for children: A team approach* (Champaign, IL: Human Kinetics).

I Can Take My Pulse!

Name _____ Date _____

Grade _____ Class_____

	Me	Class average
Resting (30 seconds)		
Walking (30 seconds)		
Jogging (30 seconds)		
Jumping jacks (30 seconds)		

Figure 9.8 Record your pulse after each activity, and then find the class average for each.

From S.J. Virgilio, 2012, *Fitness education for children: A team approach* (Champaign, IL: Human Kinetics).

(self-expression), and perceptual (experiencing the environment through the senses) needs of students. It's important to include several artistic opportunities in a thematic unit to reinforce the idea of healthy lifestyles.

- Draw a giant-sized heart on the bulletin board. Ask students to make it look like a giant puzzle by drawing small heart-healthy pictures (e.g., biking, swimming, exercising, nutritious foods or meals) and adding them to the inside of the giant heart.
- After a visit from a guest speaker such as the school nurse, a pediatrician, or a heart specialist, ask the students to create flow charts of the heart showing how the blood circulates throughout the heart and body.
- Have students construct a giant-sized three-dimensional representation of MyPlate using a variety of art materials. Display it in the hallway for other students to view.
- Invite the art teacher into your classroom to work with your students on a special project. This teamwork will benefit everyone and create a positive environment in your class and throughout the school.

Technology

Today's students are technology savvy, so what better way to incorporate the concepts of good nutrition, healthy habits, and physical activity for a lifetime than to use technology? Teachers can use computers in their classrooms, school computer labs, or school technology labs to enhance learning and create excitement among their students.

Computers

You can use numerous kid-friendly and appropriate fitness and health websites to enrich your thematic unit. For example, Discovery Education offers powerful search tools and dynamic browsing capabilities that quickly allow teachers and students to locate a variety of interesting media opportunities. Using the site's student videos, numerous activities, and interactive labs, students at the elementary level can enhance their educational experiences on a variety of topics. KidsHealth is also a great website for students to learn about a variety of health-related issues. The "Kids Site" link is appropriate and relevant to the health concerns facing students today. Both can be found in appendix B.

Interactive Whiteboards

Interactive whiteboards such as SMART Boards have been an incredibly fast-growing instructional tool to enhance class lessons. Students quickly learn how to use the interactive whiteboards, and teachers believe that they offer an additional tactile and visual learning experience. Being actively involved in the learning process is a positive way for students to add to their understanding of the concept or idea being presented in the lesson. Teachers can embed videos, graphs, charts, PowerPoint presentations, and online sites into their lessons in the SMART Notebook.

Videoconferencing

Many educational opportunities are available to teachers who have access to videoconferencing equipment in their classrooms or school. It is a dynamic way to learn about health-related concepts. Communicating with other students in your local area, state, or throughout the nation can be an exciting learning experience for all involved. Many schools are even going global with their videoconferencing plans.

Videos

Taking videos of your classes while they are working on projects or specific activities is a great way to enrich the learning experience. Many companies have developed lightweight video cameras that can make recording students in action very easy.

HEALTH-RELATED PHYSICAL FITNESS CLASSROOM ACTIVITIES

The classroom learning activities for health-related physical fitness for each developmental level described here extend the concepts discussed in chapter 8. Remember to stay in close touch with the teachers in your school so they are aware of the units you will be covering throughout the year. If you work closely with the classroom teachers, the fitness education concepts integrated in their classrooms can reinforce and complement the content you are teaching in physical education.

DEVELOPMENTAL LEVEL I CLASSROOM ACTIVITIES

I'm Important—Inside and Out

Concepts

Students learn to value their self-worth and care about others as they become more aware of their personal health.

Equipment

One pencil, one copy of the Me Tree handout, and one colored marker for each student; audio recorders; construction paper; pictures of body parts; paste

Activities

Language Arts

Incorporate language arts by having students fill in the Me Tree illustrated in figure 9.9. Have them write the names of family members on the branches and their own personal strengths on the roots (e.g., athletic, funny, good student). The first name goes on the trunk. This activity enhances students' personal feelings of self-worth.

Incorporate oral language by asking students to select their favorite physical education activity. Have each student make an audio recording, stating why they enjoy that their own particular activity. Ask them to also include the physical activity they enjoy most at home. If you wish, ask students to interview each other, asking set questions about activity preferences. (See the My Favorites section of the Sample Personal Active Lifestyle Portfolio in appendix A.)

Science

Have students make a list of their favorite body parts (e.g., knees, hands, toes). Ask them to explain what they like about these particular body parts.

Math

Ask students to solve the Body Part Addition worksheet illustrated in figure 9.10. This makes a good cooperative learning activity.

Art

Ask students to color the Me Tree and also create a scene of children playing around the tree. When the class has completed this activity, display the artwork in the classroom. After two or three weeks, send the Me Tree home with each student and have them share the activity with their families. Remind students not to color over the words on the Me Tree.

Divide students into groups of four. Provide each group with a number of body part pictures you've cut out from magazines. Ask them to select different body parts to develop an entire body by pasting the parts on a large piece of colored construction paper. (Older students or parent volunteers may help you with this activity.)

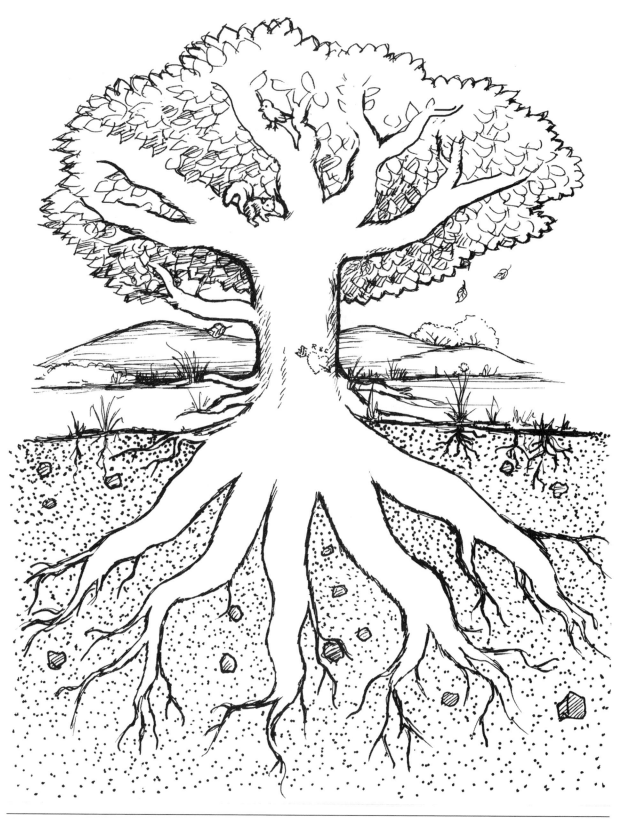

Figure 9.9   Fill in the name of family members on the tree branches. On the roots, list your personal strengths.

From S.J. Virgilio, 2012, *Fitness education for children: A team approach* (Champaign, IL: Human Kinetics).

Body Part Addition

Count the number of body parts and write the number on the blank to the right. Now add and find the total number of body parts.

Body part	How many
Ears	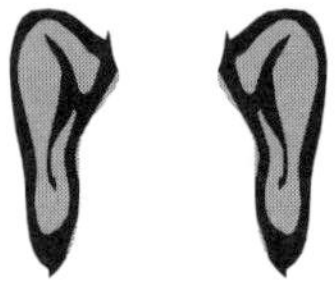 _____
Eyes	 _____
Fingers	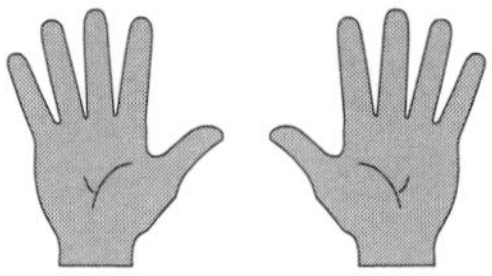 _____
Nose	 _____
Shoulders	 _____
Total number of body parts	_____

Figure 9.10 The Body Part Addition activity can help reinforce math and anatomy concepts.

From S.J. Virgilio, 2012, *Fitness education for children: A team approach* (Champaign, IL: Human Kinetics).

Safety First: Rest and Exercise

Concepts

Students learn that they need to rest periodically during vigorous physical activity. They should be aware of the basic signals of their body telling them to slow down or take a short break.

Equipment

One ruler or one large pencil, one twist tie, and one pair of scissors for each student; several magazines

Activities

Language Arts

Review the recommended responses to fatigue or overexertion:

- ◆ Slow down.
- ◆ Rest.
- ◆ Take sips of water.
- ◆ On hot days, rest under a shady tree.
- ◆ If you are experiencing sharp pains, immediately stop and tell an adult.

Have the students describe a time when they were playing vigorously and began to feel uncomfortable (tired, sick to their stomachs, pain in their sides, breathing very hard). Ask them to describe how they felt and what they did to recover.

Science

Give each student a twist tie and a pencil or a ruler. Ask them to fold the twist tie in half and place it over the pencil or ruler. Have the students hold the pencil or ruler out with the arm slightly bent (but not supported) over their desks about 1 inch (2.5 cm) high. In about 10 seconds, the twist tie will begin to move in time with the muscular jitters. This demonstrates muscle fatigue (Anderson and Cumbaa 1993).

Ask students to place one hand on their desks with the palm facing up. Have them open and chose that hand as many times as possible in a one-minute period. Ask students to describe the feeling in the hand, wrist, and forearm. They will likely mention pain, tightness, being tired. Say, "This is also called muscle fatigue." Remind them: "When your body is giving certain signals such as pain or the feeling of exhaustion, it's time to rest."

Math

Ask students to count in seconds (one-one-thousand, two-one-thousand) before the twist tie starts to dance. Have them count how many times they make a fist in the one-minute period. Record the numbers from the two experiments for each student, and then have students find the class average for each activity.

Art

Ask students to help you make a large poster or bulletin board titled Rest and Exercise. Include in the display the responses to fatigue. Have students cut out pictures from magazines of people exercising and people resting, drinking healthy liquids, exercising, and walking. Display the poster in the classroom, hallway, or gymnasium.

DEVELOPMENTAL LEVEL II CLASSROOM ACTIVITIES

Healthy Back

Concepts

Students learn that posture is the way the body is supported when they are standing, sitting, walking, or lying down. Good posture prevents or relieves strain on the neck and back. Posture is important to the way they look and feel about themselves. When body posture is correct, internal organs have enough blood supply to function properly.

Equipment

Paper and pencil, one chair, one 8.5-inch (22 cm) playground ball, one copy of figure 9.13, and one chalkboard eraser for each student; chalkboard and chalk; poster paper; four balloons; one marker; digital camera

Activities

Language Arts

Have the students sit in their chairs. Ask the students to demonstrate poor sitting posture. Ask, "Why is it harmful to sit incorrectly?" Discuss the benefits of good posture, making a list on the chalkboard:

- Keeps the neck and back supported and healthy.
- Enables you to sit for a longer time without strain.
- Keeps internal organs in place and functioning normally.
- Keeps you alert and attentive.
- Makes you feel good about yourself.

Ask the class to write a description about what people's posture tells you about the way they feel about themselves.

Science

Explain to the class that, whether sitting or standing, good posture depends on the strength and flexibility of key muscle groups.

- **Abdominal muscles:** Weak abdominal muscles allow the pelvic region to tilt forward, creating strain on the low back. Remark: "This is why people who are overweight have frequent back strain. Strong abdominal muscles will keep the back straight." (The recommended exercise is curl-ups.)
- **Back muscles:** Back muscles support the neck and shoulders. These muscles should be strong and flexible to keep the back in proper alignment. (The recommended exercise is pull-ups.)
- **Leg muscles:** Leg muscles that are inflexible—especially the hamstrings (back of thighs)—can pull the pelvic region out of alignment. Strength in the leg muscles will help support the body while standing, getting up from a seated position, and lifting. Strong legs will relieve the stress on the low back. (The recommended exercises are the back-saver sit-and-reach stretch, resistance exercising, and jogging.)

Figure 9.11 Good posture while sitting at a computer.

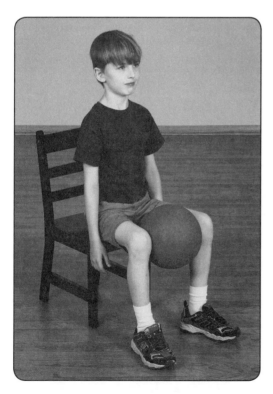

Figure 9.12 Seated ball squeeze for developing good posture.

Have one student lie on her back on a large roll of poster paper. Trace the student's body with a marker. Now place the body outline on a chair. Attach small balloons to the front of the body to represent the stomach and the heart. Attach balloons to the back of the outlined body to represent the neck and low back. Move the body into different positions. Ask, "What happens when the body is bent over?" [The stomach and heart are crunched.] "What happens to the blood supply?" [The blood cannot move freely.] (Optional: To further illustrate the point, you may use a small pin to burst the balloons when the outlined body places pressure on the organs.)

Move the outline down the chair in a backward slump. Ask, "What is stressed now?" [The neck and back.] Give the outline a name such as Slumping Steve (but do not use the name of a child in the class). Place it in the corner of the room to remind students of their sitting habits.

Ask students to volunteer to be good posture models. Photograph them as they sit with good posture at a computer (see figure 9.11). Provide a copy of the photos for each student in class. Review the major points for good sitting posture:

◆ Ears, shoulders, and hips aligned

◆ Shoulders relaxed

◆ Weight evenly distributed on both hips

◆ Chair close to desk

◆ Feet flat on the floor

Have each student take the picture home and ask their parents to post it near the computer or on the refrigerator. Ask the students to help mom, dad, sister, or brother sit correctly while eating dinner, doing homework, or watching TV.

To reinforce proper posture, have students sit up straight with their feet flat on the floor. Ask them to place their hands, palms down, directly aligned with their hips on the chair. Have them push down on the chair but not lift their bottoms and count to five. Repeat three times.

To develop the pelvic muscles and reinforce good posture, ask students to sit toward the front of a chair with the hips and knees aligned. Give each student an 8.5-inch (22 cm) playground ball. Have them place the ball between the knees (figure 9.12). Ask them to squeeze the ball between the knees, hold for five seconds, and release—all while maintaining good posture. Have them do 10 repetitions.

Give each student a chalkboard eraser to balance on the head. Have them take a walk down the hallway or outside. When you return to class, discuss how having correct posture with the head remaining over the center of gravity (trunk) helped keep the eraser balanced.

Math

Give each student the Measuring Madness activity sheet (figure 9.13). See how many they can guess. Review the answers.

Measuring Madness

Name ______________________________ Date ____________________

Grade ____________________ Class ______________________________

Try to match the amounts on the left with the items on the right.

A. 75 times	____	1. Number of new red blood cells made per second
B. 2 to 3 million	____	2. Percentage of body weight that is bone
C. 650	____	3. Number of hairs on the body
D. 1.2 to 1.6 gallons	____	4. Amount of water sweated per day
E. 2.5 pints	____	5. Amount of blood in the body
F. 16 percent	____	6. Bones in the body
G. 60 percent	____	7. Percentage of body weight that is water
H. 206	____	8. Approximate number of times the heart beats in one minute
I. 15 to 30 feet	____	9. Length of the small intestine
J. 4 million	____	10. Number of muscles in the body

Figure 9.13 How many body-related numbers can you match?

From S.J. Virgilio, 2012, *Fitness education for children: A team approach* (Champaign, IL: Human Kinetics).

Answers to Measuring Madness Activity Sheet

1. B	3. J	5. D	7. G	9. I
2. F	4. E	6. H	8. A	10. C

Art

Ask students to help develop and decorate a bulletin board titled Positive Posture. Take a photograph of each child sitting in class participating in various learning activities, such as at a computer, in a cooperative group, or reading independently. Mount the pictures on construction paper to make them look framed and display them on the bulletin board.

Body Systems: Skeletal

Concepts

Students learn that proper eating and daily exercise produce strong bones. A newborn's bones are composed of soft cartilage and become harder as the child develops into the late teens. Food choices rich in calcium and phosphorus, as well as vigorous physical activity, ensure proper bone growth and development.

Equipment

One poster of the skeletal system; two chicken bones; one jar of vinegar; one jar of water; one tape measure; one calculator, pencil, and piece of paper for each student; crayons; five pieces of colored poster paper; graphics of different bones for each group

Activities

Language Arts

Display a large poster of the skeletal system. Label only several of the major bones of the body (at this developmental level it is not necessary to review every bone). Review one bone each week. Have students feel the bone that you are discussing on their bodies. After they have studied the skeletal system, ask students to match the body part with the medical name of each bone (see figure 9.14). If you like, you can give the students a word bank from which to choose the medical terms. The answers are skull (head), clavicle (collarbone), ribs (chest), vertebrae or spinal column (back), iliac crest (hip), tibia (shin), femur (thigh), radius and ulna (lower arm), and humerus (upper arm).

Science

Strip two chicken leg bones clean and allow them to dry out for two days. Place one bone in a jar of vinegar and the other in a jar of water. Allow the bones to soak for three or four days. Remove the bones from the jars. The bone from the water jar will still be stiff, but the bone from the vinegar jar will be soft because its minerals have been dissolved by the acid in the vinegar. Reinforce to the class that when bones do not get a good supply of minerals, they become soft and underdeveloped.

Ask, "What are good food sources of calcium?" [Low-fat milk, low-fat cheese, yogurt.]

"What exercises or sports build strong bones?" [Jogging, basketball, soccer, hiking, resistance exercises—any large-muscle continuous activity.]

Math

Explain to the class that in the next few years they will begin to grow quite rapidly. Between the ages of 10 and 14, they may grow about 6 inches (15 cm) taller. Their

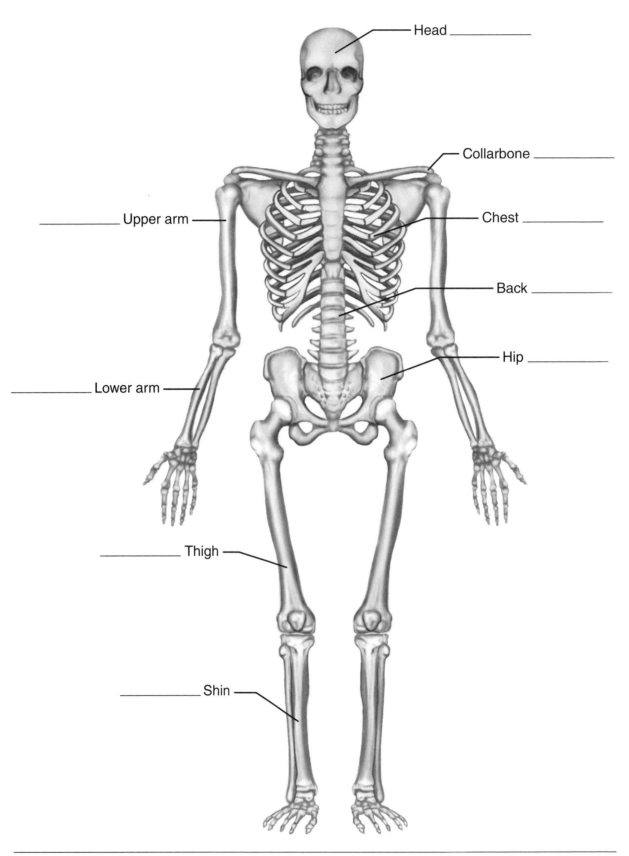

Figure 9.14 Can you identify the name of each bone?

From S.J. Virgilio, 2012, *Fitness education for children: A team approach* (Champaign, IL: Human Kinetics).

hands and feet will grow first, and they may feel awkward or uncoordinated for a short time.

Here is a method that uses bone measurements to calculate height. Using a tape measure, measure each student's arm from the shoulder joint to the bony point on the outside of the elbow. This is the length of the humerus, or upper arm bone. Follow the formula to calculate the students' height in inches (Anderson and Cumbaa 1993).

Girls:

Length of humerus = _____ inches

Multiply by 3.14.

Add 25.58 = _____ height in inches

Boys:

Length of humerus = _____ inches

Multiply by 2.97.

Add 28.96 = _____ height in inches

Help students at this level with the calculations. Compare the final calculations with each student's actual height.

Art

Divide the class into five groups. Have each group select a portion of the body, such as the legs, feet, back, shoulders, arms, or hands. Ask each student to trace the bones of the body part from the sketches you provide. Instruct them to label and color the bones. Give each group a large piece of poster paper. Have the groups create a large drawing of the body part they selected. Display the students' work around the room.

DEVELOPMENTAL LEVEL III CLASSROOM ACTIVITIES

Fitness Principles: Components of Health-Related Physical Fitness

Concepts

Students review the four components of health-related physical fitness: cardiorespiratory endurance, muscle fitness, flexibility, and body composition.

Equipment

One graph worksheet, colored markers, paper, pencil, glue, and scissors for each student; five dictionaries; 10 fitness books; several fitness magazines; one large piece of poster paper; 20 fitness index cards for every two students

Activities

Language Arts

Divide the class into four cooperative learning groups. Write the words *muscle fitness, cardiorespiratory endurance, flexibility,* and *body composition* on large chart paper or on a piece of poster board. Give each group two fitness books, one dictionary, and several fitness magazines. Ask each student to write the definition of the components of fitness on an individual learning activity sheet, using the resources to define the words. Now ask each student to look through the fitness magazines and cut out pictures of people exercising, depicting the components of physical fitness they have selected. Have them paste these on the lower portion of a learning activity sheet. Ask students to also look for a healthy food item and a picture of a person with low body fat to represent body composition.

Divide the students into pairs. Give each pair a set of 20 fitness index cards (10 cards with the fitness component and definition and 10 with the corresponding pictures). Shuffle the decks of cards for each pair of students, spread the cards out, and place them face up. Have students take turns trying to match the components with the pictures. If a student successfully makes a match, she keeps both cards. If the match is unsuccessful, she returns the cards to the table and the other student takes a turn. The student with the most cards is the winner. To avoid confusion and arguments, place a corresponding number on the back of each picture to denote the correct answer.

Science

Discuss with students the medical benefits of each fitness component, such as how cardiorespiratory endurance prevents heart disease. Then have students make a list of at least five physical activities for each fitness component. Under *body composition*, have them list five healthy snacks.

Math

Ask students to record their fitness scores for each component, using an individual bar graph labeled Pretest, Interim Test, and Posttest. Help students calculate the percentage of improvement made throughout the school year (see figure 9.15).

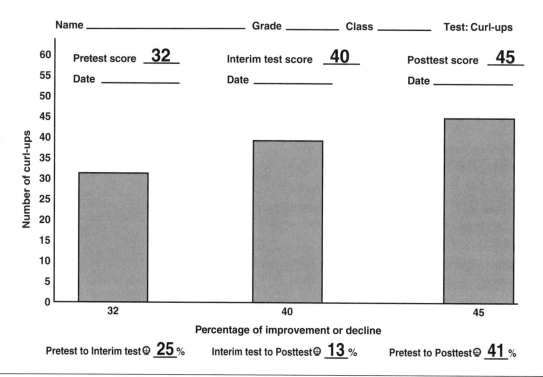

Figure 9.15 An example of a bar graph that measures curl-up progress.

Art

Divide students into pairs. Ask one student to strike an active pose (jogging, curl-up, shooting a basketball, kicking a soccer ball) while lying on a large section of colored poster paper. Have the other student trace the student performing the activity onto the paper. Have the students color the drawing and decorate it. Ask them to give the picture a name or title and the appropriate component it represents—for example, Jo Jo the Jogger, representing cardiorespiratory endurance.

Foods for Fitness

Concept

Students learn that foods that are high in carbohydrate provide the body with energy to meet the daily needs of physical activity.

Equipment

Pictures of assorted foods; five sheets of newspaper; samples of various foods (cheese, crackers, white bread, bologna); iodine solution; five eyedroppers; food magazines; 10 boxes (5 marked "GO" and 5 marked "STOP"); five pieces of poster board; several food labels; scissors, paper, graph paper, and a pencil for each student

Activities

Language Arts

Divide the class into five groups. Provide each group with a number of food pictures, such as candy, steak, pasta, cheese, carrots, and bread. Have each group decide which foods are high or low in carbohydrate by placing the pictures of the foods high in carbohydrate in the "GO" box and pictures of foods low in carbohydrate in the "STOP" box.

Science

Divide the class into five groups by pulling the desks together. Provide each group with a sheet of newspaper to place on their desks. Give each group samples of food (cheese, crackers, white bread, bologna) and an iodine solution. Ask students to place a drop of iodine on each food sample with an eyedropper. Record what happens to the food. (The foods high in carbohydrate will turn blue.)

Math

Ask students to review food labels from cereal boxes, candy bars, crackers, canned soups, and so on. Have the students design a bar graph of each label, listing the fat, protein, sodium, and carbohydrate content. Ask students to attach the label to each bar graph. Use this analysis to teach the percentages of ingredients in various food choices.

Art

Divide the class into five groups. Ask each group to look through the food magazines you have provided. Have them cut out pictures of foods high in carbohydrate and paste them on a large poster board labeled Carbo Collage. Allow each group to decide on poster colors as well as additional decorations. Display the posters in the room. You may want to give each group a name, such as Fitness Finders or Heart Smarties, or have the students in each group invent their own name.

SUMMARY

With so little time for physical education in most elementary schools, it seems appropriate to enlist the help of the classroom teacher to reach your program goals. To ensure the success of this process, first gain administrative support and the confidence of the faculty. Establish open communication channels throughout the school to properly implement your innovations.

After establishing a close working relationship with the faculty of your school, provide them with the sample cardiovascular health thematic unit for level II in this chapter to initiate your collaborative efforts. Then use the classroom learning experiences in this chapter as examples of health-related physical fitness concepts the classroom teacher can integrate into the curriculum at the three developmental levels. Work with the classroom teachers to coordinate the use of these materials to complement the content you are covering in physical education. You may want to suggest going into the classroom to team teach some of the activities described. The extra time and effort you invest will be well worth it!

Getting Parents and Your Community Involved

> While we try to teach
> our children all about life,
> our children teach us
> what life is all about.
>
> —*Unknown*

For many years studies have shown that parent involvement is critical to success in school. Simply stated, when parents are involved in their child's education, the child has a greater chance of success mentally, physically, and socially. Given the limited time you have with your students, it seems logical that the school, parents, and the community should work together to extend the time spent on physical activity and health to accomplish your comprehensive fitness education goals (Virgilio 2006).

The family has a powerful influence on a child's health and activity habits; however, few physical educators actually develop a specific plan to include parents and the community in their physical education programs. This chapter provides practical information that you can begin using today, including information on communication techniques, conducting effective parent–teacher conferences, parent education, parent volunteers, home-based activities, and community involvement. The ready-to-use instructional materials such as letters to parents, a parent survey, a family fitness contract, and family activities will get you started right away!

ESTABLISHING A PLAN OF ACTION

First, it is important to recognize that parents may have negative attitudes toward physical education and may not value the benefits of physical activity. Be sensitive to the following concerns as you plan to include parents in your program:

- Parents may have had negative experiences in physical education when they were in school.
- Parents may believe that physical education is a frill and should be eliminated from the school budget.
- Some parents may feel that physical activity is not really necessary for children, believing that they play enough at home.
- Parents may see physical education as an opportunity for athletic children to perform.
- Parents may recognize that exercise is important but do not have the time to get involved.

But don't be discouraged—move ahead with your plans! Your job is to initiate a plan to help parents recognize the importance of their involvement. Regardless of the parents' attitudes or lack of support, you must lead them to more positive attitudes about physical activity. To get started, develop and follow a specific plan of action.

First, develop a written policy. Written statements are more credible than verbal ones. Furthermore, they show the community that you are serious about enlisting their help. Finally, written policies allow school administrators to document your efforts, which may be important for yearly teacher reviews and tenure evaluations.

After you develop the policy, gain administrative support. Support from the school principal is essential. Ask him or her to allocate a small budget for guest speakers, meeting space, other facilities, audiovisual equipment, duplication costs, and mailing expenses to help you garner parent and community support. Brainstorm with the principal about other ideas that may help you find support.

Now that you have established a plan of action and have gained administrative support, you are ready to open the lines of communication to the community.

COMMUNICATION

Strong lines of communication are necessary if parents are going to feel comfortable working with the school, sharing their ideas, and contributing to their children's education. First, write a letter to the parents introducing and explaining your new fitness education program and how it will fit in with your physical education program (see figure 10.1). Explain why it is important for children to develop healthy lifestyle habits at an early age. Attach a parent survey to the letter (one survey per parent or guardian). The survey will help you gain some perspective on the parents' exercise attitudes and habits. It will also tell you whether they're willing to volunteer (see figure 10.2 on pages 138-139).

But don't stop with one letter. Keep the lines of communication open throughout the school year. Publish a newsletter three or four times a year and hold parent–teacher conferences.

Newsletters

Newsletters are an easy and efficient way to communicate with parents. Develop an eye-catching format on your computer and choose an interesting title (see figure 10.3 on pages 140-141). Choose a different theme for each newsletter. Here is a list of headlines I have used successfully:

- Fitness Is Fun
- Let's Get Heart Smart
- Jump Rope for Heart
- Heart-Healthy Month
- Family Fitness Fun
- Food and Fitness
- Active Summer Fun
- Winter Workouts
- Let's Move
- Fit for a Lifetime
- Community Connections

What should you write about? Include fitness facts, which may dispel some common myths about exercise (e.g., many believe that jogging 1 to 2 miles [1.6 to 3.2 km] is too strenuous for a 12-year-old child). Include safety tips, such as the proper use of fluids during exercise. Add home-based family activities, such as Evening's End, in which the entire family meets in the family room to exercise for 15 minutes before everyone goes their separate ways. You could also cover a major health topic each month in a three- or four-paragraph article, such as, "Shake the Salt Habit" or "Low-Fat, No-Fat, Lite—What Does It All Mean?" Finally, include dates of upcoming events such as a spring health fair or a fun run as well as reminders to parents about physical education days, proper footwear for physical education class, and medical notes, just to name a few.

Parent–Teacher Conferences

The general goal of a parent–teacher conference is to develop a partnership between home and school to benefit the child. A well-planned conference is an excellent chance for you to share your concern for the student while developing a positive relationship with the parents.

Elementary physical educators may serve up to 500 students during the school year. It may be difficult and time consuming to schedule a conference with even half of the parents at your school. You can save time by using less formal methods of conferring with parents. Use the phone or e-mail to have brief but meaningful conferences with parents that are more convenient for both you and the parents. Or have brief conversations with

(Date)

Dear Parents or Guardians,

Heart disease and stroke remain leading causes of death among adults in the United States. The American Heart Association announced that physical inactivity creates a major risk factor for heart disease along with obesity, high blood pressure, elevated blood cholesterol, diabetes, and smoking. The good news is that premature heart disease is avoidable. We can all change our lifestyles and prevent this terrible disease from destroying our happy and productive lives.

Studies show that children develop healthy habits early in life. Generally, children who are inactive in elementary school will be inactive adults; children who are overweight will tend to be overweight adults; and children who grow up on a diet high in fat and sugar will continue eating unhealthily as adults. The elementary school is a great place to start teaching positive health habits! All children will learn how to eat healthfully and balance their food intake according to the MyPlate dietary guidelines set up by the USDA.

This year I will be emphasizing health and fitness education within the physical education program through a program called _____, which I have specially designed for the children at _____ School. In every grade, children will be learning about the principles of exercise and nutrition and why plenty of physical activity and good nutrition are important to their health throughout their lives. Children will develop and maintain their own personal active lifestyle portfolios in fourth through sixth grades, and all will participate in physically active, fun activities. The basic program of skills and sports taught over the last few years in physical education will remain; however, I will make fitness education a part of every unit throughout the school year. I have developed a team of professionals and parents to help accomplish this goal. Classroom teachers, school administrators, the school nurse, the school psychologist, school lunch personnel, and parent volunteers will be working together to ensure the present and future health of your child.

You are important to the success of this effort! Throughout the school year, your child and I will be asking for your help and support. Please take a few minutes from your busy schedule to invest in your child's health. If you wish to join the parent volunteer program or request any additional information about this new, exciting approach to physical education, do not hesitate to call me at _____ (phone number).

Let's get the ball rolling! Please fill out the enclosed survey and mail it back in the self-addressed, stamped envelope.

Sincerely,

Physical Education Specialist

Figure 10.1 An example of a letter to parents that explains the fitness education program.

From S.J. Virgilio, 2012, *Fitness education for children: A team approach* (Champaign, IL: Human Kinetics).

Name of School _____

Parent Physical Activity Survey

Instructions

Each parent or guardian should fill out the survey individually. Read each statement and circle the response that best describes your current health and physical activity habit or attitude. Be honest and fair—all individual surveys will be kept confidential. For the purpose of this survey, physical activity is any large-muscle movement sustained for at least 10 minutes, such as raking leaves, washing the car, jogging, playing tennis, walking, lifting weights, and aerobics (a total of 30 minutes per day).

Yes   No   Sometimes   1. I am physically active at least three days per week.

Yes   No   Sometimes   2. I am physically active with my child(ren) at least three days per week.

Yes   No   Sometimes   3. I encourage my family to be active rather than inactive.

Yes   No   Sometimes   4. On the average, I watch more than three hours of TV per day.

Yes   No   Sometimes   5. My child(ren) is/are physically active at least three days per week outside of school.

Yes   No   Sometimes   6. Teaching children about health and fitness in the school curriculum is very important.

Yes   No   Sometimes   7. Physical education is a positive time for my child(ren).

Yes   No   Sometimes   8. My child(ren) have too many outside interests that prevent them from active play after school.

9. Parent Expertise

   I have a strong background or expertise in the following activities (please check):

   ____ Aerobic dance   ____ Jogging or walking

   ____ Yoga   ____ Cycling

   ____ Weightlifting   ____ Stretching

   ____ Dance   ____ Swimming

   ____ Hiking   ____ Team sport (specify) _____

   ____ Skiing   ____ Individual sport (specify) _____

   ____ In-line skating   ____ Other (specify) _____

Figure 10.2   The parent physical activity survey can help you gauge parents' exercise attitudes and habits.

From S.J. Virgilio, 2012, *Fitness education for children: A team approach* (Champaign, IL: Human Kinetics).

10. I would be willing to share this background with the children of _____ School through the physical education program. ____ Yes ____ No ____ Yes, if my schedule permits

11. I would be interested in attending parent health and fitness seminars sponsored by the school. ____ Yes ____ No

12. I would be interested in joining a parent–teacher advisory committee for physical education. ____ Yes ____ No

13. Comments, questions, or suggestions:

_____

_____

_____

Circle your choices:

I could attend meetings or participate in school activities on

Monday	Tuesday	Wednesday	Thursday
Friday	Saturday	Sunday	

I would like to participate:

Early bird (7:00-8:30 a.m.)   Morning   Afternoon   Evening

Parent's name _____

Address _____

Phone _____

Child(ren)'s name(s) _____

_____

*** Please return in the enclosed self-addressed, stamped envelope. ***

Thank you for your cooperation,

_____

Physical Education Specialist

Figure 10.2 *(continued)*

From S.J. Virgilio, 2012, *Fitness education for children: A team approach* (Champaign, IL: Human Kinetics).

FITNESS FACTS

Vol. 1, No. 2   January

High Blood Pressure

What Is High Blood Pressure?

Blood pressure is the force of the blood against the walls of the arteries as the heart pumps blood to all parts of the body. Normally, the blood flows easily through these vessels.

In some people, the arteries become narrow or closed off, making it difficult for blood to pass through. The heart must pump harder, and the arteries must carry blood that is moving under greater pressure. Sometimes the heart starts working overtime, pushing too much blood through with each beat. This higher blood pressure adds to the workload of the heart and the arteries.

If the blood pressure remains higher than normal for a long time, the arteries and the heart may not function as well as they should, and other body organs may be affected.

Who Gets High Blood Pressure?

No one really knows for sure what causes high blood pressure, but regular blood pressure checks are critical if you

- are overweight;
- are black (African American people are twice as likely as Caucasians to have high blood pressure and are about four times as likely to die from it);
- have a parent, brother, sister, or child with high blood pressure;
- eat too much salt;
- are on birth control pills;
- are over 30 years of age (as people get older, their blood vessels become less elastic); or
- drink too much alcohol.

What Are the Symptoms?

Approximately half of those with high blood pressure are not aware of it, because they feel no sure symptoms. That's why it is often referred to as The Silent Killer.

People with high blood pressure often associate sweaty hands, tense abdominal muscles, a fast pulse, flushing, dizziness, fatigue, and tension with high blood pressure. But these symptoms are connected with other conditions as well. The only sure way to find out if you have high blood pressure is to have it checked regularly.

What Can You Do?

If you are at a higher risk than the average person for developing high blood pressure, you should do each of the following:

- **Get your blood pressure checked regularly,** especially if you are pregnant. High blood pressure can cause serious problems for both mother and baby.
- **Get rid of excess fat.** Ask your doctor for a sensible, balanced diet and begin to develop new eating habits. Diet may be the most important change you make. Losing weight and reducing your intake of high-fat foods and salty snacks usually help control high blood pressure—sometimes without medi-

---

Sugar Facts Quiz

1. Honey is better for you than sugar.
   True   False

2. Sugar is a carbohydrate.
   True   False

3. Sugar is a source of quick energy.
   True   False

4. How many teaspoons of sugar are in a 12-ounce (360 ml) cola drink?
   2   8   14

5. Which of these ingredients mean "sugar?"
   Dextrose   Sucrose   Corn syrup

6. Which of these contain added sugar?
   Ketchup   Orange juice   French dressing

Figure 10.3 A sample newsletter.

Adapted from *Heart Smart Gazette*.

cation. Go to www.ChooseMyPlate.gov for further information.

- **Cut down on salt.** Salt contains sodium, which holds water and swells your body's tissues. Avoid foods high in salt, such as processed foods, condiments, smoked or cured meats, licorice, microwave meals, canned foods, and baking soda. Choose low-salt foods, such as fresh and dried fruits, fresh vegetables, poultry, fish, lean meat, rice, and noodles.

- **If you smoke, decide to cut down or quit entirely.** Smoking not only increases your risk for respiratory damage but also injures blood vessel walls and speeds hardening of the arteries. Heavy smoking increases the workload of the heart, increases pulse rate, and raises blood pressure. If you have high blood pressure, smoking more than doubles your risk of heart disease.

- **Exercise regularly.** Regular exercise chosen for cardiorespiratory conditioning, such as walking, bicycling, and swimming, can make your heart stronger, help relieve tension, and support your weight reduction efforts.

- **Reduce tension through activities such as yoga, reading, and walking.** These can help temporarily lower your blood pressure, but don't depend on relaxation techniques to lower your blood pressure permanently.

- **Limit alcohol consumption.** Some research links heavy use of alcohol with elevations in blood pressure.

- If you have high blood pressure, **check with your doctor before taking birth control pills.** If you do take them, you should have your blood pressure checked regularly.

If lifestyle changes alone don't lower your blood pressure, your doctor may prescribe medication to help rid your body of excess water and sodium or to widen your blood vessels. Give the medication a chance to do what it is expected to do. If you stop taking it or if you take it now and then, it will not control your blood pressure.

Treatment only works when you are faithful in using it. Even if you feel fine, you usually have to stay with the treatment the rest of your life. In return, your life will probably be a much longer and healthier one.

Figure 10.3 *(continued)*

Adapted from *Heart Smart Gazette.*

Answers

1. False.

Honey contains fructose, a sweeter sugar digested differently than table sugar. These differences, however, have little actual effect because fructose, just like table sugar, ends up as glucose—the food substance your body needs for energy. Unrefined sugars such as honey, raw sugar, and turbinado ("washed" raw sugar) have no special benefits. Their mineral content is so low that you would have to consume all your day's calories in sugars to get a significant amount. These sugars provide only sweetness and calories, just like refined (table) sugar.

2. True.

Sugars are called simple carbohydrates, and starches are called complex carbohydrates. Compared to starches, sugars have a simpler chemical structure. Foods high in sugars and starches are our basic sources of carbohydrate.

3. True . . . but . . .

Using sugar as a quick pickup—like eating a candy bar—will backfire. Your body uses the sugar very rapidly. You'll get a quick pickup and then a quick letdown. You can often end up feeling hungrier as well.

4. 8 teaspoons.

Remember that most of the sugar in our diets is from the sugar in processed foods such as soft drinks or baked goods, rather than from naturally sweet foods such as fruit.

5. All three.

Besides dextrose, sucrose, and corn syrup, common label terms include *sugar, invert sugar, honey, molasses, sucrose, fructose, lactose, maltose,* and *galactose.*

6. Ketchup, French dressing

Look for *sugar* (and its many other names) on the ingredient label. Before you add table sugar to foods, remember that many foods such as fruits, vegetables, dairy products, and grains already contain sugar naturally.

parents about their child's progress when you see them at school, after PTA meetings, or at athletic events. Ensure, however, that you include positive comments and maintain the family's privacy. You may be surprised by what good public relations informal conferences are for your program.

Initially try to reach the parents of students who are high risk; for example, those who have low fitness scores, lead inactive lifestyles, are obese, have elevated cholesterol levels, have a family history of heart disease or diabetes, or have disabilities. Develop a special program for these students, schedule additional class time, and arrange family health promotion nights to get parents motivated and involved in improving their children's health status. In this way, you can reach several families at the same time, thereby streamlining your efforts.

Sometimes, however, a situation calls for a more formal, yet nonthreatening, traditional conference. If, like most of us, your time is limited, concentrate on the parents of primary students (kindergarten through third grade). These parents are usually highly motivated, and their enthusiasm may permeate the school. Perhaps most important, children in the primary grades and their parents are usually more open to considering changes in exercise, nutrition, and lifestyle habits.

Before the Conference

Send home a Fitness Flash a few weeks before conference time to give parents an idea of how their child is doing in physical education (see figure 10.4). The Fitness Flash is simply a progress report of the health-related physical fitness scores with comments attached. Place an asterisk next to each score that indicates that the student is in the healthy zone. Leave scores in need of improvement without an asterisk. Provide the student with specific exercises and recommendations when a score is not within the healthy zone. The Fitness Flash should be accompanied by a letter that explains that fitness tests are just one aspect of a physical education program. Emphasize that participation, effort, and physical activity levels are equally important, and that progress and improvement are your main goals.

When scheduling a conference, be sensitive to busy working parents by accommodating their schedules. If after school is not convenient, then an early bird or evening appointment may be necessary. Being flexible will show that you really care about the child.

Take advantage of regular conference days at your school as well. Make sure that the administration has included you when making room assignments and schedules and when signing up parents. Explain that you need a setting for the conference that will be more conducive to individual parent–teacher discussions than a cramped, noisy gym office; request an administrative office, conference room, or empty classroom. Once you have scheduled a conference, send a simple, yet professional, letter of confirmation stating where you'll be holding the conference and your willingness to work with the parents during the school year. Arrange to have a translator nearby if necessary.

Prepare for the conference by updating the student's personal active lifestyle portfolio for parents to review. Make notes about the student's specific needs based on your assessments and observations.

Don't plan to sit behind a desk or arrange chairs in a teacher–student lecture format. Arrange the chairs in a semicircle to project the message that you are all equal members of the same team and that information should be shared to help support the children.

During the Conference

Begin the conference by attempting to relax the parents with a calm, nonthreatening voice. Greet the parents by saying, "It's wonderful to get the chance to talk with you about [Joseph's] progress over the last few weeks."

Use direct, plain language, avoiding educational jargon. For example, parents may not understand the difference between static and ballistic stretching but may be too embarrassed to ask you to explain.

Lead, but don't dominate, the conversation. If a child is obese, ask a few leading questions rather than lecturing about the ills of overweight children—for example, "What does [Joseph] usually do after dinner each night?" Or, "What types of snacks are usually available in the house?" Put the parents at ease by acknowledging that many poor habits are quite common.

Use concrete examples from the student's active lifestyle portfolio. For example, discuss the student's activity log to show that the only exercise he is getting is in physical education class, twice per week. Then ask the parents how they think they can help increase the child's activity level after school and during the weekend. Next, review the Fitness Flash you sent home a few

 **Fitness Flash**

To the parent or guardian of _____ ,

Your child's fitness status was recently examined as a part of the physical education program. Listed below are your child's results of the Fitnessgram test and the date of the assessment.

An asterisk (*) next to the score denotes a healthy fitness zone (HFZ) in the particular component. Scores that appear without an asterisk are in need of improvement. I will provide specific exercises to help develop the specific fitness components that need improvement.

Fitness component	Date: _____ Score:	Date: _____ Score:	Comments
Flexibility • Sit-and-reach • Shoulder			
Cardiorespiratory endurance • One-mile run • PACER			
Muscle fitness • Push-ups • Curl-ups			
Body composition • Percent fat • BMI			
Additional comments:			

Figure 10.4 A Fitness Flash keeps parents updated on their child's progress in physical education.

From S.J. Virgilio, 2012, *Fitness education for children: A team approach* (Champaign, IL: Human Kinetics).

weeks before the conference. Ask the parents if they have any questions about the scores or your recommendations.

Asking leading questions and discussing the student's portfolio are nonthreatening ways to guide parents toward making their own conclusions about their child's health and fitness needs. At this point, they may be more interested in hearing your suggestions for improvement than before the conference.

Be honest, truthful, and concise when discussing the child and making suggestions. Parents may listen more closely to suggestions that begin with, "It may be helpful for [Joseph] to. . . ." than with, "You need to. . . ." However, try not to overwhelm the parents with too much information in one meeting.

To close the conference, summarize the discussion and ask if they have any further questions. Provide a few action items to help follow up and reaffirm what you have discussed. For example, ask the parents to review and sign the physical activity log each week for the next four weeks.

After the Conference

Documenting the conference is very important. Develop a conference file for each student and keep it in your office. Include the day and time and which parent(s) attended. Add copies of any materials you reviewed. Note the main points of the conversation and any follow-up action you recommended. File a parent–teacher conference form in the school's main office if this is a requirement. Keeping an accurate account of what transpired can save you time and trouble later.

Finally, send a follow-up note or make a phone call to the parents when the student shows signs of improvement. This will indicate that the conference was worthwhile and that you still care.

PARENT EDUCATION

Parent education is a natural extension of parent–teacher communication. Parents must understand what you are trying to accomplish and why it is so important. If you educate parents with up-to-date health and fitness information, they'll be more inclined to participate with you and their children during the school year. But what can you do beyond newsletters? Parent seminars, a PTA demonstration, a parent–teacher wellness room, and a health and fitness fair all educate parents in fun and practical ways.

Parent Seminars

Schedule a brief seminar as part of the monthly PTA meeting or schedule lengthier seminars before school, at lunchtime, directly after school, or in the evening. Schedule them at different time slots during the school year so different parents may be able to attend. You can even repeat the same seminar at more than one time slot. If possible, schedule guest speakers to lecture about a variety of health and fitness topics. Contact the local university, the American Heart Association, medical schools, and health clubs for possible speakers. Remember to advertise the parent seminars in the newsletter. Be specific and concise: topic, speaker, place, time, and date.

PTA Demonstration

Each year arrange to showcase your program at a PTA meeting. Select a theme, such as North Side Elementary School Is Heart Smart. Here are a few suggestions to help you design your PTA night:

- Decorate the gym or cafeteria with the children's work, such as fitness posters, artwork, murals, exercise logs, the MyPlate image, and snapshots of children engaged in physical activity.
- Introduce yourself. State the basic goals and philosophy of your new fitness education program.
- Have a guest speaker such as a professor, medical doctor, or health educator. Ask the speaker to be brief (8 to 10 minutes is usually enough time) and very direct.
- Select about 25 children and give a physical activity demonstration. Music will help keep the activity upbeat (e.g., aerobics, jump rope workout, exercise bands and tubes, parachute play, Zumba dance).
- Narrate a PowerPoint slide show. Slides should show your students exercising, having fun, doing family workouts, or eating healthy foods. Finish with an upbeat song as you continue to show slides of children exercising and cooperating with each other.
- Video record students at several grade levels exercising and participating in the fitness education program. Set up three video monitors around the room so everyone can see the video. You can also include a few video clips within the PowerPoint presentation.

Parent–Teacher Wellness Room

Remember the staff wellness room we discussed in chapter 2? Why not expand it to include parents? Convert an empty classroom or turn the staff lounge into a combination wellness room and lounge. Include a reading area with a small reference space for books, DVDs, magazines, brochures, and cookbooks. Use another section of the room for exercise. One mat and an exercise bike or a treadmill facing a television and a few dumbbells and exercise tubes on a shelf are all you need. And why not add a DVD player and exercise DVDs? Decorate the room with American Heart Association posters, and place a small stereo on a shelf with soft rock music playing throughout the day. No time to develop this idea? Delegate the responsibility to interested parents. The PTA could supply the funds and request the space from the principal. Ensure that the hours for using the wellness room are flexible for busy parents and teachers. A wellness room that includes parents creates excellent public relations.

School Health Fair

Schedule a school health fair during a school day, on a weekend, or in the evening. Set up individual booths on the school grounds—for example, for posture analysis, body composition testing, healthy snack hints and samples, blood pressure and cholesterol screening, flexibility measures, and grip strength. Make each station a practical learning experience for the entire family. Plan this event with a local university, a local hospital, and the business community. (See also chapter 15.)

PARENT PARTICIPATION DURING SCHOOL HOURS

Parents and grandparents (who may have more time) can help support your program during the school day. Your parent survey will give you a sense of the willingness of parents to get involved during school hours. You can use the following approaches to bring the parents into the school:

- **Parent aides:** Parents can help you with attendance, marking a field, recording fitness scores, and organizing large classes.
- **Guest speakers:** Schedule parents who are knowledgeable in specific subjects to speak or demonstrate to your classes.

- **Volunteers and monitors:** Ask parents to supervise recess workouts, to video record classes, to record fitness scores on the computer, or to act as chauffeurs or chaperones for special events.
- **Facilities and equipment:** Ask handy parents to help build or repair physical education equipment. Painting lines on your court or putting up equipment room shelves are activities that some parents would feel very comfortable doing. Organize a Fitness Factory in which parents meet on a Saturday morning every three months to help you repair, build, and maintain your facilities and equipment.
- **School governance:** Establish a special committee of the PTA to help you with public relations, special events, fundraising, and curriculum decisions. This committee can also serve as an advocacy group, which may be the support you need in uncertain economic times.
- **Guests and observers:** Select certain days each month during which you open your classes to unscheduled parent visitors. Also, invite them to special event days as well as typical class periods. Parents will appreciate your openness and will be more likely to get involved. In addition, they'll see you in action and begin to develop an appreciation for the benefits of physical education.

HOME-BASED ACTIVITIES

The home is the most influential environment in a child's life. Take advantage of this by suggesting creative family fitness activities. (*Caution:* Many parents are not accustomed to playing or exercising as a family. Begin slowly and don't expect too much progress at first. If you are persistent and follow some of the recommendations in this chapter, you will be quite successful.) Use your newsletter to communicate the following home-based activity possibilities.

Family Game: Fitness Fortune

Parents and children accumulate fitness dollars by engaging in moderate to vigorous physical activity. Give each physical activity a specific dollar value. For example:

Jogging 1 mile (1.6 km) = $1,000

Walking 30 minutes = $500

Step aerobics 30 minutes = $1,500

Resistance training 30 minutes = $1,500

Raking leaves 15 minutes = $500

Vacuuming the house 15 minutes = $500

Biking 30 minutes = $1,500

The family totals each member's dollars at the end of each week. Each family member describes how he or she would spend the hypothetical dollars. Dad may purchase a new entertainment system! This activity may be logged in the active lifestyle portfolio and shared with the rest of the class in a brief discussion.

Family Playacting

The family spends one evening writing and casting a miniplay based on a health and fitness theme. For example, the miniplay may at first depict how an unhealthy, tired, lazy family acts on a typical day. The second portion of the play depicts how, through exercise and nutritious foods, a healthy, active family responds to the day. Another evening, the family could perform their play for neighbors or video record it and show it later to grandparents, friends, or teachers.

Family Fitness Contract

A family fitness contract asks the family to make a commitment to exercise or engage in physical activity together. Create a contract that allows the family to decide what type of exercise they would like to do and when they would like to do it (see figure 10.5). If the family completes the contract, the physical education department gives them a reward, such as YMCA passes, frozen yogurt certificates, spa visits, or T-shirts.

Homework Helpers

Physical education homework assignments that involve parents can provide an exciting learning experience for the entire family. Select activities that support your module goals but that don't duplicate class activities. For example, send home the Heart Thump homework assignment (level II; see figure 10.6). Children and parents can graph their heart rates, using an X for parents and a dot for children. Have children explain to their parents how exercise makes the heart beat faster, making the heart stronger, and how after resting the heart rate is lower.

Neighborhood Fitness Trail

In this assignment, children and parents design fitness stations throughout the neighborhood. They draw a map and plan exercises at each station (see figure 10.7). Ask parents to calculate the total distance of the course with their car's odometer. For safety's sake, emphasize that participants should jog and exercise on the sidewalk (level III).

Wake-Up Workout or Evening's End

A Wake-Up Workout or Evening's End is a 10-minute exercise routine that parents and children design and perform before school or after dinner. Ask the family to keep track of their workouts on a large calendar placed on the refrigerator.

TV Time-Out

Ask parents and children to watch a sporting event together. After the game, have the family answer questions such as the following:

- What specific exercises would be important for this sport?
- Did the players use good sporting behavior?
- Did physical conditioning play a role in the outcome of the game?
- Name two players who used strength, endurance, or speed to gain an advantage in the game.

Fitness Minute

Each time a commercial is aired during a favorite prime-time show, the family does one to two minutes of exercise. Family members take turns leading and selecting the exercise for the group.

COMMUNITY INVOLVEMENT

The community can be a gold mine for your physical education program. First, to establish a good relationship, organize a school–community wellness committee. (This can be a subcommittee of the school wellness committee discussed in chapter 2.) Invite local business leaders, parents, and senior citizens to join your program; each will be a link to a different segment of the

Family Fitness Contract

We, the _____ family, promise that today _____ (date) we will adopt an active lifestyle and become more physically active.

We acknowledge that general physical activity is very important to the health of all family members. We promise to devote _____ minutes on Monday, Tuesday, Wednesday, Thursday, Friday, Saturday, Sunday (circle at least three days) toward making positive changes in our physical activity levels. The best time of day for us to work on this change is _____ a.m./p.m.

We will try our best to fulfill this one-month contract as we develop our family physical activity goals. We understand that fulfilling this contract will entitle us to receive YMCA passes or frozen yogurt certificates from the school physical education program.

Family members (sign):

_____

_____

_____

_____

_____

_____

This promise was witnessed by

_____

Figure 10.5 The family fitness contract allows families to commit to physical activity together.

From S.J. Virgilio, 2012, *Fitness education for children: A team approach* (Champaign, IL: Human Kinetics).

Heart Thump

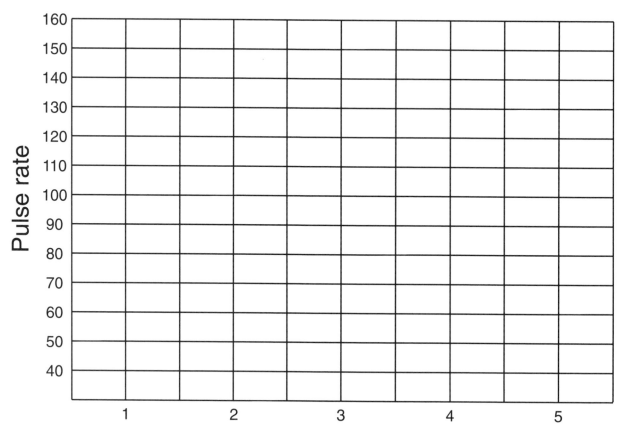

● Child
X Parent

1 Pulse at rest
2 Pulse after 30 seconds of jogging in place
3 Pulse after 30 seconds of jumping jacks
4 Pulse after one minute at rest
5 Pulse after two minutes at rest

Figure 10.6 Use the Heart Thump homework activity to graph your family's heart rates.

From S.J. Virgilio, 2012, *Fitness education for children: A team approach* (Champaign, IL: Human Kinetics).

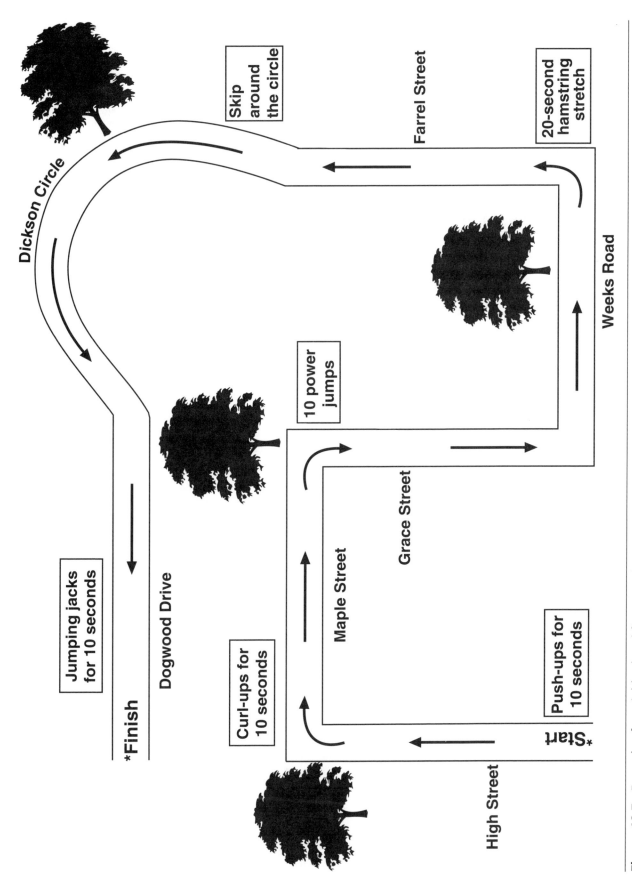

Figure 10.7 Example of a neighborhood fitness trail.

community. The following are guidelines for committee selection:

- Select individuals from different social and cultural backgrounds, reflecting the ethnic and religious makeup of your community.
- Encourage a gender balance.
- Involve people from various age groups.
- Choose volunteers who value health and fitness—for example, runners, fitness leaders, and spa owners.
- Invite proven community leaders to join.

The committee should meet once a month to discuss a variety of topics, including how to educate the community about healthy lifestyles and how they can help the school fitness education program plan special events such as a community health fair or fun run. It may also be helpful to identify your approach by giving it a name, such as the East Williston Heart-Healthy School–Community Program. One special event in the fall and one in the spring will keep the committee active throughout the school year.

With the help of a strong committee, you will be able to network throughout the community. The community support gained will strengthen your program and provide you with many advantages, such as the following:

- The city or another organization may let you use its swimming pool for classes or after-school programs.
- Sporting goods stores may donate athletic and fitness equipment.
- A local health club or YMCA may supply you with free passes to use as incentives for your students.
- Bowling facilities may give free or low-cost alley time for your classes or the opportunity to develop an intramural program after school.
- Restaurants may offer heart-healthy choices and give your students special discounts.
- The local American Heart Association or American Cancer Society may provide workshops, brochures, videos, or educational kits for your school.
- Frozen yogurt stores may donate buy-one-get-one-free certificates for you to use as incentives.

- Local newspapers or radio stations may advertise your program and special events.

Give Back to the Community

The school–community relationship is a two-way street. It is very important to provide the community with a number of benefits and services in return for its support. Consider the following suggestions:

- Each year provide two or three community health seminars in the school cafeteria from 7 to 9 p.m. Possible topics include Heart Disease—The Facts, Exercise—For the Health of It, and Eat to Your Heart's Content. Schedule medical doctors, university professors, or nutritionists to speak.
- Provide space for local clubs and organizations to meet during the evening.
- Help clean up and maintain the softball and Little League fields at your school or in your town's public parks.
- Begin an exercise class for senior citizens in your community. Your compensation should come from the school district's budget because many seniors pay local school taxes.
- Have students keep the school grounds and surrounding streets clean. Plant flowers in the spring to show your community pride.
- Patronize the local businesses that support your school.
- Distribute flyers to your students about community programs such as summer camps, Little League teams, recreation centers, exercise classes, bowling leagues, and swimming activities.
- Start a Saturday morning walking club. Meet at the school and walk through the neighborhood. Give your club a name—for example, The Fitness Walkers.
- Provide your help and expertise to local youth sports teams.

Fall Community Health Fair

Form a subcommittee to plan and carry out a fall community health fair. Plan to hold it on the school grounds on a Saturday or Sunday. First, it is vital to the success of the event to begin by establishing a budget. Ask local businesses such as banks and grocery stores to sponsor the event; in return, you place the businesses' names on the brochures that will be distributed throughout the day. To defray any unexpected costs, sell heart-healthy refreshments during the event. Donate a portion of the profits gained from selling refreshments to the American Heart Association or a similar organization to give back to the community.

Make sure the committee remembers to advertise. Committee members can approach your local or regional newspapers and TV and radio stations with public service announcements. Two other effective advertising tools are distributing flyers throughout the school and community and designing a poster advertising the fair and asking local merchants to display it in their windows. Students may also design and make posters for display at the public library and local businesses.

Establish a wellness booth as the focus of your fair, locating it in the middle of the fair. Let this booth serve as the general administrative area for questions, problems, or emergencies. You may also wish to include an array of information about a number of health topics, perhaps in the form of free brochures that clearly explain basic health principles. In addition, consider including a small bookstore at which community members may purchase more substantive books and materials related to healthy lifestyles. Locally owned bookstores may set this up and give the school a portion of the profits.

Finally, be certain you have planned for setup, cleanup, security, and road supervision. Contact the local police several weeks before the event to inquire about traffic and security issues.

Following are possible health fair participants and ideas:

Local restaurant	Heart-healthy foods
Physical therapists	Posture screening
Health club owner	Equipment demonstration
Dance studio	Zumba dancing
Nurses	Blood pressure screening
Nutritionist	Healthy snacking
Medical school	Cholesterol screening
University Health and Physical Education Department	Body composition testing
Sports apparel store	Selecting the correct physical activity shoe
Exercise physiologist	Myths about exercise
Parents	Family fitness workouts
PTA	Personal hygiene

For ways to include children in developing a health fair, see chapter 15.

Spring Fun Run

As with the fall health fair, form a subcommittee to organize a spring fun run. If possible, route the run through the school's neighborhood. Contact local police to provide supervision and traffic control.

Sample fun run schedule (printed on flyer):

8:00 a.m.: Group warm-up with physical education teacher

8:30 a.m.: 5K Community Fun Run/Walk (ages 7 and older) (Everyone receives a ribbon!)

9:30 a.m.: Little Tykes Run (ages 2 to 6; 200-yard run) (Everyone is a winner! Each child receives a ribbon!)

11:00 a.m.: Awards for each age division

12:00 noon: Community picnic

1:30 p.m.: Parent–child softball game

Grocery Store Tour

Arrange to visit the local grocery store just before it opens in the morning. This is a great field trip for your fifth- or sixth-grade classes. Give each student $50 in play money to spend on food they would purchase for the family if they were a parent. Meet as a group and introduce the store manager, who may speak for a few minutes about the grocery business, how they order the food, and the basic store operations. Then have students get carts and go food shopping for 20 minutes. Ask students to shop for one day's food: breakfast, lunch, dinner, and a snack. After checking out, students get computer readouts of exactly what they purchased. Later that day, have students analyze and compare their purchases to the healthy choices recommended by MyPlate. Ask students to note any major discrepancies in their selections. You might ask students to take their shopping lists home and discuss their purchases with their parents.

Village Visits

Arrange to have a class review several businesses in your community. You may arrange to visit a frozen yogurt shop and study how yogurt is made and what it is made of. A health food store is another good place to visit. Ask students to analyze the fat, sugar, and sodium contents of the various foods on the shelf. Then arrange to view a local health club. Perhaps the children could participate in a step aerobics class. Finally, visit a local restaurant that offers heart-healthy items, and review how the chefs prepare the items and what makes them heart healthy. Then students could sample the food and discover how tasty healthy items can be.

Young at Heart

Young at Heart enlists the help of the senior citizens in your community, matching them to first- or second-graders as exercise partners. Attend local seniors' meetings to explain your purpose and major objectives. During the first and third Fridays of each month (or whatever works for your schedule), the seniors visit the school and walk and exercise with their partners. While exercising, they discuss how they are feeling and what is going on in their lives. When the walk is completed, the class returns to the classroom, where the senior reads to the student for about 30 minutes. This program may be especially meaningful for children who have lost their grandparents or have grandparents who live out of town. This is also another way to give back to your community.

Can It

Collect canned foods from the community to help the homeless or natural disaster victims. Taking civic responsibility to help a charity is good public relations. Announce that you are interested in healthy foods that are low in fat, sugar, and sodium, reinforcing your support of healthy foods. Students may also use healthy canned foods for resistance exercises such as arm curls, or study and analyze the labels.

Fund-Raising

When people in the community at large are aware of your physical education program, they will be more inclined to help you financially. Individuals and businesses that have participated in the community-based activities will gladly sponsor children for such fund-raising events as Jump Rope for Heart, Step for Heart, and raffles to buy equipment. The American Cancer Association and the American Heart Association have various fund-raising events during the year. The school may join these events and share a percentage of the donations.

Once you have developed a comprehensive community involvement program, it's much easier to apply for local, state, or national grants for your school. Speak to the Department of Health and Physical Education at the local university. Professors may be interested in using your school as a health and fitness intervention model for their research. Funds may be available for graduate assistants, equipment, and instructional materials through the university. As we have already touched on, local businesses may be interested in sponsoring community-based programs. They may volunteer to adopt a grade level at your school to support the cost of curriculum materials, fitness equipment, cholesterol screening, and special events. For additional information, see *Promoting Physical Activity: A Guide for Community Action, Second Edition* (Centers for Disease Control and Prevention 2010).

SUMMARY

Work with your students' parents and community organizations to expand your opportunities to develop physically active and healthy lifestyles in children. Keep in mind that family and community influences have a significant impact on the health behaviors of children. Channel these influences by including parents and the community in your fitness education plans. Indeed, never underestimate the power of parent and community involvement. The time you invest in communication and building bridges to parents and your community will ultimately bring tremendous dividends to your physical education program. Remember, it takes a village to raise a child.

Fitness
Activities

Developmental Exercises

> What a disgrace it is for a man
> to grow old without ever seeing
> the beauty and strength
> of which his body is capable.
> —*Socrates*

As you well know, cardiorespiratory endurance, muscle fitness, flexibility, and body composition are each critical to the health and well-being of children—indeed, to all of us. As you design your program, include a variety of developmental exercises from these health-related physical fitness components while also focusing on the need for a physically active lifestyle throughout the school year. I recommend that you review the background information of each component in chapter 4 as well as the specific exercise guidelines so that you can safely implement the activities in this chapter in your physical education curriculum.

The cardiorespiratory endurance, muscle fitness, and flexibility exercises described in this chapter are only some examples among many that are developmentally appropriate for children. Present these exercises in an open, personalized manner, allowing students to make decisions and assume individual responsibility for their progress. This gives them the decision-making practice they need to become lifelong fitness advocates. In contrast, emphasizing rigid class structure and regimentation may cause negative attitudes about exercise and therefore may have an adverse effect on long-term participation in physical activity.

As discussed in chapter 4, exercise prescription recommendations and formal workout schedules often advised for adults may not be appropriate for school-aged children. Children respond better to interval-type activities, spontaneity, and group play, which are all fun ways to increase their physical activity levels and therefore their overall fitness.

Tailor exercises and activities to meet the individual needs of your students. Furthermore, be certain that every child in your class feels truly included and has an opportunity to become successful in each task. Let's start by examining specific exercises for developing cardiorespiratory endurance.

CARDIORESPIRATORY ENDURANCE

First, let's quickly review the four basic techniques used to enhance cardiorespiratory endurance: continuous activity, interval activity, fartlek course, and circuit course, along with specific related activities.

Continuous Activity

As the name implies, continuous activity refers to large-muscle movements sustained for an extended period of time. The activity may vary in intensity but remains continuous for several minutes. Activities appropriate for elementary students include jogging, walking, rope jumping, dancing, aerobic dancing, step aerobics, and basketball and soccer games. Physical activities that you may wish to recommend to children and parents outside of school include the following:

- Biking
- Swimming
- Hiking
- Skating (ice and in-line)
- Rowing
- Family walks
- Exercising to DVDs
- Jogging and walking
- Dancing

See additional examples of continuous activity in chapters 12 and 13.

RANDOM RUN

Ask children to walk or jog in any direction for a specified period of time. At your signal, the class returns to the starting point.

BUDDY WALKS

Have students find a friend in class to walk with for a specified period of time. If both agree, allow them to also jog or run. Encourage students to stay together, interact with each other, and work as partners in this cooperative learning activity.

LINE CHANGE

Arrange students in straight lines of five or six, facing the same direction. Have them begin jogging or walking in any direction, staying in lines. At the signal, have the last student in line jog to the front to become the leader. Continue until everyone has had a chance to lead the line.

ESTIMATION

Inform students that you will be timing them as they walk or jog three times around the course you have outlined. Have students write down the times they estimate the course will take them on index cards before they start. Declare the student who comes the closest to guessing her final time as the winner. The bases around a softball infield work well as the route for this activity, and moving around the bases is a nice warm-up activity before a softball class. You could also select a random landmark on your field to define the route (e.g., run to the large oak tree and back).

Interval Activities

Interval activities enhance cardiorespiratory endurance in school-aged children. Children normally work hard, rest, and recover quickly during physical activity. As you may recall, this approach uses continuous large-muscle movements that you alternate by lowering and raising the intensity, varying the distance or recovery time, or modifying the number of repetitions or sets. You can choose from a variety of activities. The following is an example of a jogging interval workout appropriate for level III.

JOGGING INTERVALS

Warm up.	5 minutes
Walk briskly.	50 yards (46 m)
Jog at 75 percent speed.	150 yards (137 m)
Walk briskly.	50 yards (46 m)
Jog at 75 percent speed.	150 yards (137 m)
Walk briskly.	50 yards (46 m)
Jog at 75 percent speed.	150 yards (137 m)
Walk briskly.	50 yards (46 m)
Cool down.	5 minutes

JUMP ROPE INTERVALS

Rope jumping is a particularly fun interval routine. Provide a rope for each student (the plastic beaded ropes are the most common and most appropriate for children because they are easy to control). The following example is appropriate for level II:

Warm up.	3 to 5 minutes
Ask students to design various letters with the ropes and imitate the letter shapes with their body parts.	3 to 5 minutes
Ask students to place the rope in a straight line on the floor. Have them walk, jog, skip, and then hop once around the rope.	2 minutes

Play music during the next set of activities (124 beats per minute). When the music stops, have children pause and listen for the next direction.

With ropes still on the floor, jump back and forth over the ropes.	15 to 20 seconds

Jump on one foot back and forth.	15 to 20 seconds
Walk around the playing area as if your legs are pieces of spaghetti.	15 to 20 seconds
Walk around the playing area as if your legs are stiff as steel.	15 to 20 seconds
Do side swings: Hold the rope with both hands on the left side of the body and swing the rope in rhythm.	15 to 20 seconds
Do a two-foot basic step: Jump with two feet (include a rebound step while the rope is overhead).	15 to 20 seconds
Do side swings: right side.	15 to 20 seconds
Do a two-foot basic step.	15 to 20 seconds

Do side swings: left to right in a crisscross motion.	15 to 20 seconds
Do a two-foot basic step.	15 to 20 seconds
Cool down.	3 to 5 minutes

If students feel uncomfortable performing the two-foot basic step, allow them to hold the rope in one hand at one side and turn the rope while jumping in rhythm to the music, or to use lines on the gym floor to jump over.

Fartlek Course

A fartlek course is similar to interval activity; however, the intensity and speed are not controlled. The activity course varies to place stress on different muscle groups by changing the levels and the direction often. Figure 11.1 shows a fartlek course adapted for elementary school levels II and III. The course includes eight different movements.

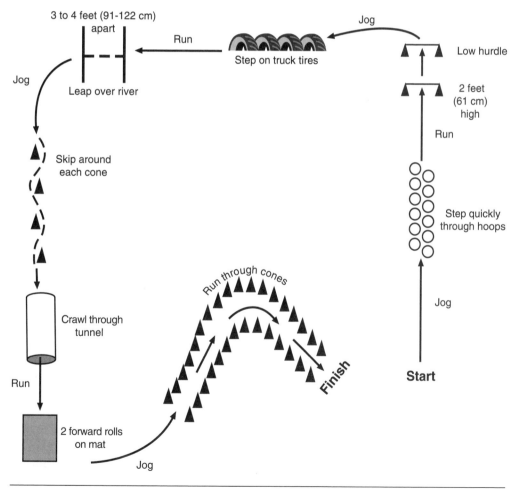

Figure 11.1 An example of a fartlek course for levels II and III.

Place task cards at each new movement area to identify the activity as well as arrows to remind students of the direction to go in next.

Circuit Course

A circuit course is a continuous activity that includes a general body workout, developing various components of health-related physical fitness, such as cardiorespiratory endurance, muscle fitness, and flexibility. Once again, place task cards at each station, describing the specific task and the proper techniques. Pictures may be helpful at some stations to remind students of proper form and body alignment (e.g., curl-ups). Separate the stations by 15 to 20 yards (14 to 18 m). Encourage students to move at their own paces, but remind them that speed is not the major objective (see figure 11.2).

MUSCLE FITNESS

As you know, muscular strength and muscular endurance are not the same thing. Muscular strength is the capacity of a muscle or muscle group to exert maximum force against a resistance. Muscular endurance is the capacity of a muscle or muscle group to exert force over a period of time against a resistance that is less than the maximum you can move. I use the term *muscle fitness* to avoid confusion because children should not perform strength-related exercises. Because of the danger of overuse injuries, stress to major joints, and muscle imbalance, carefully supervise elementary students who do engage in resistance exercising. (See chapters 1 and 4 for a complete explanation of resistance exercising.)

You can choose from a broad range of exercises to enhance muscle fitness. The activities

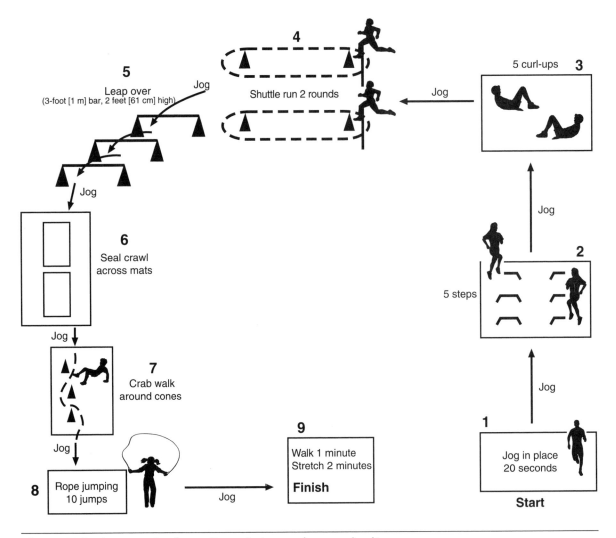

Figure 11.2 An example of a cardiorespiratory endurance circuit course.

described here will broadly develop muscular endurance. To maintain muscular balance, it's important to cover all the major muscle groups: shoulders, arms, chest, back, trunk, and legs. Furthermore, ensure that students perform exer-cises equally on each side of the body as well as properly align their bodies for each activity.

Table 11.1 lists the appropriate developmental level to begin each activity. The checkmarks denote the most appropriate levels to incorporate.

Table 11.1 Muscle Fitness by Developmental Level

Activity	Level I	Level II	Level III
EXERCISES			
Seal crawl	✔		
Crab crawl	✔		
Arm saw	✔		
Turtle walk	✔		
Push-up		✔	✔
Inchworm	✔		
Problem-solver	✔		
Stork stand	✔		
Treadmill	✔	✔	
Curl-up	✔	✔	✔
Curl-up and twist			✔
Diagonal crunch			✔
PARACHUTE ACTIVITIES			
Curl-up	✔	✔	✔
Chute down	✔	✔	✔
Wrist roll	✔	✔	✔
Push-up		✔	✔
Hurricane	✔	✔	
Superdome	✔	✔	✔
Bubble	✔	✔	✔
Floating cloud	✔	✔	✔
Popcorn	✔	✔	✔
Parachute golf			✔
Tug-of-war		✔	✔
MEDICINE BALL ACTIVITIES			
Chest pass			✔
Curl-up and throw			✔
Overhead pass			✔
Half-twist pass			✔

(continued)

Table 11.1 *(continued)*

Activity	Level I	Level II	Level III
EXERCISES WITH RESISTANCE TUBES AND BANDS			
Arm curl		✔	✔
Triceps extension		✔	✔
Lateral deltoid raise		✔	✔
Upright shoulder row		✔	✔
Arm extension		✔	✔
Chest press		✔	✔
Ball/band squeeze		✔	✔
Big band march step		✔	✔
Kickback		✔	✔
Crossover lift		✔	✔
BODY SUPPORT EXERCISES			
Heel raise	✔	✔	✔
Wall seat	✔	✔	✔

Exercises

Incorporate the following muscle fitness exercises throughout your physical education program. Where possible, I have written the instructions as you might speak them directly to the students, making them easy for you to begin using immediately. Study the photos carefully, and demonstrate proper technique to ensure that your students perform the exercises safely.

SEAL CRAWL

Lie on your abdomen with your hands directly under your shoulders, pointing slightly outward, and your arms straight, feet 3 to 4 inches (8 to 10 cm) apart. Move your hands left, right, left, right while dragging your legs along the floor. (Muscle groups: arms and shoulders; see figure 11.3.)

CRAB CRAWL

Lie on your back with your weight supported on your hands and feet. To begin, move your right hand and left foot forward at the same time; then move your left hand and right foot forward. Be sure the hands are pointed toward the feet to relieve stress on the shoulders. Move your body sideways, forward, or backward. (Muscle groups: arms and shoulders; see figure 11.4.)

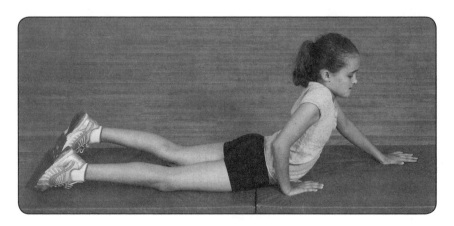

Figure 11.3 Seal crawl.

Figure 11.4 Crab crawl.

ARM SAW

In pairs, stand 8 to 12 inches (20 to 30 cm) apart, facing each other. Clasp hands, keeping the wrists stable. Begin with each of you pushing your right hand and pulling with your left at a steady, controlled pace. Pretend to be sawing a tree. (Muscle groups: arms and shoulders; see figure 11.5.)

Figure 11.5 Arm saw.

TURTLE WALK

Lie facedown with your hands flat on the floor, your arms straight, and your knees off the floor. Keep your arms and legs slightly wider than shoulder-width apart. Move the right arm and leg together; then the left arm and leg. Move forward, backward, or sideways. Make small movements to reduce the stress on your muscles and joints. (Muscle groups: arms and shoulders; see figure 11.6.)

Figure 11.6 Turtle walk.

PUSH-UP

Lie on your chest on the floor (or mat). Place your hands under your shoulders with your body in a straight line. To begin, raise your body by extending your arms; then go down until your chest is 3 inches (7.6 cm) from the floor or your elbows are at a 90-degree angle. (Muscle groups: arms and shoulders; see figure 11.7.)

Figure 11.7 Push-up.

Use the modified bent-knee push-up to decrease difficulty (see figure 11.8).

To increase difficulty, try these modifications:

- Open-hands (wide-stance) push-up
- Closed-hands (4 in. or 10 cm apart) push-up
- Hold in upright position for 10 seconds
- Slow-motion push-up
- Only one foot on floor
- Push up and clap hands
- Chair push-up (hand on each seat) (see figure 11.9)
- Box push-up (see figure 11.10)
- Wall push-up (Stand 2 to 3 ft, or 0.6 to 0.9 m, from the wall, hands flat, legs straight, and back straight. Push away from the wall.)

═══ **PROBLEM-SOLVER** ═══

Ask students a series of questions, such as these: "From a supine position [demonstrate] with both knees bent, can you raise your left leg, place it down, raise your right leg, place it down? Can you raise your left knee to your chest? Now can you raise your right knee to your chest? Can you raise both knees to your chest? With knees bent, can you raise your head while looking straight up? Can you raise your shoulders off the mat a few inches [or centimeters]? Can you raise your head and bring your left knee to your chest?" (Muscle group: abdominals.)

Figure 11.8 Modified bent-knee push-up.

Figure 11.9 Chair push-up.

Figure 11.10 Box push-up.

Figure 11.11 Inchworm.

Figure 11.12 Stork stand.

═══ **TREADMILL** ═══

Begin in a crawling position. Bring one leg up to the chest and extend the other leg backward. Begin moving by alternating your legs in a steady, rhythmic pattern. Keep your upper body still and your head up. I'll start by timing you for short intervals (20 to 30 seconds). (Muscle groups: legs and abdominals; see figure 11.13.)

═══ **INCHWORM** ═══

Sit on the floor with your arms folded across your chest. To move, pull your bottom and hips forward while pushing down into the floor with your heels. (Muscle groups: hips and legs; see figure 11.11.)

═══ **STORK STAND** ═══

Stand straight and tall with your hands on your hips. Bend your right knee slightly. Place your left foot gently against the inside of your right knee. Hold for 5 to 10 seconds. This activity helps strengthen your legs and may also develop your balancing skills. (Muscle group: legs; see figure 11.12.)

Figure 11.13 Treadmill.

CURL-UP

Lie on your back with your knees bent to approximately 140 degrees with your feet flat on the floor [demonstrate]. Place your arms alongside your body with your palms down. Lift your head and shoulders to a 45-degree angle (demonstrate; see figure 11.14). Slowly lower your head and shoulders until your shoulder blades touch the floor. (Muscle group: abdominals.)

Figure 11.14 Curl-up.

CURL-UP AND TWIST

Lie on your back with your knees bent and feet flat on the floor. Fold your arms across your chest. Begin with a curl-up; then twist to one side by rotating the upper torso, go back to a straight position, and then down. Repeat, alternating sides. (Muscle groups: abdominals, obliques, and hip flexors; see figure 11.15.)

Figure 11.15 Curl-up and twist.

DIAGONAL CRUNCH

Lie on your side with one leg on top of the other, knees bent. Make sure your bottom shoulder blade is flat against the mat. Place one hand behind your head to support your neck. Crunch up by raising the bottom shoulder blade off the mat. Repeat, alternating sides. (Muscle groups: upper abdominals and obliques; see figure 11.16.)

Figure 11.16 Diagonal crunch.

Parachute Activities

The parachute can be an excellent piece of equipment to promote muscular strength and endurance. Through teamwork and cooperation, the entire class will be able to participate in highly active games, locomotor movements, shape formations, and exercises.

CURL-UP

Everyone, sit with knees bent, holding the parachute at your waist with an overhand grip. [Divide the class in half.] This half, lie back to perform the curl-up. The other half, lean forward to give slack. Then do the opposite. (Muscle group: abdominals.)

CHUTE DOWN

Everyone, hold the parachute at waist level with an overhand grip, feet at least shoulder-width apart. Now, all together, lift the chute overhead. At my signal, pull the chute back to your waist, using only your arms and shoulders. (Muscle groups: arms and shoulders.)

WRIST ROLL

Everyone, hold the chute straight out with an overhand grip. Now slowly roll the chute toward the center, keeping it tight by leaning slightly backward. (Muscle groups: wrist and forearms.)

PUSH-UP

Everyone, raise the chute overhead. Pull the chute down to the floor. Place your hands on the edge of the chute with your legs extended away from the chute. Perform as many push-ups as possible before the chute deflates. (Muscle group: arms.)

HURRICANE

Everyone, grasp the parachute with an overhand grip. Begin by making moderate (medium-sized) waves, moving the chute up and down. [Describe an approaching storm as students move the chute in response to your description.] The sky gets black, the wind picks up, the waves get larger with deep swells. Now the wind is swirling; the waves get short and choppy. Oh no, the hurricane is here! Move the chute up and down as fast as you can. [Have them cool down by describing how the storm is passing and everything is safe and back to normal.] (Muscle groups: arms and shoulders.)

SUPERDOME

At the signal "Up," everyone lifts the chute overhead. At the signal "Down," everyone brings the chute down to the floor. Watch the chute form a dome. (Muscle groups: arms and shoulders.)

BUBBLE

This activity begins with the parachute on the floor. Everyone, squat down and grasp the chute with an overhand grip. At the signal, lift the chute overhead and at the same time walk quickly into the center forming a large bubble. (Muscle groups: arms and shoulders.)

FLOATING CLOUD

Everyone, grasp the chute with an overhand grip. At the signal, raise the chute overhead. At the command "Release" let go of the chute. (Muscle groups: arms and shoulders.)

POPCORN

I'm going to place several types of balls in the parachute. Everyone, grasp the parachute with an overhand grip. On the first signal, "Simmer," shake the chute, creating small ripples. On the second signal, "Cook," make the balls move more rapidly by shaking the chute harder. On the last signal, "Popcorn," make large, fast ripples by waving your arms and jumping up and down to pop the balls straight up—but try to keep the popcorn in the pan. [To culminate the activity, ask students to pop the balls outside the parachute.] (Muscle groups: arms and shoulders.)

PARACHUTE GOLF

[Divide the class into a red and a yellow team around the parachute. Place all students of each team on one side of the parachute. Place a red and yellow ball inside the parachute.] At the signal, as a team, try to move the parachute to get your team's ball in the center hole. Do not use your hands to move a ball. The first team to score three points wins. (Muscle groups: arms and shoulders.)

TUG-OF-WAR

[Divide the class in half.] At the signal "Pull," each side pulls straight back. The team that pulls across the curved line, marked 3 to 4 feet (0.9 to 1.2 m) directly behind them, is the winner. The entire team need not cross the line. [Use your own judgment to decide when a team has won.] Take care not to damage the parachute. [Check for tears or holes before each use.] (Muscle groups: arms and shoulders.)

Medicine Ball Activities

Medicine balls come in various colors and sizes and are weighted to develop hand, arm, and upper-torso strength. The new and improved balls are soft, pliable, and stuffed with a special fiber padding. Following are the three most appropriate medicine balls for the elementary school level:

- 4-pound (1.8 kg), 7-inch-diameter (18 cm) medicine ball
- 2.2-pound (1 kg), 6-inch-diameter (15 cm) PVC plastic ball
- 2-pound (0.9 kg), 6-inch-diameter (15 cm) Powerball with handle

The following exercises may be used in a medicine ball routine.

CHEST PASS

Stand, with feet shoulder-width apart, two steps from a partner. Push the ball slowly from your chest with palms facing outward. Keep your knees

Figure 11.17 Chest pass with medicine ball.

and back slightly bent. The catcher receives the ball with the palms facing upward, knees bent and hands shoulder-width apart. (Muscle groups: chest and arms; see figure 11.17.)

CURL-UP AND THROW

Lie on your back with knees bent, holding a medicine ball at your chest, arms slightly bent.

Slowly perform a curl-up, lifting your head and shoulders off the mat, contracting (tightening) the abdominal muscles. Gently toss the medicine ball to your partner. The partner tosses it back in one smooth motion without losing the continuity of the curl-up movement. (Muscle groups: abdominals, shoulders, and arms; see figure 11.18.)

Figure 11.18 Sequence for curl-up and throw with medicine ball.

OVERHEAD PASS

Stand back-to-back about 8 inches (20 cm) from a partner with knees slightly bent. The student with the ball passes it directly overhead. The partner accepts the ball with palms facing upward and hands shoulder-width apart. (Muscle groups: arms and shoulders; see figure 11.19.)

Figure 11.19 Overhead pass with medicine ball.

HALF-TWIST PASS

Stand back-to-back with your partner with your knees bent. The student with the ball holds it at waist level. At the signal, both of you perform a gentle half-twist. The student with the ball twists to the right; the partner twists to the left to accept the ball at waist level. Repeat the exercise, alternating sides. (Muscle groups: abdominals and obliques; see figure 11.20.)

Exercises With Resistance Tubes and Bands

The use of rubberized resistance equipment is an innovative and creative way to increase muscular strength and endurance in the elementary school.

Figure 11.20 Half-twist pass with medicine ball.

The tubes and bands are light and durable and add variety to your program. The rubberized resistance equipment is color-coded to denote the levels of resistance, allowing you to tailor specific exercises to individual fitness needs. In addition, this equipment provides moderate resistance without placing undue stress on the muscles and joints common in other weighted exercise products. Remind your students of the following guidelines when using resistance equipment.

- Never tie pieces of tubing together.
- Inspect the tubes carefully before each class for cracks.
- Breathe normally—never hold your breath.
- When standing, exercise in slow, controlled movements with proper body alignment, with your knees slightly bent.
- Perform an equal number of repetitions with each arm or leg to avoid muscle imbalance.
- Rest at least 10 seconds between sets of exercises.
- When standing, step firmly on the tube with the middle of your foot to secure the tube, keeping your knees slightly bent.
- Space students about 4 feet (1.2 m) apart when exercising to avoid accidents.

The following are examples of exercises performed with exercise tubing and bands. Remember to make sure students always anchor the tube under the instep of one foot or both feet (to increase resistance), slightly bending both knees.

ARM CURL

Grasp one handle in each hand with palms facing up, arms straight at your sides and elbows against the sides of your body. Curl both arms toward your chest while keeping your elbows at your sides. Return slowly to the starting position. (Muscle group: biceps; see figure 11.21.)

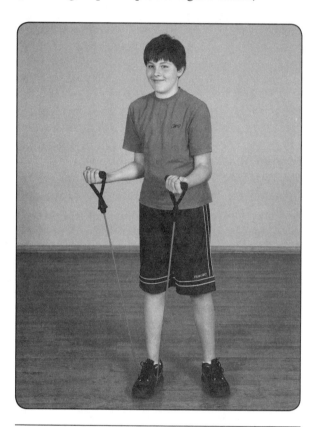

Figure 11.21 Arm curl with exercise tubing.

TRICEPS EXTENSION

Stand in a lunge stance [demonstrate] and place the tubing under your front foot. Cross the tubing and grasp the handle with the hand of the nonexercising arm and rest it on the upper leg. Bend forward at the waist, resting the weight of your upper body on the nonexercising arm. Grasp the handle with the exercise arm next to your hip with your palm facing backward. Keeping your wrist firm, slowly straighten the exercise arm and end with

Figure 11.22 Triceps extension with exercise tubing.

your palm facing up. Return slowly to the starting position. (Muscle group: triceps; see figure 11.22.)

LATERAL DELTOID RAISE

Grasp one handle in each hand. Keep your elbows slightly bent at the sides of your body. Raise your elbows away from your sides while keeping your

Figure 11.23 Lateral deltoid raise with exercise tubing.

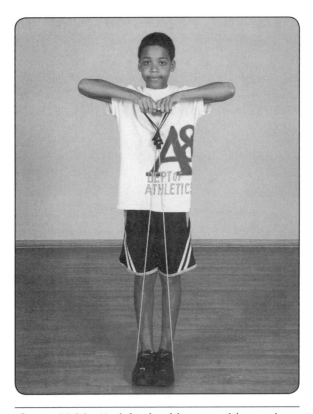

Figure 11.24 Upright shoulder row with exercise tubing.

wrists and forearms firm. Slowly return to the starting position. (Muscle group: deltoids; see figure 11.23.)

UPRIGHT SHOULDER ROW

Grasp the handles with both hands and position your arms straight in front of your thighs. Bend your elbows and pull your hands up to chest height. Slowly return to the starting position. (Muscle group: deltoids; see figure 11.24.)

ARM EXTENSION

The arm extension and the chest press are shown using the toner rubberized resistance equipment from **SPRI** Quik-Fit for Kids (see the website in appendix B), but you can use any type of resistance band.

Grasp the toner with your left hand and position it behind your back with your elbow bent and palm facing outward. Position the exercise arm over the shoulder with the palm facing up. Grasping the toner handle, slowly pull the exercise arm (right) away from the shoulder, and return. Do the same number of repetitions on each side. (Muscle groups: triceps and shoulders; see figure 11.25.)

Figure 11.25 Arm extension with toner.

CHEST PRESS

Stand with your feet slightly wider than shoulder-width apart with your knees bent. Position the toner behind your back with the rubber pad squarely in the middle. Grasp the handles with the palms facing outward. Extend your arms outward. Keep a slight bend in your elbows. Slowly return to the starting position. (Muscle groups: chest and triceps; see figure 11.26.)

Figure 11.26   Chest press with toner.

BALL/BAND SQUEEZE

[Provide each student with a dead rubber ball about the size of a tennis ball.] Squeeze the ball with your right hand and hold for three seconds. Alternate hands. Or fold up an exertube into a few sections, grasp the tube with one hand, and squeeze. Alternate hands. (Muscle groups: hands, wrists, and forearms.)

BIG BAND MARCH STEP

Position the resistance band around both ankles, with your knees slightly bent. Bend the leg you're exercising and lift it off the floor several inches

(or centimeters). Place your hands on your hips, keeping the hip and trunk muscles tight. Slowly return to the starting position. (Muscle groups: quadriceps and hip flexors; see figure 11.27.)

Figure 11.27   Big band march step with exercise band.

KICKBACK

While standing, position the exercise band around both ankles. Balance on the leg you're not exercising, bending your knee slightly. Bend the leg you are exercising and lift that heel from the floor. Slowly lift and press the exercising leg backward, keeping the knee slightly bent. Point the toes and allow the hip to rotate outward slightly. Avoid overarching the low back. Return slowly to the starting position. Adaptation: Move the band up higher on the leg to increase the resistance. (Muscle group: hamstrings; see figure 11.28.)

CROSSOVER LIFT

Position the band around the lower leg. Balance on the leg you're not exercising, bending your

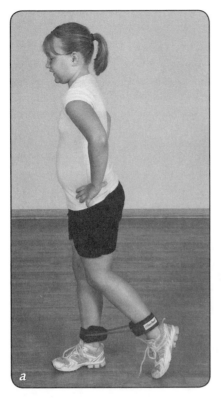

Figure 11.28 Kickback with exercise band.

knee slightly. Place your hands on your hips to keep them and your low back from moving too much. Keep your shoulders and hips stable (still). Slowly lift and sweep the leg you are exercising up and across the front of your body, keeping your knee slightly bent. Return slowly to the starting position. Rest your toes on the floor between repetitions. Adaptation: Move the band up higher on the leg to increase resistance. (Muscle groups: inside of thighs and hip flexors; see figure 11.29.)

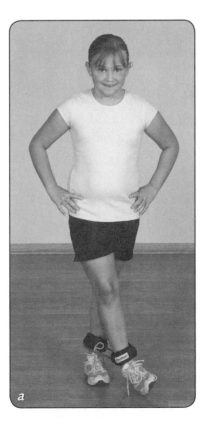
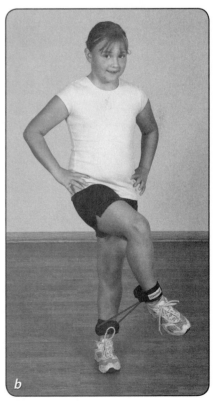

Figure 11.29 Crossover lift with exercise band.

Body Support Exercises

Body support exercises can be an easy and efficient way to include muscle fitness exercises without added equipment. Students can also practice these exercises at home.

═══ HEEL RAISE ═══

Stand on a board or a book with your heels resting on the floor. If you need to, use a chair for support and to help keep your body aligned. Slowly rise onto your toes, hold for three seconds, and return to the starting position. (Muscle group: calves; see figure 11.30.)

Figure 11.30 Heel raise.

═══ WALL SEAT ═══

Stand with your back against the wall, feet slightly wider than shoulder-width apart, hands on your hips. Slowly bend your knees, sliding your back 4 to 6 inches (10 to 15 cm) down the wall. Keep your body lined up so that your hips and the rest of you face straight ahead. Hold for 10 to 15 seconds and slowly slide back up to the starting position. Repeat. (Muscle group: quadriceps; see figure 11.31.)

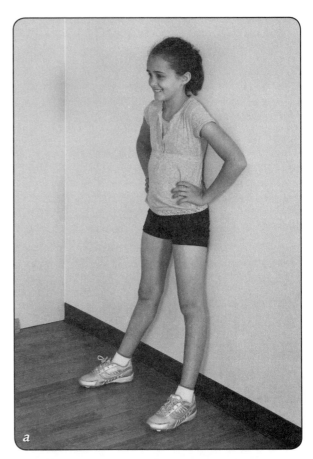

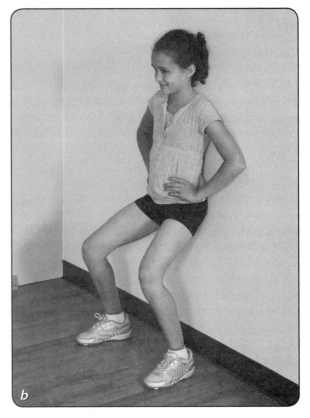

Figure 11.31 Wall seat.

FLEXIBILITY

Remember, flexibility is the ability to move the joints in an unrestricted fashion through a full range of motion. The best time to enhance flexibility is during the cool-down period following 15 or more minutes of continuous physical activity when the muscles are already warm.

Keep in mind that flexibility is joint specific, which simply means that a student with flexible hamstrings may not have the same degree of flexibility in the shoulder region. For this reason, flexibility exercises in your program should cover a wide range of muscle groups.

The following exercises illustrate static stretching movements—the safer, more controlled approach to enhancing flexibility, which is appropriate for all elementary school children. For safety reasons, avoid the bouncing, jerky movements of ballistic stretching.

Baseline Assessments

According to Corbin, Welk, and colleagues (2011), the following six exercises can serve as baseline assessment measures of the low back, calves, quadriceps, hip flexors, neck, and shoulders.

LOW BACK

Using both hands, pull your thighs to your chest. (Thighs should gently touch the chest; see figure 11.32.)

CALVES

Place one heel on the floor. Raise the rest of your foot. Repeat with your other foot. (The ball of the foot should be at least 2 in., or 5 cm, from the floor; see figure 11.33.)

QUADRICEPS

Grasp your right foot with your right hand. Bend your right leg so that the heel touches your buttock. Repeat with your left leg. (Heel should touch buttock; see figure 11.34.)

HIP FLEXORS

Pull your left thigh into your body. Your right leg should remain straight and flat on the floor. Change legs and repeat. (See figure 11.35.)

NECK

Bend your neck forward. (The chin should move to about 2 in., or 5 cm, from the upper chest; see figure 11.36.)

SHOULDERS

Place your right hand over your right shoulder as far as possible. Take your left hand and reach back and touch your right hand. The fingers of the right hand should at least touch the fingers of the left. Reverse hands to assess the left shoulder. (See figure 2.5 on page 22.)

Flexibility Exercises

Have students perform the following exercises with a static stretching technique. Each stretch should be held for about 15 seconds and should be done in a slow, deliberate fashion with the

Figure 11.32 Baseline assessment of low back flexibility.

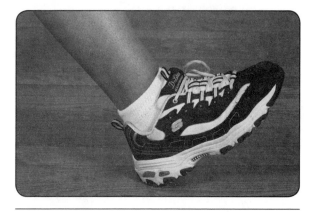

Figure 11.33 Baseline assessment of calf flexibility.

Figure 11.34 Baseline assessment of quadriceps flexibility.

Figure 11.35 Baseline assessment of hip flexor flexibility.

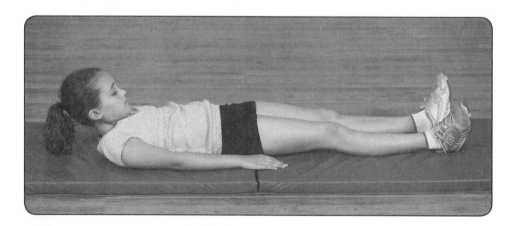

Figure 11.36 Baseline assessment of neck flexibility.

body in proper alignment. Always complete the exercises from both left and right sides. Never have children do full head circles or hyperextend the neck. (For additional flexibility exercises, see Corbin, Welk, et al. 2011.)

FORWARD HEAD DROP

To increase neck flexibility, drop your head, placing the center of your chin on your chest (see figure 11.37).

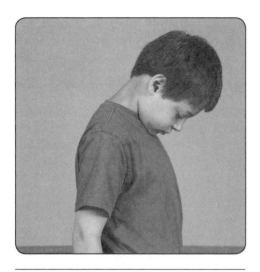

Figure 11.37 Head drop.

LOOK-OVER

This exercise stretches the neck muscles. Keeping your shoulders stable, turn to the left and look over your left shoulder and then turn to the right and look over your right shoulder. (See figure 11.38.)

NECK TILT

Place your ear to your shoulder (see figure 11.39).

STRAIGHT-UP

To increase shoulder flexibility, extend your arms overhead and press your palms together. Stretch your arms straight up, then slightly backward. (See figure 11.40.)

Figure 11.39 Neck tilt.

Figure 11.40 Straight-up.

Figure 11.38 Look-over.

ARM-CROSS STRETCH

This exercise stretches the shoulders. Place your right arm across your chest while supporting your right elbow with your left hand. With your left hand, pull your right elbow gently across your chest (see figure 11.41). Repeat on the other side.

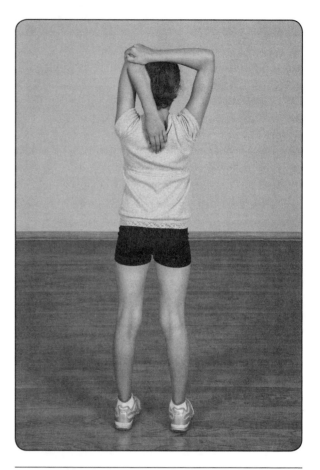

Figure 11.42 Overhead arm stretch.

Figure 11.41 Arm-cross stretch.

OVERHEAD ARM STRETCH

To stretch your shoulder and the back of your arm, raise one arm overhead with the elbow bent. Hold the elbow in position with your opposite hand. Gently pull the elbow of the arm you're exercising behind your head. Hold; then repeat the stretch with your opposite arm. (See figure 11.42.)

CAT AND CAMEL STRETCH

This exercise helps make your back more flexible. Sit on the mats [or grass]. To do the camel part, arch your back slightly by relaxing your low back muscles, lifting your chin, tucking your abdominal muscles, and expanding your chest. The cat part begins on your hands and knees in line with your hips. Gently round your upper back while tightening and tucking your abdominal and pelvic muscles. At the same time, lower your head, keeping your neck and shoulders relaxed. Hold. (See figure 11.43.)

SIT-AND-TWIST BACK STRETCH

This stretches the midback, the trunk, and outside of the hips. Sit with your right leg extended, knee slightly bent. Cross your left leg over your right knee, bending your left leg. Bring your right arm across your left leg, rotating your trunk. Push your right elbow against your right knee. Repeat on the opposite side. (See figure 11.44.)

LEG HUG

To stretch your low back, pull your knees to your chest. Hold on behind your knees. Curl up into a ball, bending your chin slightly toward your chest. (See figure 11.45.)

Figure 11.43 Cat and camel stretch.

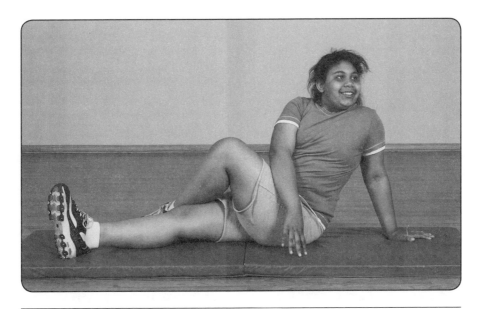

Figure 11.44 Sit-and-twist back stretch.

Figure 11.45 Leg hug.

Figure 11.46 Inside leg stretch.

INSIDE LEG STRETCH

To stretch the muscles of the inside of your thighs, sit with the bottoms of your feet together. Press your knees gently toward the floor and hold. (See figure 11.46.)

HAMSTRING STRETCH

Lie on your back with one foot flat on the floor, knee bent. Pull the other knee to your chest. Place one hand on the calf and the other hand on the thigh. Slowly straighten the knee until the hamstring becomes tight. Never completely straighten and lock the knee. Repeat with the opposite leg. (See figure 11.47.) You may use a towel around the foot you're exercising to help keep your leg in place.

QUADRICEPS STRETCH

To stretch the quadriceps (front of thigh), stand upright with the top of one foot resting on a chair, bench, or low-standing support behind you. Bend your front knee, keeping your hips and back stable and lined up with the support leg, and hold. Repeat with the other leg. (See figure 11.48.)

LUNGE

To stretch your hip flexors and quadriceps, bend your right leg, keeping your right knee directly

Figure 11.47 Hamstring stretch.

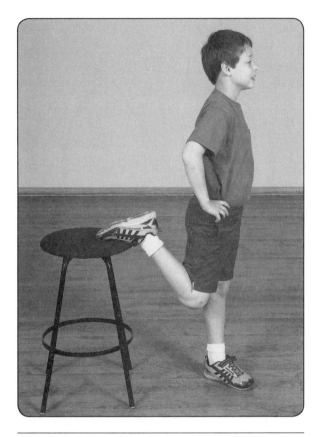

Figure 11.48 Quadriceps stretch.

above your right ankle. Stretch your left leg backward and touch your left knee to the floor. Press your hips forward and down and hold. Repeat with your other leg. (See figure 11.49.)

Figure 11.49 Lunge.

CALF STRETCH

To stretch the calf, face something sturdy to lean against for support such as a wall. Bend one knee and bring it toward the support. Keep your back leg straight with the foot flat and toes pointed straight ahead. Slowly move your hips forward while keeping your back leg straight and your heel down. Repeat with your other leg. (See figure 11.50.)

Figure 11.50 Calf stretch.

EXERCISES TO AVOID

The following exercises are unsafe to perform. Many of them place undue stress on the major joints and may have an adverse effect on students' physical health.

PLOW

The plow may stress the nerves and disks in the neck and back area (see figure 11.51). Alternatives: leg hug and cat and camel stretch.

TOE TOUCH

The standing toe touch may cause severe low back strain (see figure 11.52). Alternative: hamstring stretch.

Figure 11.51 Plow.

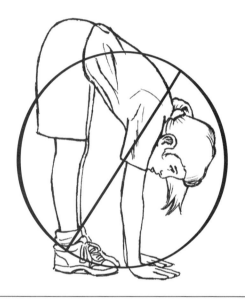

Figure 11.52 Toe touch.

Figure 11.53 Full squat.

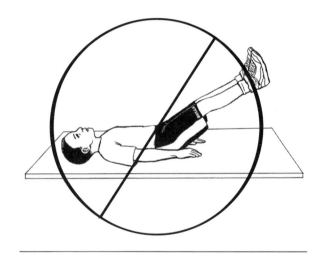

Figure 11.54 Leg lift.

FULL SQUAT

Full squats may place excessive strain on the knee ligaments (see figure 11.53). Alternative: wall seat.

LEG LIFT

Leg lifts cause stress on the low back by compressing disks (see figure 11.54). Alternative: curl-up.

NECK CIRCLE

Neck circles may pinch the nerves in the neck and irritate the disks (see figure 11.55). Alternatives: forward head drop, look-over, and neck tilt.

Figure 11.55 Neck circle.

ARM CIRCLE

Arm circles with palms down stress the shoulder ligaments and joint (see figure 11.56). Alternative: use backward rotation with palms up.

Figure 11.56 Arm circle.

WINDMILL

The windmill causes low back strain and irritates disks (see figure 11.57). Alternatives: hamstring stretch and sit-and-twist back stretch.

Figure 11.57 Windmill.

FULL SIT-UP

Full sit-ups with hands locked behind the neck place stress on the back and the neck (see figure 11.58). Alternative: curl-up.

Figure 11.58 Full sit-up.

SUMMARY

Use the numerous examples of cardiorespiratory endurance, muscle fitness, and flexibility exercises in this chapter to offer a wide but well-balanced variety of physical activity opportunities to your students. Try to incorporate these exercises into any skill- or sport-related unit in your curriculum to maintain fitness and physical activity levels throughout the school year. Moreover, use the photos in this chapter as visual reminders of proper form and body alignment. Finally, avoid the dangerous exercises listed, opting for the safer alternatives to provide developmentally appropriate physical activity.

Active Games

> It should be noted that children's games are not merely games; one should regard them as their most serious activities.
>
> —*Michel de Montaigne*

Games are an excellent way to increase physical activity levels in the elementary school. Most children view playing an active game as recreation—it's fun! For this reason, games are a great way to motivate children to become more physically active. Your task is to maintain the enthusiasm children feel for games without compromising sound educational principles. Therefore, you should avoid games that eliminate players, otherwise embarrass children, include low activity levels, or do little to develop your objectives.

CHARACTERISTICS OF DEVELOPMENTAL GAMES

To maximize your students' learning experiences, match the game to their developmental level. You can do this by changing the boundaries or the formation of the game, the method of tagging, the rules, and so on. For example, to increase the level of physical activity, you can increase the distance children have to move within the game by expanding the boundaries. Or you can vary the locomotor movements to change the tempo and develop various muscle groups (e.g., have students skip, then hop, instead of always running). Moreover, you can change the rules of a game so that everyone feels included and has the opportunity to succeed. For example, awarding points for each successful task within a game encourages student participation. When choosing and modifying games, keep in mind the following characteristics of developmentally appropriate games.

Objective Based

Each game should have an educational objective, providing you with an instructional focus instead of allowing the game itself to become the sole purpose of your class. For example, the primary objectives for a game may be to promote social interaction, to enhance a skill, to apply problem-solving techniques, to increase physical activity levels, or to accomplish a combination of objectives.

Humanistic

Choose games that develop positive feelings in students. Activities that foster cooperation and good sporting behavior will help your students see the value of physical activity. For example, use physical education equipment such as balls, Frisbees, and beanbags to develop skills—not to kick or throw at other students as a condition of a game.

Inclusive

A game should include each child in the class at all times. Modify the rules, equipment, or procedures of the game to ensure that every child is an active participant capable of success. Never eliminate students from the game because they are somehow unsuccessful.

Engaging

Students should spend most of their time on task. Children who spend an inordinate amount of time waiting in lines or standing inactively cannot fully reach their physical potentials. Indeed, a high percentage of time off task is a form of exclusion. Organize a game so that children truly benefit from the lesson because they are actively and continually involved in kicking, running, throwing, catching—whatever you have structured the game to accomplish.

Active

Don't forget to be inclusive when it comes to the activity level. Ask yourself, Do all of my students have the opportunity to continuously move throughout the game? If a game is dominated by a few active students, change the procedures to allow others to participate more actively. For example, you may rotate positions or player responsibilities to ensure activity for the entire class. Then, to help keep children interested in participating, vary the activity levels of the games you incorporate into your program as well as the health-related physical fitness components you focus on.

Success Oriented

The best way to ensure that a game is humanistic, inclusive, engaging, and active is to structure it so that everyone can feel like a winner. Within the game, provide many opportunities for scoring points or completing a task that may assist the team. This approach will reassure all students that they have made a positive contribution to the team. For instance, in the game VBS (pages 190-191), you may award a point for each base successfully passed rather than only when a student makes it home. Beyond this, make certain that each student in class has the skill or the physical development to successfully participate in the game. If not, teach the skill or modify the game further.

Positive Competition

Most games require a certain amount of competition; however, you can structure this aspect of a game to provide a positive experience for children. First, don't focus on the team, group, or individual who is successful but on the skills learned and the enjoyment of the game. Teach children how to compete in the spirit of fair play by promoting cooperation, teamwork, and sensitivity to others in class. Furthermore, work to reinforce to your students the concept that we play active fitness games primarily for the health-related benefits. For example, ask students to monitor their heart rates before and after the game and discuss what muscles were most involved in the activity. Help your students view games as healthy and fun activities, rather than as competitive experiences between classmates.

Appropriate Equipment and Facilities

The equipment should match the developmental level of the learners. Provide the class with a range of equipment to match the sizes and strengths of your students. Adjust standard equipment, such as basketball goals, to a suitable height (7 to 8 ft, or 2 to 2.4 m). Constantly assess playing areas and game boundaries for compatibility with the developmental level of each class.

Safe

Safety first! Always make the safety of your students the top priority in game situations. When I was a teacher, the first thing on my list every morning was to check the playground equipment and field area for hazards. It is important to arrange safe, wide-open spaces for highly active games. Specifically, in the gymnasium, leave at least an 8- to 10-foot (2.4 to 3 m) buffer zone between the playing area and walls, stages, doors, and the like. Mark your field clearly with orange-colored cones. Make sure that any playing surface is level, dry, and free of debris. Check daily to ensure that children are wearing proper footwear (sneakers and sport socks) and are not wearing jewelry. Teach children to move in their own personal spaces and respect the spaces of others by reviewing the techniques of body management, such as how to stop, change direction, and accelerate.

Fun

To children, a game isn't a game unless it's fun. We should never lose sight of this essential aspect. Although children do not have to be yelling, cheering, and screaming to have fun, a well-developed, challenging game can be a positive and exciting addition to your curriculum.

PROMOTING PHYSICAL ACTIVITY THROUGH ACTIVE GAMES

I have selected the games in this chapter to help you increase the activity levels of your students throughout the school year in humanistic and fun ways. Use them as warm-up activities or as closing segments for skill-oriented lessons, not as the core of lessons. Help children recognize how games promote healthy physical activity. To avoid unnecessary frustration, however, first teach any specialized manipulative skills the game requires.

The primary purpose of the games in this chapter is to promote physical activity levels. To make planning easier for you, I have divided the games by developmental levels and have used the following symbols to indicate the physical intensity level of each game:

 Warm-up

Moderately active

Highly active

DEVELOPMENTAL LEVEL I GAMES

Remember, developmental level I activities are for kindergarten and first-grade students. When adding new games to your curriculum, remain mindful of the developmentally appropriate characteristics on pages 183-184.

HOOPSCOTCH

Arrange 60 or more standard hula hoops in six configurations (three illustrated in figure 12.1). Ask children to each toss a beanbag into one of the hoops. Ask them to "hoopscotch" through the hoops, hopping on one leg, picking up their beanbags along the way. They should hop once in each hoop as they hop through the arrangement.

Adaptation: Increase the difficulty by having students quickstep through the hoops.

ZOOWILD

Arrange students in two parallel lines, 40 to 50 feet (12 to 15 m) apart. Put two identical sets of pictures of different animals in two boxes, one for each team. Students in each line select a picture of an animal from their team's box. At the signal, have the students begin to walk slowly toward

Figure 12.1 Possible hoop arrangements for Hoopscotch.

each other making the noises of the animals they selected (e.g., pig, cow, dog, horse, snake, monkey, cat, lamb, tiger), trying to find their matches. Once students find their partners, they must imitate the animal sounds and their physical movements. Repeat the procedure. This game also promotes expressive movement and creativity.

SHAPE UP

This game promotes flexibility as well as body awareness and creative movement. You'll need a box full of various pictures mounted on 3-by-5-inch (8 by 13 cm) index cards (e.g., chair, pencil, television, couch, washing machine, blender, ball, desk, car). Make sure you have at least 10 more picture cards than the number of students in the class. Ask each student to select a picture card from the box. Then have them try to shape their bodies to imitate the selected pictures in their personal spaces. Provide enough time for everyone to create the special formation selected. Then say, "Shape up!" to signal small groups of children to come over to the box and exchange their cards for new ones.

HOPPING THE ISLANDS

Scatter hoops 10 feet (3 m) apart throughout the playing area, making sure you have one hoop for every student. At the beginning of class, ask students to each find a home island by stepping inside a hoop. Ask students to perform one movement activity of their choice inside their hoops. Now ask them to perform a movement outside their hoops. Then have them hop back on their islands. Next, play a popular children's song. Ask them to walk, jog, or skip throughout the playing area without stepping inside the islands. When the music stops, tell the children to hop inside a different island. Then allow 10 to 15 seconds for them to perform an exercise, movement, or stretch of their choice. Play the music and repeat the procedure. To add variety, use music with different beats and ask the students to match the pace of their movements to the tempo of the music. Alternate the physical activities each turn, or have a student decide for the class. For closure activities, ask the students to return to their original home islands. Because this game allows for plenty of personal choice, it also develops physical activity decision-making skills.

LIFELINE

Divide the students into groups of three or four. In each group, have one student hold the end of a standard jump rope (the lifeline). At the signal "Go!" the student with the rope runs throughout the playing area dragging the rope along the ground and shaking it. The students in the group try to pick up the end of the jump rope. The student who picks up the lifeline then gets to run with the rope. Allow each student in the group to have a turn running with the lifeline. Remind the class: "The reason the rope is called a lifeline is that jumping rope is a good exercise for the heart, and exercise will improve your life and keep you healthy." Remind children to keep the rope on the ground.

THE WHEEL OF FITNESS

Use chalk or gym tape to design two large circles, one inside the other. (The exact size of the circles depends on how many children are in each group.) Arrange an equal number of children around each circle. Say: "At the signal 'Go!' the outside circle runs clockwise [point], and the inside circle runs counterclockwise [point]. At the signal 'Stop!' turn and face your partner." Have them greet their partners with high fives. Now, allow 10 to 15 seconds for the children to choose and perform an additional exercise with their partners. Repeat the procedure.

Adaptation: Vary the locomotor movements (e.g., walking, skipping, hopping).

BACK-TO-BACK

Have an uneven number of students scatter around the playing area. Say: "On the signal 'Go!' find a partner and stand back-to-back. The student without a partner calls out the next class movement activity, such as hopping, skipping, or walking. The student claps twice to start the next round." If you have an even number of students, have students find a different partner each round and alternate the students who call out the next type of movement. Modify the game by calling out different body parts (e.g., elbow-to-elbow, foot-to-foot, wrist-to-wrist).

This is a great game to reinforce good standing posture. When students find their partners, remind them to stand straight, with head and shoulders back, chest out, and feet pointing straight ahead. Demonstrate or show a picture of good standing posture. Ask, "What types of jobs require workers to stand most of the day?" [Police officers, waiters, cashiers, toll booth operators, teachers.] Remark, "Good posture is especially important to these adults." As a closing activity, have each student perform the twin walk: "Stand back-to-back with a partner and gently lock elbows and walk together forward and backward." Encourage cooperation and unity (see figure 12.2).

Figure 12.2 Twin walk.

 === **VEINS AND ARTERIES** ===

Review the basic concepts that veins carry blood to the heart and arteries carry blood away from the heart. Reinforce that exercise will keep the veins and arteries healthy. Design a heart with chalk or gym tape about 10 feet (3 m) in diameter, including veins and the two main arteries. Mark an area inside the heart and a safe area outside the heart, each with four cones. Select two to four "its," designating them with red jerseys. Explain: "Begin walking around the playing area. At the signal 'Veins!' everyone tries to run back to the inside of the heart (marked by the cones) without getting tagged by the its. At the signal 'Arteries!' run away from the heart to the safe area (marked with cones). Tagged students become its and get red jerseys." (This game may be more appropriate for advanced level I students.)

DEVELOPMENTAL LEVEL II GAMES

Developmental level II games are for grades 2 and 3. Using slight modifications, you might also try these games with level III students.

=== **LAS VEGAS FITNESS** ===

This is a motivating activity that works especially well as a five-minute warm-up routine. Have students form a large circle. Select a student to roll one large foam die. Each number (1 through 6) represents a different exercise.

1. Hopping around the gym
2. Push-ups or push-up stance
3. Vertical jumps
4. Toe raises
5. Seconds in the seal crawl position
6. Curl-ups

After the first student rolls and chooses the exercise, have the student roll two dice for the number of repetitions or seconds to be performed by the class. After the repetitions of the first exercise are completed, select another student to roll for exercise and repetitions or seconds.

=== **FITNESS GUESS** ===

Replace the old squad formation calisthenics routine with this great warm-up activity. Have students form a large circle. First, select a fitness guesser and have her leave the gym or turn away from the circle and close her eyes. Now select a fitness leader who will change the exercise by miming a new one before the group every 10 to 15 seconds. Bring the guesser, with eyes opened, back to the middle of the circle. The class begins exercising, and the guesser must try to name who the fitness leader is. Keep track of the students who did not get a turn as fitness guessers and leaders and reassure them that they will get a turn in the next few classes.

=== **SHAPE-A-ROUND** ===

Try this interesting warm-up activity. Divide the class into circles of seven or eight students. In each circle, give each student a number, 1 through 8. Have students spend a few minutes deciding on an exercise or physical movement to perform as individuals. Then have students demonstrate their choices to the class, beginning with number 1 and moving up. The other students jog in place in their small group circles. When they hear their number called, they first perform the exercise just finished by a student in their own group followed by their own individual exercise. Everyone else continues to jog in place. The student who begins this game may copy an exercise you demonstrate first.

FIND A FRIEND

This is a great activity to do at the beginning of the school year. Have the students scatter throughout the playing area. Select two students as "its," and have them wear colored jerseys. Explain: "On the signal 'Go!' the its choose a number from 1 to 5 and call it out, telling you how many students should be in a group holding hands. If the number 4 is called, for example, form groups of four by holding hands. The its try to tag any students who are not in groups. The its may start chasing as soon as a number is called. The first two students who were tagged become the new taggers. Once you are in a group, shake hands and introduce yourselves to each other. This game is called Find a Friend because everyone in class is a friend working and playing together."

KICKOUT

Children are divided into six or seven groups around the gymnasium. Each group is given two 8.5-inch (22 cm) soft cushion balls and a goal placed against the wall marked with two cones about 6 feet (1.8 m) apart. Each group is given a specific color and a small 10-inch (25 cm) marker cone. In the middle of the gym about 15 plastic cap cones are lined up and numbered 1 through 15. You will also need a music player for music.

At the signal "Go," the first student from each line tries to score a goal from a line marked 10 to 12 yards (9 to 11 m) from the goal. The student who kicks also retrieves the ball for the next player. Students who score goals run to the middle of the gym and advance their colored marker cones one level along the numbered plastic cap cones. Then, when the music is turned on, all students find a line in the gym and perform ski steps (short hops, side to side, with both feet together) over the line (usually for 10 to 15 seconds). When the music is off, they then go back to their kickout teams and continue to score goals taking turns. Use the music throughout the game or every three minutes or so.

Variation: Place a bowling pin in each corner of the goals. Players who knock down a pin move their markers two places in the middle of the gym.

CIRCLE CIRCULATION

Explain to students that this game will elevate the level of intensity in a manner similar to jogging. By increasing their heart rates, students are increasing their circulation. Ask the students to take their heart rates before, during, and after the game.

Have the class form a large circle around a plastic bowling pin. Divide the circle into two equal halves, called teams A and B. Have the students on each team count off starting with 1 so that every person shares a number with someone on the other team. Begin the game by asking everyone to walk around the circle. After a few seconds, call out a number. Explain: "The two players with the same number run out and try to steal the plastic bowling pin and run back with it to any part of the circle without getting tagged by the other player. If a player succeeds, her team gets two points. If the player stealing the pin gets tagged by the other player before getting back to the circle, the player who successfully tagged the other gets one point for his team. All the while, the other players continue to walk in a circle."

To add variety, change the locomotor movement each round (e.g., walking, jogging, skipping, hopping). Or call out simple addition problems with the answer forming the number called (e.g., call out 3 + 2, and students with the number 5 must try to steal the pin). Ask students to check their heart rates halfway through the class period and also at the end of the class period and then compare the two. Point out that their movement around the circle is similar to the blood circulating in their bodies and that exercise improves circulation.

HEARTY HOOPLA

Discuss the fact that running helps decrease the bad cholesterol (LDL) and increase the good cholesterol (HDL). Divide the class in four equal groups and position one group in each corner of the playing area. Place a hoop in each corner with five beanbags and five tennis balls. Label the beanbags LDL (bad cholesterol), and label the tennis balls HDL (good cholesterol). Say: "On the signal 'Go!' run to another team's corner to get as many tennis balls (good cholesterol) as possible and bring them back to your home. At the same time, try to clean out the beanbags (bad cholesterol) from your corner and place them in another team's hoop. But you can grab only one tennis ball or beanbag at a time. You may not guard your home or steal tennis balls from other students, and you may not interfere with someone placing beanbags in your home." After two to three minutes of playing time, call out "Freeze!" The team with the most good cholesterol (HDL) and the least bad cholesterol (LDL) is the winner. Remark: "Exercise helps build the amount of good cholesterol (HDL) and reduce the bad cholesterol (LDL) that can develop if you don't exercise and you eat too much fat."

TRIANGLE TAG

Divide the students into groups of four. Have three of the students in each group hold hands in the shape of a triangle. One of these three is an "it." The student outside of the group is also an it. Explain: "The it outside of the triangle tries to tag the it in the triangle. Students in the triangle must stay together in the triangle formation as they are being chased." Rotate the its until each student has had a turn. You may vary the activity—for example, the triangle students may hop on one foot, walk briskly, run on their toes, or run on their heels. At the end of the activity, point out that everyone in class performed about 7 to 10 minutes of healthy, vigorous physical activity in this game. Remind them that a total of 30 minutes is recommended each day. Ask, "What will you be doing for physical activity after school today?" (Allow a few minutes for this important discussion.)

FITNESS TAG

Have students scatter throughout the playing area. Select six "its." Each it wears a different-colored jersey and a sign denoting a heart disease risk factor and an exercise name.

- Smoking: curl-ups (10 seconds)
- Inactivity: jog in place (10 seconds)
- High cholesterol: sit-and-reach (5 seconds each leg)
- High blood pressure: vertical jumps (5 times)
- Obesity: march steps (10 steps)
- Diabetes: jumping jacks (5 times)

Students who are tagged must stop and perform the exercise that is assigned to the risk factor, and then continue to play. After three or four minutes, change the taggers. If students have trouble remembering the exercise for each risk factor, tape a card on the jersey that has the name of the risk factor, the name of the exercise, and the number of repetitions or the duration of the exercise.

CATCH THE DRAGON'S TAIL

This is a great activity to help bring the class closer together. Divide students into groups of seven or eight, and have each group stand in a straight line holding hands. The last person in line tucks a scarf behind him in his waistband. The scarf should fall at least 18 inches (46 cm) below the waist. Say, "At the signal 'Go!' the student in the front of the line tries to catch the last student by grabbing the dragon's tail without the line breaking apart." Rotate positions and repeat the activity. As a closing activity, try putting the entire class into one line. Emphasize the teamwork and cooperation needed for succeeding in this game. (Have a few elastic belts for students wearing dresses without waistbands.)

CRAZY CONES

Take 10 more cones than you have students in class and scatter them throughout the playing area. Knock over half of the cones. Divide the class into two even groups: lumberjacks and farmers. Explain: "When the music begins, the lumberjacks try to knock over the standing cones while the farmers try to pick up the cones that are lying down. After one minute, we'll change roles and repeat the activity."

Adaptation: Ask the lumberjacks to knock down cones with different body parts (e.g., knee, elbow, foot). Use plastic milk containers or two-liter soda bottles if you do not have enough cones.

CRABS AND CATFISH

Explain that crabs and catfish are scavengers and eat just about anything on the bottom of the ocean floor. Divide the class into four groups, two marked crabs and two marked catfish, and position them at the four corners of the gymnasium or court area. Place a large hula hoop at each group. Throughout the open space area (the ocean) scatter beanbags and plastic hockey pucks. At the signal "Go," all students (crabs and catfish) move throughout the ocean collecting their food.

The crabs move in a crab walk manner; when they collect a piece of food, they place it on their abdomens and return it home to their hula hoops. The catfish move in a bear walk motion on their hands and feet with hips slightly elevated. The catfish place the food on their backs and return to their home in the hula hoops.

Students may collect only one piece of food per turn. At the end of one minute, the students in each team count the number of beanbags or hockey pucks they have accumulated. Add the two catfish numbers together and likewise for the crabs. Now have students change roles: catfish become crabs and vice versa for the next round. Allow at least one minute between rounds. Explain to children that this was a fun game, and that they were also getting great exercise for their arms and shoulders.

DEVELOPMENTAL LEVEL III GAMES

Developmental level III games are for children in grades 4 through 6. Continue to reinforce the health-related physical fitness concepts throughout the games.

 ## KNOTS OF PROBLEMS

This activity develops group problem-solving skills and may enhance flexibility. Divide the class into circles of five to seven children standing shoulder to shoulder. Have each player reach forward and grasp the hands of other players in the circle as shown in figure 12.3. Students may not hold both hands of the same person or hold the hand of a student to the left or right of their positions. Have students work to unravel the hands into a circle. Remind students not to release their grips. In addition, caution them to be careful not to twist another student's wrist or shoulder.

 ## SPORT LINEUP

Before class, set up a minicircuit course adjacent to the playing field. Divide the class into two teams. Have the defensive team play traditional softball fielding positions. Assign the offensive team a batting order. Say: "Before playing offense each inning, the offensive team must complete the timed minicircuit course. To take a turn, you step up to home plate and either throw, punt, or placekick the Nerf football; then run all four bases without stopping. The defensive team's job is to line up behind the player who catches or retrieves the ball. The lead player then passes the ball overhead until it gets to the last player, who must run to the front of the line so everyone can then sit down. The base runner scores one point for each base successfully passed before the defensive team completes the lineup." Have students change sides after each player on the first offensive team has had a turn. Adaptations: Use other sport skills such as soccer kicks, hitting a Wiffle or rubber ball off a tee, or serving a volleyball.

Circuit Course

1. Curl-ups on mat (15 seconds)
2. Push-ups (15 seconds)
3. Rope jumps (15 seconds)
4. Jog to the tree and back in right field (total of about 100 yd or 91 m)
5. Three arm curls using an exercise tube (color choices: yellow, green, red)

 ## VBS (VOLLEYBALL, BASKETBALL, SOFTBALL)

For this game, you'll need six to eight volleyballs, six to eight tennis balls, six to eight basketballs, four bases, and one basketball goal. Set up the game as a softball field in the gymnasium with home plate directly in front of a basketball goal.

Figure 12.3 Knots of Problems.

Have the defensive team play traditional softball fielding positions. Assign the offensive team a batting order. Explain: "To take a turn, you step up to home plate and properly serve the volleyball; then run around all bases without stopping. The objective for the defensive team is to catch the ball, throw to any two bases—in any order—and then throw back to the catcher at home plate. Then the catcher must try to score a basketball layup before the runner passes home. If the catcher is unsuccessful, the runner scores. A player is out if the catcher makes a layup in time, if the player serves the ball in foul territory, or if a defensive player catches a fly ball."

Have students play two or three outs per inning. Each inning rotate the defensive positions to allow everyone a chance to practice fielding skills and layups. To keep everyone active and involved, have players waiting their turns perform a series of different, but related, skill drills off to the side of the playing field—for example, volleyball (bump and set), softball (catch and throw with tennis balls), or basketball (chest and bounce passes).

Adaptation: Teams score a point for each base a runner passes before the catcher makes the layup.

SOCCER GOLF CHALLENGE

For this game, you'll need two cones, three bowling pins, one large garbage pail, one hula hoop, one hockey goal, one cardboard box, and one index card and pencil for each student. Divide students into groups of three. Have one group, each student with a soccer ball, begin at station 1 as illustrated in figure 12.4. Say: "Keep track of how many kicks it takes to complete the task at each hole (station). Record the number after each station on an index card. If you do not complete a task in five kicks, record a score of six and move on to the next station. Try to improve your personal best." When the first group has completed station 2, have the next set of players begin. You may even choose to have a small part of your class work on this activity while the rest of the class plays a soccer game on the adjacent field.

Here is a list of possible stations you should set up 30 yards (27 m) apart:

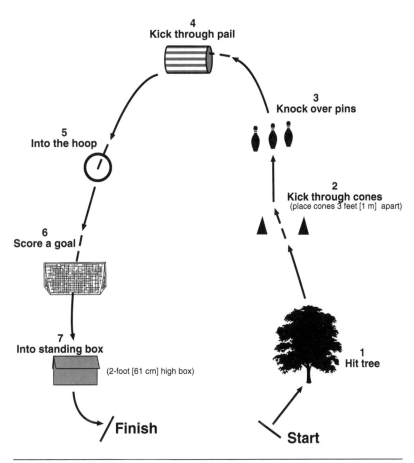

Figure 12.4 Station setup for the soccer golf challenge.

1. Kick a ball at a tree.
2. Kick a ball through cones set 3 feet (1 m) apart.
3. Kick a ball to knock over bowling pins.
4. Kick a ball into a large garbage pail lying on its side.
5. Pass a ball into a hula hoop.
6. Score a point in the hockey goal.
7. Lift a ball with foot kick into a cardboard box.

CHUTE THE BALL

This game increases muscle fitness and promotes cooperation and teamwork. Divide the class into two teams and have them stand around a large parachute, with one team on one side and the other on the other side. Place a large inner tube and two different-colored balls on top of the chute near the center. Say: "At the signal 'Go!' each team tries to shake the parachute to get its colored ball through the inner tube. The first team to score three points wins the game."

Adaptation: Place more than one ball for each team inside the parachute.

NATURE WALK WITH PEDOMETERS

Instruct children on the use of pedometers. Provide each with a pedometer, and check to see that they are positioned and fastened correctly. Now, divide the class into groups of four. Provide each group with a clipboard and a list of nature items you want them to collect on their nature walk (e.g., leaf, pebble, rock, twig, branch, weed, acorn). Provide each group with a plastic bag in which to store the items. After they have completed their nature walks, groups should report back to a designated area. Students record their individual step counts and then add up the total of all four students to get a sum for the group. Now ask them to divide that number by four to get an average step count per student. Be sure to set boundaries and always remain in clear sight of all students throughout the nature walk. This is a great activity to integrate math skills, the appreciation of nature, and enjoyment of physical activity with friends.

FITNOPOLY

This game develops teamwork, math skills, and general physical fitness. Design a large game board or individual 8.5-by-11-inch (216 by 279 mm) laminated cards spaced around the middle of the court area in the shape of a rectangle. You will need about 30 spaces marked 1 through 30. On each card write an exercise (e.g., jumping jacks, half squats, power jumps, curl-ups). On several spaces write instructions such as *Go back 2 spots, Go forward 3 spots,* and *Perform double the repetitions on the die.*

Now divide the class into four teams and place them in the four corners of the gym next to a large cone and a hoop. Each team has a die and a small, colored marker cone. At the signal "Go," the first student in each group rolls the die and then runs to the middle of the court to advance the team's small cone the number of spaces according to the die. The student then runs back to the home spot and the entire group performs the exercise activity stated on the spot the cone landed on, completing the number of repetitions from the die (1 through 6). Then the next student rolls the die. Have them continue until each student has taken at least one, two, or three turns. The first team to travel two times around the board wins.

ESTIMATION RUNNING

To help students become more aware of pacing during distance runs, design a 0.75- to 1-mile (1.2 to 1.6 km) route throughout your school and playground area for students to jog around, positioning large cones with arrows pointing the way. Be certain the ground is level and clear of any obstacles. Before starting, have students estimate the time it will take them to finish the route and write it down on their index cards. Walk them through the course so that they understand how far it is. Send two groups of 10 to 15 students each, separated by 30 to 40 seconds to avoid route congestion. Time the students with a stopwatch. The student closest to the estimated time is the winner.

HEART-SMART LOTTERY

Write various heart-smart food items (e.g., carrots, yogurt, brown rice, chicken, turkey, low-fat milk) on separate pieces of plain white paper. On two pieces of paper write a junk food item (e.g., candy, cookies, potato chips, cheeseburger). Crumple the pieces of paper into individual balls and place them in a box. Have each student select a paper ball and start jogging in the circle. Explain: "At the signal 'Heart-smart lottery!' unfold your paper balls and read the food item. The students with the junk food items are it and try to tag the other students. If tagged, you freeze and yell 'I'm heart smart!' Another player comes over and performs 10 jumping jacks with you to release the junk food from your body. You're in a safe zone when you're performing the jumping jacks and cannot be tagged." Every two or three minutes, begin a new round of play. Reinforce the difference between heart-smart foods and unhealthy foods at the beginning and end of the activity.

 ## HOOP DRIBBLE

Have students scatter in pairs around the playing area. Fasten a standard jump rope securely to a hula hoop for each pair. Explain: "One student drags the hoop around the court at a slow to moderate pace. The other partner tries to dribble or bounce a ball in the center of the hoop as it moves."

 ## BUMP AND RUN

Divide students into groups of eight. Have seven students in each group form a circle, which is marked with small cones or gym tape. Direct the eighth student to stand in the middle. Say: "To warm up, bump a volleyball around the circle playing Keep It Up. Next, the students in the circle begin sidestepping around the circle, and the student in the middle with the volleyball calls, 'Bump and run.' Each time a player on the outside of the circle bumps the ball back to the middle, he runs completely around the circle back to his original spot." Add more players to the circle to keep the drill continuous. Have students count how many times members of their group bump and run. Encourage groups to compete against themselves for their best scores, not against the other groups.

SUMMARY

Incorporating active games into your physical education curriculum can be an exciting way to promote higher levels of physical activity. Children love well-designed, dynamic games and often remark that they have great fun when they are playing with classmates. Take advantage of this natural enthusiasm for games to teach children about the benefits of physical activity as well as to prove that fitness is fun, that cooperation is a team effort, and that we can include everyone in all physical education activities.

To maximize the learning experiences for your students, keep in mind the characteristics of developmentally appropriate games discussed in this chapter. Avoid games that eliminate players, embarrass children, and have low activity levels. Instead, sensitively promote moderate to vigorous physical activity levels to reach your class objectives. Use the active games described in this chapter to augment your lessons as you strive to increase the degree of physical activity in your physical education classes.

Dance and Rhythmic Activities

> Dancing is the loftiest, the most moving,
> the most beautiful of the arts,
> because it is no mere translation
> or abstraction from life; it is life itself.
> —*Havelock Ellis*

Dance and rhythmic activities naturally contribute to the goals of a balanced physical education program in the elementary school. They are an excellent way to develop motor skills, self-expression, creativity, and aesthetic appreciation as well as to increase physical activity levels. Whether you are teaching creative dance, tinikling activities, parachute dances, or step aerobics, the purpose remains the same: children actively moving in rhythm.

Dance and rhythms inherently help children enhance their self-concepts, express their feelings, and understand their bodies' potential. Certainly, dance and rhythms can develop body awareness as children explore space through locomotor movements such as walking, hopping, and skipping and through nonlocomotor movements such as bending, stretching, twisting, and swaying.

Teaching a variety of dance and rhythmic activities is an excellent strategy for communicating cultural and ethnic awareness. For example, if you have students of Hispanic descent, teach a variety of Latin dances and rhythms. This will help these students feel more comfortable in class. As an additional benefit, you will foster a personal bond with these students that will carry over to the rest of the school year. But teach a number of American folkdances, too, so everyone—regardless of their cultural heritage—will develop an understanding and appreciation of this country's rhythmic heritage. Indeed, provide a variety of experiences to encourage students to appreciate other cultures and ethnic groups, thereby promoting better communication and understanding among them.

SAFETY PRECAUTIONS

You need to be aware of safety precautions as you plan dance and rhythmic activities for school-aged children. First, include proper warm-up and cool-down activities in each dance and rhythmic class session. Then, allow for intermittent rest periods within the class activity, taking these opportunities to reinforce the benefits of dance as a healthy physical activity.

Next, avoid movements that result in hyperextension of any joint because this places a significant amount of stress on the joint. Do not repeat a movement more than four consecutive times on one leg; instead, vary the movement at least every four counts. Avoid any quick, jerky movements of the arms, head, or legs, which may cause muscle strain in transitions between advanced steps and may require a movement sequence before changing direction. Moreover, it's important to avoid movements that include forward trunk flexion, which can place undue stress on the low back. Be cautious of dance moves that use a crossover step because this may be stressful on the pronators, the muscles strained during the weight-bearing phase of the crossover. Ensure that students maintain proper posture and body alignment while performing the various dance movements to avoid structural imbalances. Initially, teach a dance at a slow tempo without music and gradually increase to the normal level, moving from the simple to the advanced.

Advise children well in advance of each class about appropriate attire. Do not allow children to wear jewelry of any kind, and insist that they wear a general cross-training shoe to provide support and proper socks to absorb sweat and provide support while reducing friction on the feet during dance and rhythmic activities. Don't allow children to wear running shoes because these can constrict lateral movements and may cause ankle or knee injury.

PLANNING DEVELOPMENTALLY APPROPRIATE ACTIVITIES

One of the most important ways to ensure safety and enjoyment is to introduce dance and rhythms in a developmentally appropriate progression similar to how you approach the other areas of your program. Study the activities for the three developmental levels in this chapter to discern what types of dance and rhythmic activities are appropriate and motivating for students at each level.

I have designed and field-tested the activities in this chapter to ensure that they are user friendly and developmentally appropriate. Use and adapt these simple instructions for your lessons. Keep in mind that you don't have to be a dance instructor to incorporate rhythmic activities into your physical activity program!

DEVELOPMENTAL LEVEL I DANCE AND RHYTHMIC ACTIVITIES

Music and dance are not always necessary to enhance rhythmic development in your curriculum. Skipping, hopping, throwing a ball—most large-muscle movements are inherently rhythmic, providing the foundation for the begin-

ning experiences of rhythmic movement. At this level, emphasize children moving through space, exploring variations, and developing body awareness through locomotor and nonlocomotor movements. To demonstrate how enjoyable physical activity can be in a child's life, incorporate creative dance, singing games, and rhythmic activities using streamers, hoops, Lummi sticks, wands, and balls at this level.

THE BEAT GOES ON

This activity enhances expressive movement related to rhythm, tempo, and basic locomotor skills. Explain to the class that they will be moving in time to the beat of a drum. Allow the students to decide how to move based on their interpretations of the beat (hard, soft, fast, slow, even rhythm, or uneven rhythm). Here are some suggestions:

1. Beat the drum in an even four-count rhythm.
2. Tap the drum lightly four counts.
3. Beat the drum heavily four counts.
4. Combine light and heavy beats.
5. Have students move to the beat of the drum, one step for each beat (an even four-count beat).
6. Have students move to an uneven beat.
7. Have students move to a fast beat (change tempo).
8. Have students move to a slow beat.
9. Have students make a variety of quick, angular movements with arms and legs on each beat in a four-count rhythm.
10. Have students move to the beat of the drum in various ways (e.g., heel walking, toe walking, sidestepping, march steps, crawl movement).

THE SUNDAY TRIP

This creative activity is a dramatization of a Sunday trip using physical activity to promote self-expression and locomotor skills. Tell the class they will be taking a Sunday trip through the countryside. Give each student a scarf for bad weather (ask them to tuck it in their pockets) and a hoop to use as a steering wheel for a car. Use the following dialogue or create something similar: "Walk briskly throughout the playing area using your hoop to turn your car. Now place your hoop on the floor. OK—that was a long trip. Let's stretch. Stand inside your hoop and get as tall as you can." Continue as follows:

> Get as small as you can.
>
> Get as wide as you can.
>
> Let's park our cars here and go for a hike in the country.
>
> Show me how you would walk up a hill . . . down a hill.
>
> How would you walk if you were carrying a heavy backpack?
>
> Let's take a break and have a snack and some water. What kind of snack are you eating? Nuts, a banana, carrot sticks . . . good!
>
> OK, let's get moving.
>
> It's starting to get cold. Everyone place your scarf on your head.
>
> How would you walk on a cold day?
>
> Can you feel the wind blowing? How would you walk on a cold, windy day with the wind blowing hard in your face?
>
> Stretch one hand out and check for raindrops. Yes! It's starting to rain. Let's go over to that cave (standing mats in corner of gym)!
>
> Is everyone here? Good, let's wait until the rain stops.
>
> Look, there's a rainbow! What colors do you see?
>
> OK, the sun is out now. Let's continue.
>
> Look at the trees gently blowing in the breeze.
>
> Let's pretend we are trees. Our arms and fingers are branches swaying in the breeze.
>
> Let's start back to the cars. Walk carefully.
>
> Let's take a big leap over the puddles.
>
> Look, there's a rabbit hopping in the grass.
>
> Everyone try to imitate the rabbit hopping through the grass.
>
> OK, we're back at our cars. Everyone find your own hoop.
>
> Start your engines. Let's drive home! That was a great Sunday trip through the country!

RHYTHM STREAMERS

This rhythmic movement activity reinforces manipulative skills and shape formations while developing arm and shoulder muscle endurance. Give each student a streamer and have students scatter around the playing area, reminding them to stay in their personal spaces facing you. Encourage the students to keep time to the music as they twirl the streamers (see figure 13.1).

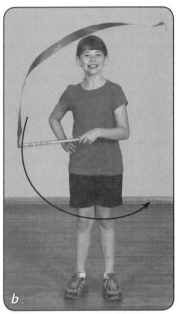
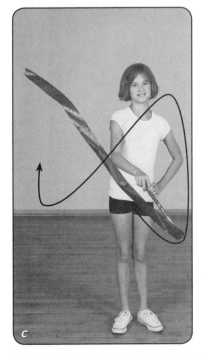

Figure 13.1 Rhythm streamers.

Four-count rhythm suggestions:

Left-side circles (four times; figure 13.1*a*)

Right-side circles (four times)

Front circle with left hand (four times; figure 13.1*b*)

Front circle with right hand (four times)

Figure eight (four times; figure 13.1*c*)

Lasso overhead with left hand (four times)

Lasso overhead with right hand (four times; figure 13.1*d*)

Repeat

Once students are familiar with this routine, vary the movements. For music, use the song "Firework" by Katy Perry (Capitol Records).

FREEZE DANCE

This activity develops decision-making skills and agility by encouraging continuous physical activity in short segments. Have students scatter around the playing area. Encourage students to move to the rhythm of the song "Turn the Beat Around" (Gloria Estefan, Epic Records) using any locomotor movements they select (walking, hopping, skipping, galloping) throughout the playing area. Explain: "When you hear me beat the drum (with two quick beats), change direction. When the music stops, freeze like statues and hold the freeze for five seconds." Repeat.

OLD MACDONALD

Try this old favorite with updated active, healthy lyrics. Use it to help children identify body parts and as an interesting warm-up activity. Have students stand in a large circle facing the center. Use the traditional song "Old MacDonald" and develop lyrics such as the following:

Old MacDonald had a healthy body, E-I-E-I-O. And on his body he had healthy arms, E-I-E-I-O. With a bend, bend here and a bend, bend there, here a bend, there a bend, everywhere a bend, bend, Old MacDonald had healthy arms, E-I-E-I-O. Old MacDonald had a healthy body, E-I-E-I-O. And on his body he had healthy legs, E-I-E-I-O. With a march, march here and a march, march there, here a march, there a march, everywhere a march, march, Old MacDonald had healthy legs, E-I-E-I-O. Old MacDonald had a healthy body, E-I-E-I-O. And in his body he had a healthy heart, E-I-E-I-O. With a jog, jog here and a jog, jog there. . . .

DEVELOPMENTAL LEVEL II DANCE AND RHYTHMIC ACTIVITIES

You can introduce simple combinations of locomotor and nonlocomotor movements at this level. Make sure, however, that the combinations include no more than three different motor skills. Introduce a variety of activities that use individual, partner, small group, and entire class experiences. Try activities such as tinikling, parachute dances, expressive dance movement, jump ropes, simple folkdances, and basic dance steps.

THE CHICKEN DANCE

Have students scatter around the playing area facing you. First, practice the movements to the song "The Chicken Dance." Describe and demonstrate the movements to the children: "Begin with four finger snaps with your hands up to shoulder height, then you do four wing flaps with arms up, elbows bent, and an up-and-down motion. Now you do four wiggles with knees bent and back bent, gently wiggling the waist and trunk area. Finally, you do four claps while standing in place. We'll repeat the four movements three times." After the third time through the sequence, have the students find a partner and hold hands and perform 16 walking steps or skips in a circle, moving counterclockwise.

CALIFORNIA DREAMIN'

This rhythmic activity includes walking, jogging, sidesteps, arm movements, and expressive movements. To begin have students form a single line.

California Strut
(a single line dance to the song "California Dreamin'," Mamas and Papas, Capitol Records)

- Walk forward (4 counts); clap.
- Walk backward (4 counts); clap.
- Sidestep right (4 counts); clap.
- Sidestep left (4 counts); clap.
- Jog in place (16 counts); clap.
- Repeat sequence.

Surfin' Dudes
(to the song "Surfin' U.S.A.," The Beach Boys, Capitol Records)

Have the students scatter around the playing area. Tell them to pretend they are each on a surfboard (see figure 13.2). Participate with the class by leading the actions:

- Wax down your imaginary surfboard.
- Hop on your boards.
- Bend your knees to go low.
- Lean to the right.
- Lean to the left.
- Surf on the right leg . . . now on the left.
- Move around the gym, pretending to surf.
- Hop off your surfboards and swim
  - the front crawl,
  - the backstroke, and
  - the breaststroke.
- Repeat swimming motions.
- To finish, jump up and down and splash in the water!

Figure 13.2 Surf movements.

EVERYBODY CONGA

This activity emphasizes Latin rhythms as well as walking and changing directions. Have students form two lines, resting their hands on the shoulders of the student directly in front of them. Use the songs "Conga" and "Rhythm Is Gonna Get You" (Gloria Estefan, Epic Records). Explain the dance: "When the music begins, everyone starts on the right foot and walks together. Take three steps and kick with the left foot. Take three steps and kick with the right foot. Take three steps left, then three steps right. At the signal 'Change,' everyone turns around and goes in the opposite direction. The conga line continues, and the last student in line now becomes the leader." End the activity with the entire class in one large line. Have students leave the gym and conga around the school campus, being careful not to disturb other classes.

MEXICAN HAT DANCE

In this dance, students learn to do the La Raspa step in time to the music. Have students stand in a circle grasping a large parachute. Explain the La Raspa step: "Hop on your left foot and quickly step with your right heel on the floor, toes up. Hop on your right foot with your left heel on the floor, toes up. Hop on your left foot with your right heel on the floor, toes up, and hold. So it was left-right-left and hold. The next La Raspa step is right-left-right and hold." Have students perform eight La Raspa steps while standing in place. During the chorus, have students jog around counterclockwise, grasping the parachute with their left hands. Repeat, changing the locomotor movements during each chorus (e.g., skipping, hopping, galloping). At the end of the song, have everyone raise the chute straight up and walk to the center to make a cloud.

TINIKLING

Years ago a rice bird from the Philippine Islands developed the strange habit of hopping and kicking its legs so as not to get tangled in the weeds of the swampy marshlands. The tinikling dance steps were created to replicate the tinikling bird's movements and improve agility and rhythmic timing. Divide students into groups of four (two dancers, two bangers), and have the students scatter around the playing area. Tell the bangers to kneel while holding two 7- to 8-foot (2.1 to 2.4 m) bamboo poles (3 in., or 7.6 cm, in diameter), about 15 inches (38 cm) apart, resting the poles on two wooden crossblocks, 2 inches (5 cm) by 2 feet (61 cm) long. If desired, play a waltz, in three-quarter time. Say: "The pole movement is the same throughout the dance. The bangers hit the poles twice against the crossblocks; then slide the poles together and tap once." Demonstrate the action and allow bangers sufficient time to practice (see figure 13.3).

Figure 13.3 Tinikling dance.

Explain and demonstrate: "With your left side to one pole, touch your toes between the poles twice; then bend that leg up, and hold. Repeat this six times. Then leading with your left foot, hop into the middle of the poles on your left foot, hop into the middle of poles on your right foot, and hop out of poles with your left foot to the opposite side. Repeat leading with the opposite foot."

With partners, have students move in opposite directions across the poles but jump together into the middle of poles. After practicing the partner dance, have dancers and bangers switch roles. Adaptation: You can modify the tinikling steps to be a 4/4 rhythm with the poles open for two counts and closed for two counts (close, close, tap, tap). You may also use jump bands to replicate similar dance step movements.

DEVELOPMENTAL LEVEL III DANCE AND RHYTHMIC ACTIVITIES

Group activities characterize level III. Given enough time to practice, students at this level can learn advanced steps such as the grapevine or the two-step. Most students will be motivated to participate in up-to-date dances as well as more traditional activities such as aerobic dance, step aerobics, and line dancing (such as the Electric Slide and the Macarena).

LOW-IMPACT AEROBIC DANCE

The term *low-impact* simply means that one foot is always in contact with the floor, placing less stress on the joints and creating continuous physical activity through basic dance movements performed to music. Have students scatter throughout the playing area, facing you. Be sure to select the tempo of the dance music carefully. If the music is too fast, students will become frustrated and give up; if it is too slow, you will not elicit a desirable level of activity, and students will become bored. The following guidelines will help you gauge the appropriate tempo:

- Warm-up (3 to 5 minutes): 120 to 125 beats per minute (BPM)
- Main event (15 to 20 minutes): 128 to 145 BPM
- Cool-down (3 to 5 minutes): 120 to 125 BPM

Choreograph the following basic dance steps to popular music. Keep the dance steps simple, building your routines throughout the school year as the students gain experience and confidence.

Warm-Up Dance Steps

1. Step touches: Begin with the weight on the left foot, and step to the side with the right foot. Close with the left foot, touching the ball of the foot to the floor. Reverse. (See figure 13.4.)

2. Touchbacks: Begin with the weight on the right foot and the left foot touching back on the ball of the foot. Step to the side with the left foot. Bring the right foot back behind you. Repeat. (See figure 13.5.)

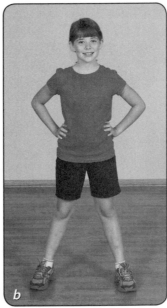

Figure 13.4 Step touches.

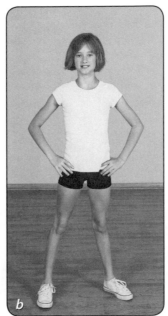

Figure 13.5 Touchbacks.

3. Heel touches: Alternate heel touches in front of the body, keeping the knees slightly bent. Repeat. (See figure 13.6.)

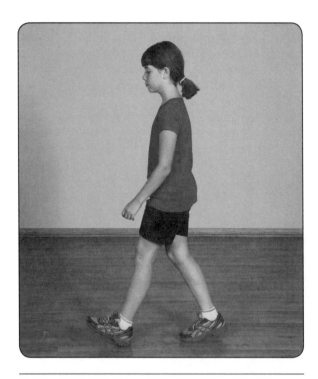

Figure 13.6 Heel touches.

Dance Steps

1. March step: Raise one knee up parallel to the floor with the toes pointed down and swing the arms in opposition to the legs (the left arm is up when the right knee is up), keeping the head up and shoulders back. (See figure 13.7.)

2. Jog step: Hold the arms at waist level with the elbows bent and the hands in half-fists. Contact the floor with the heel, roll to the outside of the foot, and push off with the ball of the foot last. (See figure 13.8.)

3. Plié touches: Reach the arms to the right side while touching the left foot out to the side, bending both knees. Swing the arms in front of the body, and then stretch them to the left side, touching the right foot out to the side. (See figure 13.9.)

4. Simple grapevine step: Step to the right on the right leg, arms bent to the shoulders. Step behind with the left leg while pushing the arms above the head. Step to the right on the right leg, arms bent to the shoulders. Touch to the left side with the left heel while pushing the arms above the head.

Figure 13.7 March step.

Figure 13.8 Jog step.

Figure 13.9 Plié touches.

Figure 13.10 Simple grapevine step.

Then reverse and step to the other side. (See figure 13.10.)

5. Cross-elbow touch: Step up on the right foot, lifting the left knee up and touching the left knee to the right elbow. Reverse. (See figure 13.11.)

6. Step-kicks: Step with the left foot; then kick the right foot with the toes pointing downward, keeping a slight bend in both knees. Stretch the arms out to the side, elbows slightly bent. Reverse. (See figure 13.12.)

Figure 13.11 Cross-elbow touch.

Figure 13.12 Step-kicks.

7. Heel tap and snap: Bring the left leg behind the body and touch the right hand to the left leg. Now, stretch the leg outward and snap the fingers of the right hand. Reverse. (See figure 13.13.)

Cool-Down

You can use the warm-up steps for the cool-down.

STEP AEROBICS

Step aerobics is an adaptation of aerobic dance and is usually considered low impact. The intensity levels may exceed aerobic dance, however, because the students are stepping up and down on and off a bench while performing various dance steps (see figure 13.14).

You may use popular or oldies music with tempos of 118 to 122 BPM. Select songs with a clear beat. The step bench should be 6 to 8 inches (15 to 20 cm) high. Teachers have been using alternatives to the step bench; however, for safety reasons, I recommend that you use a manufactured step from a reputable company.

Have students consider the following guidelines:

- Maintain good posture.
- Keep the knees soft (never locking the joint) and centered over the toes.
- Keep the buttocks tucked under the hips.
- Line up the shoulders over the hips.
- Step up lightly and with control.
- Stay close to the bench when stepping down.
- Do not twist or pivot the knee or the weight-bearing leg.
- Do three to five minutes of both warm-up and cool-down.

Use this key when studying the following directions: R = right and L = left.

1. Basic single lead: Beginning from the front of the step, move R foot up, L foot up, R foot down, L foot down for four counts while arms extend, punch-

Figure 13.13 Heel tap and snap.

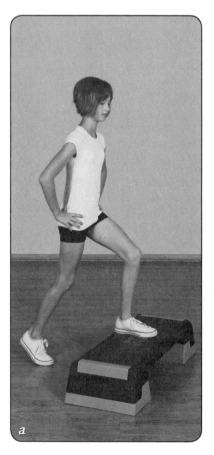

Figure 13.14 Technique for stepping on a step bench.

ing forward as you step up, and pulling your fist back as you step down (see figure 13.15); repeat, leading with L foot.

2. Single lead tap up, tap down: Beginning from the front of the step, move R foot up, L foot tap up, L foot down, R foot tap down while snapping the fingers with arms bent at the elbows, hands just below the shoulders for four counts; repeat, leading with L foot.

3. V-step: Beginning from the front of the step, move L foot up wide step, R foot up wide step, L foot down center, R foot down center while curling the biceps on the same side as the leading leg (see figure 13.16) for four counts; repeat, leading with R foot.

4. Kickback step: Beginning from the front of the step, move R foot up, L leg kicks back, L foot down on floor, R foot down on floor while doing biceps curls with both arms on the kickback movement (see figure 13.17) for four counts; repeat, leading with L foot.

5. Side leg lift step: Beginning from the end of the step, move R foot up, L foot side leg lift, L foot down on floor, R foot down on floor for four counts; repeat with L foot leading. (Raise both arms when lifting a leg to the side and lower arms when stepping down. See figure 13.18.)

6. Over the top: Beginning from the side of the step, move L foot up, R foot up, L foot down on the opposite side, R foot down for four counts. Arms move as follows: first beat—elbows up; second beat—cross arms; third beat—elbows up; fourth beat—cross arms (see figure 13.19). Repeat, leading with R foot.

Figure 13.15 Basic single lead on step bench.

Figure 13.16 V-step on step bench.

Figure 13.17 Kickback step with double-arm biceps curl.

Figure 13.18 Side leg lift step on step bench.

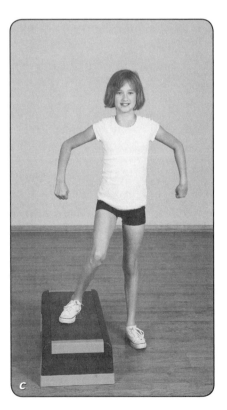

Figure 13.19 Over the top with step bench.

THE ELECTRIC SLIDE

This is a line dance that includes moderate physical activity and simple dance steps. It is helpful to play the song "The Electric Slide." Divide students into three lines spaced about 3 yards (2.7 m) apart facing you. Have them start with feet together and weight evenly distributed.

Measures

1 through 4: Step sideways right, close left to right.
Step sideways left, close right to left.
Step-touch with left toe.

5 through 8: Repeat same movements, beginning on the left.

9 through 12: Moving backward, lead with the right foot.
Close left to right.
Step right and click left heel to right foot.

13 and 14: Rock forward on left foot, touch right foot in place, making a digging movement (may swing right arm in arc).
Bend over and touch floor in front of left foot on "dig" (knees bent).

15 and 16: Rock backward on right foot.

17 and 18: Step left (count one); pivot one-quarter turn left and brush right foot forward (count two).

Repeat measures 1 through 18.

ZUMBA

Zumba is a high-impact aerobic dance that incorporates a number of Latin rhythms and dance movements. Zumba is a combination of easy-to-follow steps that alternate among slow, moderate, and fast rhythms to maintain an elevated heart rate throughout the routine. The Salsa, Merengue, and Cumbia are traditional Latin dances incorporated into a Zumba dance pattern. Zumba is a form of interval activity because the dance sequences vary from slow to fast throughout the session.

For children at developmental level III, start with simple dance steps to popular music they might be familiar with, performed by well-known performers. As the children become more confident and experienced, include more advanced Latin steps and body movements to upbeat Zumba music. Try this beginners routine in your next physical education class.

Warm-Up

Suggested song: "Waka Waka (This Time for Africa)," the Official FIFA World Cup Song by Shakira

- March to the beat of the music at the start, 12 steps (figure 13.20a).
- Verse 1
  - Two steps to the left while pulling the right arm up to the chest (figure 13.20b).
  - Two steps to the right while pulling the left arm up to the chest (figure 13.20c).
  - High knees march, high intensity; all remaining verses and bridge (figure 13.20d).
  - Repeat warm-up sequence.

Figure 13.20 Warm-up steps for Zumba.

Main Event

Suggested song: "Let's Get Loud" by Jennifer Lopez

- Three steps to the right; lift the left foot (figure 13.21*a*).
- Lift the right foot (figure 13.21*b*).
- Lift the left foot (figure 13.21*c*).
- Keep hands in a fist and pull the arms into the chest when lifting each leg.
- Three steps to the left; lift the right foot (figure 13.21*d*).
- Lift the left foot (figure 13.21*e*).
- Lift the right foot (figure 13.21*f*).

- Keep hands in a fist and pull the arms into the chest when lifting each leg.
- Verses and bridge
  - Straighten arms to the left of the body, point the left foot, and bring the arms straight down (figure 13.21, *g* and *h*).
  - Straighten the arms to the right side of the body, point the right foot, and bring them straight down (figure 13.21, *i* and *j*).
- Do 10 hip rotations.
- Straighten the arms above the head and swing the hips around (figure 13.21*k*).

Figure 13.21 Main event steps.

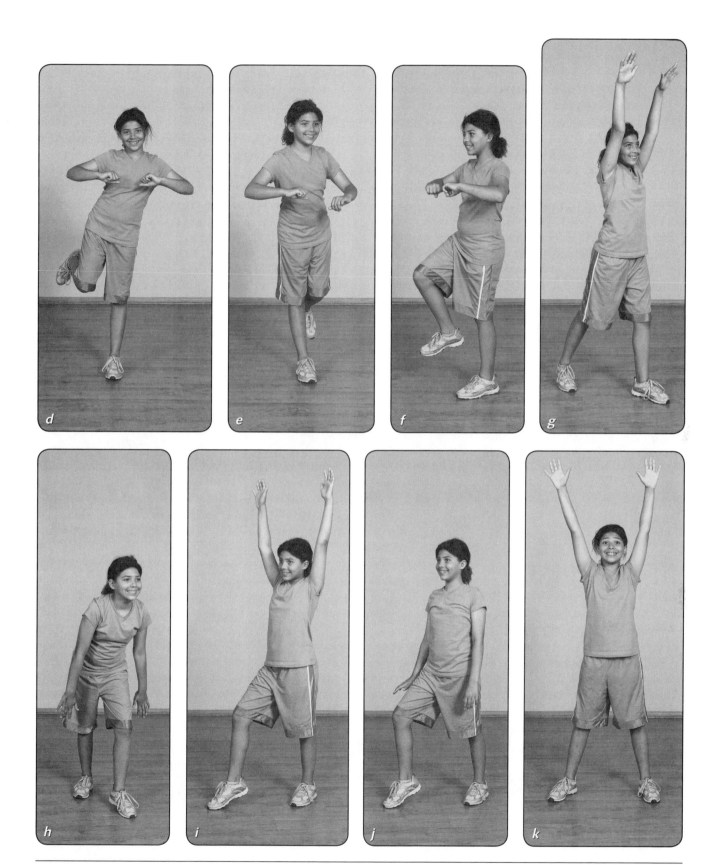

Figure 13.21 *(continued)*

Cool-Down

Suggested song: "Smooth" by Santana

- Face to the left, step forward with the right foot (figure 13.22*a*).
- Step backward with the right foot (figure 13.22*b*).
- Step forward with the right foot four times (figure 13.22*c*).
- Face to the right; step forward with left foot (figure 13.22*d*).

- Step backward with the left foot (figure 13.22*e*).
- Step forward with the left foot four times (figure 13.22*f*).
- Chorus
  - Two steps to the left (figure 13.22*g*).
  - Two steps to the right (figure 13.22*h*).
- Verse and bridge

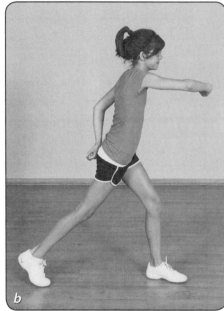

Figure 13.22 Cool-down moves.

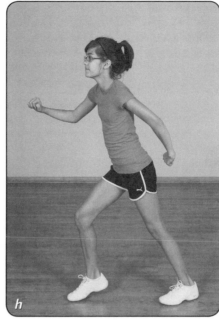

Figure 13.22 *(continued)*

Additional Steps

As students become more familiar with Zumba, add the following steps: the Zumba Shuffle, the Merengue March, and the Cumbia.

- **Zumba Shuffle:** Stand with your feet shoulder-width apart and knees bent, palms in front of you with your left palm facing down and your right palm facing up. Swing your hips out to the left, while simultaneously pointing your hands to the right. Then switch sides by swinging your hips to the right, now with your right palm facing down, and your left hand pointing to the left. Repeat this shuffle to the right twice, switching back to the left. (See figure 13.23.)

- **Merengue March:** Begin by marching in place with very small steps: right-left, right-left. The front (or the ball) of the foot should touch the floor first, then lower the heel. As the heel is lowered on one side, the opposite hip points outward. Now swing your hips from side to side in rhythm with the march steps. Raise your arms to chest level. Extend your left arm out to

the side and bend your right arm at the elbow. Now extend your right arm out to the side and bend your left arm at the elbow. [To vary the step, change the arm movements or have children move in different directions.]

Figure 13.23 Zumba Shuffle.

- **Cumbia:** Cumbia moves are performed by starting with the feet together and arms at each side, bent at the elbows. Tap the right foot behind you, followed by tapping the left foot in place. Bring the right foot back to the starting position, and repeat the same movements on the left side. As you step back, rotate your body to the side.

MACARENA

This is a Latin line dance with its origin in Spain. Instructors in Miami, Florida, popularized this dance, which has migrated throughout the world. Arrange students in three lines, shoulder to shoulder, facing you. Have students dance to the song "Macarena Club Cutz," RCA Records.

Measures

1. Put out the right hand; then the left hand, palms down (figure 13.24a).
2. Turn up the right palm; then the left palm.
3. Place the right hand on the left arm; then the left hand on the right arm (figure 13.24b).
4. Place the right hand behind the head.

Figure 13.24 Macarena steps.

Figure 13.24 *(continued)*

5. Place left hand behind the head (figure 13.24*c*).

6. Put the right hand on the right hip; then put the left hand on the left hip (figure 13.24*d*).

7. Sway the hips gently from side to side, repeating three times (figure 13.24*e*).

8. Jump up (figure 13.24*f*).

9. Do a quarter turn to the right and start over.

Have students try the Macarena dance from the push-up position, eliminating steps 8 and 9.

SUMMARY

Incorporating these developmentally appropriate dance and rhythmic activities into your fitness education program is an excellent way to promote higher physical activity levels. Use the brief overview for planning dance and rhythm activities in this chapter and follow the specific safety precautions to create productive lessons. Make dance and rhythmic movement an integral component of your physical education curriculum. And don't forget to teach children the joy of moving to music—for fun and fitness!

Yoga for Children

> Yoga is invigoration in relaxation.
> Freedom in routine.
> Confidence through self-control.
> Energy within and energy without.
>
> —*Ymber Delecto*

Since the early 1990s, parents, teachers, and administrators have been increasingly aware of the benefits of yoga for children. In light of our fast-paced society, high-stakes testing in schools, and emphasis on sport competition, many professionals have discovered the positive educational experiences that yoga brings to children.

The word *yoga* means "union"—the union between the mind and body to create a sense of balance and harmony in one's life. For many years, yoga was perceived as a more adult activity to help relieve stress and anxiety. Recently, educators have accepted yoga as a refreshing addition to the traditional movement and exercise activities taught in school.

Yoga is a noncompetitive physical and mental experience that can be used by individuals, in small groups, in pairs, or in large groups. It can be done in the gymnasium or the classroom and requires little space and equipment.

Practitioners have reported the following educational advantages to yoga:

- Increased attention span
- Body awareness
- Self-confidence
- Increased concentration skills
- Creativity
- Inner peace or calm

- Stress reduction
- Improved social interaction skills

Yoga may help children to recenter their energy, value their bodies, and reflect on their lives on a daily basis. Yoga is being used in schools to help children with various challenges, such as autism and ADHD, as well as a number of other emotional and physical issues.

From a physical perspective, yoga has a cross section of benefits and uses. In general, it can enhance the following:

- Muscle fitness
- Balance
- Stability
- Flexibility
- Coordination
- Body awareness

Yoga was originally developed around a series of poses imitating animals. The notion was that if people did the same exercises and performed the same movements as animals, they too would be strong, flexible, and healthy. More recently, yoga has advanced to include numerous interpretations. Try to design your own or have the children help you create different images leading to new poses. Provide them with pictures, such as of a mad cat, a mountain range, a tree, and the like, that they can imitate.

This chapter is adapted, by permission, from Virgilio, 2006, *Active start for healthy kids* (Champaign, IL: Human Kinetics), 191-205.

Students at developmental levels I and II (grades K through 3) enjoy using fantasy and imitation to explore their emotions and create physical movement. Help them enjoy yoga through stories or by imitating animal movements. Encourage them to create poses of objects at school, on the playground, or at home. Children are learning to cooperate at this level, so plan yoga poses they can do in pairs and small groups to show them how much fun it is to work together. If you are working with students at these developmental levels, consider planning various themes through your yoga class—such as honesty, cooperation, getting to know other cultures, and generosity.

At developmental level III (grades 4 through 6), the fantasy stage begins to fade, and children are more interested in real-life experiences. They want to know more about what happens outside of the home and the elementary school. This is a great stage at which to teach yoga techniques. Children are able to perform a number of poses and movements that are more difficult for those at levels I and II. Consider teaching poses such as the dancing peacock (page 225). Children at this developmental level enjoy the physical, mental, and emotional challenges of yoga. However, be mindful of their enthusiasm and pace the exercises in a developmentally appropriate manner. Remind children at this age that yoga is not competitive or a sport. The goal should be to enjoy the yoga class and work more on self-improvement. You might include large-group activities of six or more students, such as Bouquet of Flowers (page 221), or games such as Frozen Yoga (page 226) or Air Hockey (page 227).

Caution! Many of the poses found in popular books on yoga and yoga for children include contraindicated exercises or movements that may have harmful effects. Some yoga movements place undue stress on the neck, back, and other major joints such as the knee (see Exercises to Avoid in chapter 11).

HELPFUL HINTS

Keep in mind the following helpful hints for making yoga a positive experience for young children (Virgilio 2006):

1. Plan yoga for an entire class, or infuse the poses or games into your curriculum.
2. Yoga activities should begin with a large muscle warm-up, such as marching steps or jogging in place, followed by several dynamic arm and leg movements (see chapter 11). Then, move to a calming segment, followed by breathing exercises, a series of poses from simple to more advanced, relaxation poses, and finally, meditative movements.
3. Present the yoga movements in a positive, sensitive manner. Be flexible and understanding about students' varied needs and abilities. Try to be accepting of their ideas and comments. Ask children to create their own poses and animal imitations.
4. Develop a positive social atmosphere in class. Help children get to know each other through simple yoga games (see Chanting Names, page 226).
5. All poses should be performed using slow, controlled movements. Each pose should be held for several seconds, or as long as the children feel comfortable.
6. Encourage children to relax, breathe slowly, and think positively. Use background music.
7. Make sure children do not force the movements or go beyond their limitations.
8. Never compare children; some may be more flexible than others. Continued practice will make the movements easier. Remember, all pose interpretations are correct.
9. Yoga should be performed on a mat or carpeted surface, and children should remove their shoes, if possible, and jewelry. They should also avoid eating for at least an hour before performing yoga movements so their bodies are settled and calm.

The poses in this chapter are arranged starting with breathing exercises and then in order of body positioning (standing, kneeling, sitting, lying), ending with support movements. The last section describes a few games that may add some fun and excitement to yoga activities.

BREATHING POSES

The following poses focus on breathing to help regulate the heart rate and bring the body into balance.

CANDLE

Have the children sit with their legs folded and in good posture, with their chins slightly lowered and their shoulders and neck relaxed. Next, have them adopt the pose by raising their hands to head level with their fingers spread, pointing up. Tell the children to pretend that their hands are a candle and their fingers are the flame. Have them close their eyes, take in one deep breath, and gently release it by bringing their arms down slowly. They should continue to breathe evenly for one to two minutes and stay very quiet, with their hands resting on their legs. Ask the children to think of something they like and why it makes them happy. (See figure 14.1.)

Figure 14.1 Candle pose.

BALLOON BREATHING

Have the children lie on their backs and relax. Ask them to pretend that there is a balloon on their abdomens, and when they breathe in, the balloon is slowly filling their abdomens with air. When they breathe out, the balloon empties and their abdomens flatten out. Try placing a balloon on each child's abdomen and have them practice slow, relaxed abdominal breathing. Ask the children to control the balloon on their abdomens with their breathing. (See figure 14.2.)

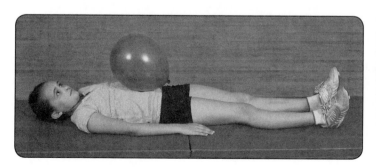

Figure 14.2 Balloon breathing pose.

STANDING POSES

The following poses are performed from a standing posture, which will enhance balance and body symmetry.

STANDING TALL

Attach helium balloons (enough for each student to have one) to pieces of string. Fasten the end of the string to each student's waist area (use belt loops or masking tape) so the string runs straight up the spine. Ask students to imagine their spines extending as they stand straight and tall with their shoulders back and their hands at their sides. This will help them to remember how it feels to stand straight. At any time when they begin to slump, they can go back to the balloon pose and recall how it felt. (See figure 14.3.)

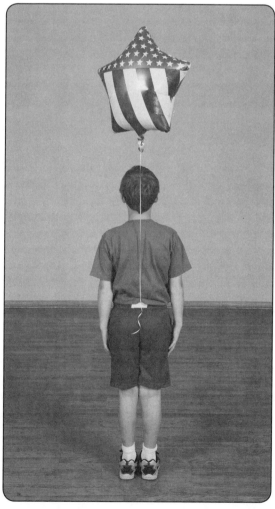

Figure 14.3 Standing tall pose.

TREE

From a standing position, the children bend the right knee outward and lift upward. Next, have them slide the right foot into the inner thigh and gently rest it in that position. Then have them raise their arms out to the sides to imitate the branches of a tree. (See figure 14.4.) After reaching stability, they should raise both arms straight overhead to represent high-level branches.

Younger children may have more success by crossing one leg in front of the support leg in the junior tree pose.

Figure 14.4 Tree pose.

MOUNTAIN

Instruct the children to stand as tall and straight as they can, keeping their feet firmly on the ground. Ask them to pretend that their shoulders are mountains and their heads are the peak of the mountain. They should keep their arms at their sides and point their fingers straight at the ground. Have them take in a deep breath and then breathe out and relax. Tell them to stand very still and very straight—just like a mountain. (See figure 14.5.)

Figure 14.5 Mountain pose.

HERO

Have the children stand with their feet spread wide apart. Instruct them to turn the left foot toward the left side, slightly bending the knee and turning the body in that direction (the knee should not move past the left foot). Then have them raise both arms out to their sides, hold, and then change to the opposite side.(See figure 14.6.)

Figure 14.6 Hero pose.

BIRD

Have the children stand with their arms at their sides and raise both arms backward with the palms facing up toward the sky. Then have them rise up onto their toes, keeping their heads up, and pretend they are birds flying through the air. Instruct them to look straight ahead and focus on an object; then balance and hold. (See figure 14.7.)

Figure 14.8 Cat pose.

Camel

Starting from the cat position, the children should gently relax their backs and flatten out, keeping their backs straight. They should then arch their backs slightly by relaxing their lower backs, lifting their chins, and gently pressing their abdomens toward the floor. (See figure 14.9.)

Figure 14.7 Bird pose.

KNEELING POSES

The following poses are performed from a kneeling position to enhance balance using various body parts on a low level.

CAT AND CAMEL

Cat

Have the children begin on their hands and knees. Ask them to gently round their upper backs while tightening and tucking their abdominal muscles. Then have them slowly lower their heads, keeping their backs and shoulders relaxed. (See figure 14.8.)

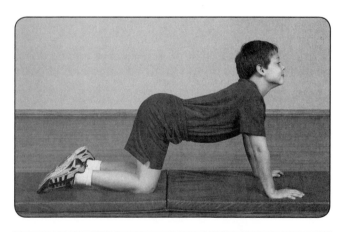

Figure 14.9 Camel pose.

SQUIRREL

Instruct the children to begin by sitting back on their heels and then slowly raising up to a kneeling position. Next, have them bend both arms and bring their hands up just beneath their chins, with the palms facing outward and the fingers cupped. Ask them to hold and then slowly repeat the movement. (See figure 14.10.)

OSTRICH

From a starting position on their hands and knees, have the children place their hands in front of them, about shoulder-width apart. The

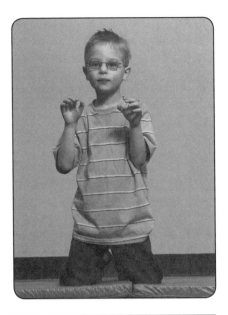

Figure 14.10 Squirrel pose.

palms should be flat and facing inward with the fingers pointing toward each other. Instruct the children to keep their knees together. Next, have them slightly bend their elbows and lean forward. Then tell them to lift both feet while keeping their knees on the floor and their heads and backs straight. Have them hold the pose, release by slowly sitting back on their heels, and then repeat the movement. (See figure 14.11.)

Figure 14.11 Ostrich pose.

SITTING POSES

The following poses are performed from a sitting position to enhance stability and creativity.

═══ STAR ═══

Ask the children to sit with their knees bent and the soles of their feet together. Have them overlap their fingers behind their heads and point their elbows out to the sides. Make sure they maintain good posture. (See figure 14.12.)

Figure 14.12 Star pose.

═══ FLOWER ═══

Have the children begin by sitting with the soles of their feet together. Instruct them to slowly bring one arm at a time underneath their lower legs (left arm under the left leg and right arm under the right leg) and gently hold the front of their shins. Next, have them slowly straighten their backs and keep their heads up, hold, and then release one arm at a time. (See figure 14.13.)

Figure 14.13 Flower pose.

PARTNER TWISTS

Ask partners to sit facing each other, cross-legged with four knees touching. Each child places the right arm behind the back. Now, have them reach out with their left hands and grab their partners' right hands. Now, have children gently twist by looking over their right shoulders and sit tall, breathing naturally. Have them hold for five to seven seconds, come back to a neutral position, and release.

Now, have them change sides (left arm behind the back, right hand reaches across and grabs the partner's left hand). (See figure 14.14.)

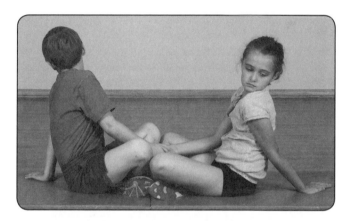

Figure 14.14 Partner twists pose.

BOUQUET OF FLOWERS

Arrange three to five children in a circle, sitting close together. Begin by having them practice the flower pose. Remind the children that a group of flowers is called a bouquet. Next, have them raise their legs and slowly lean back; then grasp hands with the children on either side of them—the left hand grasping the right hand of the child on the left and the right hand grasping the left hand of the child on the right—between their legs. Tell them to lean back and relax with their heads up so that the entire group can balance. (See figure 14.15.)

Modification: You can tie a large rope in a circle for the children to hold on to so that they can lean back with their legs up and stay balanced.

PEACOCK

Have the children begin from a sitting position and straighten their legs outward as far as possible. Instruct them to point their toes straight up and keep their backs straight. Next, have them place their hands on the floor in front of them, close to their bodies, with the palms down. Then have them press downward gently to widen their shoulders. (See figure 14.16.)

Figure 14.15 Bouquet of flowers pose.

Figure 14.16 Peacock pose.

LYING POSES

The following poses are performed from a lying position to enhance low-level activity as well as concentration and stability.

=== **CLOUD** ===

Have the children lie flat on the carpet or mat, facing up, with their hands at their sides. Their arms and legs should be spread wide apart. Remind the children to relax (eyes may be open or closed) and stay calm and quiet. Ask them to pretend that they are clouds floating in the sky as you say the following: "Your body is very light as it moves around the sky. You are floating in the air, feeling very happy and relaxed." Then have the children take a deep breath and exhale slowly. (See figure 14.17.)

=== **BUTTERFLY** ===

Ask children to lie on their backs. Now, have them separate both knees wide with the soles of their feet touching. Next, ask them to stretch their arms overhead and extend their hands, palms

Figure 14.17 Cloud pose.

upward and fingers extended. Have them relax in this position for three breaths. Now ask them to move like butterflies, moving their knees (wings) up and down in a gentle, controlled, rhythmic movement and wiggle their fingers (antennae). (See figure 14.18.)

═══ STARFISH ═══

Direct the children to lie flat on the carpet or mat, facing up, with their eyes closed. Then have them spread their legs as wide as feels comfortable and spread their arms out to the sides with the palms either facing up or facing down while resting on the mat. (See figure 14.19.) Ask them to pretend they are starfish, floating on the water in the ocean, as you say the following in a soothing voice: "Feel the waves move you gently up, down, and around. Relax and breathe quietly. Now you have reached the shore." Then have them slowly bring their legs and arms in and gently roll themselves up.

Figure 14.18 Butterfly pose.

Figure 14.19 Starfish pose.

MODIFIED COBRA

Ask the children to lie on their abdomens with their legs together and straight. Have them place their palms down on the mat and rest on their elbows, keeping their hands close to their chests. Then have them raise their chests, keeping their shoulders straight and wide. They should try to keep their heads up and their necks long and straight. (*Note:* Do not allow children to arch their necks backward.) (See figure 14.20.)

SUPPORT POSES

The following poses are performed in various support postures to enhance balance and stability.

RAINBOW

Ask the children to lie on the left side, supporting the body with only the left arm. Instruct them to keep the arm straight and stable with the fingers spread slightly apart and keep both legs together with the right foot on top. Then have them gently swing the right arm up to the sky as you tell them: "You're a rainbow—full of color and beauty." (See figure 14.21.)

TABLE

Have the children begin in a seated position with their knees bent and their feet flat on the floor, about 3 inches (8 cm) apart. Next, ask them to place their hands several inches (centimeters)

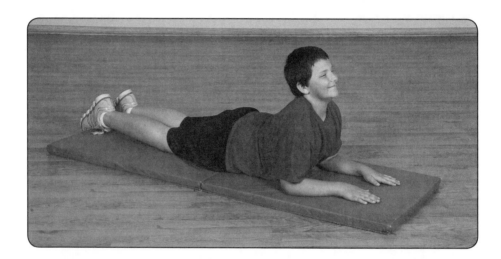

Figure 14.20 Modified cobra pose.

Figure 14.21 Rainbow pose.

behind them, fingers pointing toward their feet. Then have them press their hands and feet into the floor and lift their hips, making their abdomens as flat as possible. Ask them to hold the position and then release gently. (See figure 14.22.)

Figure 14.22   Table pose.

═══ DANCING PEACOCK ═══

This pose is a sequence of three poses.

1. Have children kneel down and sit back on the mat, hips to heels. Have them place their forearms flat on the mat facing forward. They then spread their fingers wide just like a peacock's feet with thumbs touching each other. Remind them to keep good balance, eyes looking straight ahead. (See figure 14.23a.)

2. Have children remain supported on the forearms. Now, have them lift their hips slowly, keeping their heads up. They should then stretch both legs behind them while lifting their hips just a little higher. They are now supported on the balls of their feet. Have them breathe and hold for three to five seconds. (See figure 14.23b.)

3. Now, have them slowly lift the right leg upward off the mat, with the knee slightly bent, and try to point the toes while still supported on the forearms, head facing downward. (See figure 14.23c.) Have them hold for two breaths; then lower the right leg slowly back to the original position.

Now, have them repeat using the left leg with the same movements. Explain that they are imitating the peacock in full plumage. Have them return to the start position and repeat the three-step sequence.

Figure 14.23   Dancing peacock poses.

GAMES

The following games help bring the yoga poses to life and add fun and social interaction to the learning experience.

FROZEN YOGA

Play background music and instruct the children to move in various ways throughout the play area. After 30 seconds or so, stop the music and call out a yoga pose (e.g., "Tree!"). The children must all stop what they are doing and pose like a tree. Start the music again and call out a different pose (e.g., "Cobra!"), and continue on in that manner.

GROWING FLOWERS

Ask the children to form a circle. Explain that everyone will become a small seed that will be planted in the early spring, and by the middle of summer the seed will become a beautiful flower. Then ask the children to make themselves as small as possible, just like a flower seed (show them an example of a flower seed to reinforce how small they are). Instruct them to kneel down and sit back on their feet with their foreheads on the floor, keeping their arms bent and close to their knees.

Ask the children to imagine that they are flower seeds as you say the following in a soft voice: "As the weather gets warmer, you slowly lift your head. Then the sun gets even warmer and you start to rise, higher and higher. Now the spring turns to summer and you rise from your knees while sitting back on your heels. Open your arms from the side; then gently raise your arms overhead. Now slowly stand up as your arms greet the sun. Stand straight and tall and stretch as high as you can—reach for the sun and breathe in. Now lower your arms and breathe out. Think of a beautiful flower that you enjoy." Repeat the activity. (See figure 14.24.)

POSING PICTURES

With a small group of children (three or four), have each child, one at a time, select a yoga pose from a bag or box and demonstrate it. The others must try to guess the name of the animal or the yoga pose.

CHANTING NAMES

This a great game to help you get to know your students' names and have the class participate. Pronounce each child's name very slowly and clearly as if you were singing it, accentuating each syllable.

Ask students to sit in a circle. Go around the circle and ask each child to announce his or her first name. Then chant the name. Now, have the other children repeat the name before moving on to the next child. This is a good technique to teach controlled breathing. Remind children to breathe in before beginning a name, and breathe out slowly as they chant each name clearly.

Figure 14.24 Children pretending they are growing flowers.

Here are examples:

Barbara: Ba-r-r-r-b-a-r-r-r-a-a-a

Anthony: A-a-a-a-a-n-t-h-o-o-o-n-y-y-y

AIR HOCKEY

Arrange four or five children on a mat, in a circle, lying on their abdomens. Give each child a plastic drinking straw. Using the straw will teach them about inhaling and exhaling breathing techniques.

Place a small cotton ball or small piece of paper (the size of a marble) in front of one player. The first activity calls for each student to pass the cotton ball around the circle, clockwise, so that every player has a turn. Children may only use their breath from the straw; they may not use their hands or the straws to move the cotton ball. Reverse the sequence moving counterclockwise.

Next, place the cotton ball in the middle of the small circle. At the signal, "Go," children try to blow the cotton ball through an opening on the right or left side of another student to score a goal (figure 14.25). Don't keep score. The children should play for a few minutes. Reinforce breathing methods such as the use of the diaphragm and abdominal muscles to create a strong breath as the children exhale.

SUMMARY

Use yoga throughout the school year in your classes. Add new poses and breathing exercises as your students become more skilled and confident in the use of yoga techniques. Teach them the general philosophy behind yoga as they gain the physical benefits of muscle fitness, balance, stability, flexibility, and coordination. Incorporating yoga in your curriculum can also help children deal with various physical, mental, social, and emotional challenges in their lives.

Figure 14.25 Children playing air hockey.

Schoolwide Events

> Education is not preparation for life;
> education is life itself.
> —*John Dewey*

Schoolwide events bring additional attention to your efforts to promote physical activity. When the entire school is involved in a well-organized physical education project, children's morale and spirits are heightened, which often permeates the entire school atmosphere. Classroom teachers usually report that students seem to be more alert and interested in learning when a physical education special event is conducted at their school. Successful schoolwide events are often highly organized, well-planned projects that include the entire school community. Gaining administrative support and approval as well as securing a budget are all essential for the event to run smoothly. Furthermore, it would be important to communicate your project early in the school year and have it placed on the master calendar so that all may plan accordingly.

You and your colleagues can also use schoolwide events to integrate classroom learning activities with fitness education activities (e.g., Geography Run; see later in this chapter). You might also choose to help classroom teachers coordinate a health-related thematic unit with a special schoolwide event (see chapter 9). Whatever you choose to do, conducting various schoolwide projects provides many opportunities to communicate and network with the faculty, staff, and administration at your elementary school. This will not only strengthen your physical education program itself but also make clear to your colleagues that you are truly willing to collaborate.

Schoolwide events are also excellent opportunities to enlist the help and support of parents and the community (see chapter 10). If your school organizes an event committee, be sure to ask at least one parent to serve. Seeing this parent on the committee will encourage other parents or community members to participate. And don't forget another wonderful resource: senior citizens. They are highly capable, eager, and available during the school day.

Study the brief descriptions in this chapter of schoolwide events to promote physical activity and maintain positive public relations for your physical education program. As you read, think about what you can use, or modify the contents to suit your situation and needs. But don't limit yourself to only one schoolwide event. Incorporate these exciting activities throughout the school year. Change the special schoolwide events each year so that they don't become monotonous or routine. The same events repeated each year simply will not be special after a while; they will certainly lose their impact and that vital sense of excitement.

FITNESS FIELD DAY

A fitness field day is ideal for the spring or early fall. Promote it with the central theme of physical activity for health and fun. It helps to identify the event with a special title—for example, The Fun, Food, and Fitness Field Day! Unlike traditional field days that focus on competition in various events, your field day should emphasize participation, physical development, and social interaction.

Form a field day committee to help organize this event. Include a few classroom teachers, special area teachers, and at least two parents.

Contact the local university for student volunteers. Health, physical education, and elementary education majors at a nearby university make ideal personnel to help manage this event. Of course, parents, grandparents, and members of the community can also assist. In addition, ask the local American Heart Association or the American Cancer Society to work with a few teachers at the school to help develop a display.

Ensure that each class has an opportunity to participate in each activity by using a station approach. Set up at least 10 stations throughout the outdoor physical education area (see figure 15.1).

Organize the field day into two phases: kindergarten through third grade and fourth through sixth grades. Consider this sample schedule: 8:30 to 9:00, set up; 9:00 to 11:00, kindergarten through third grade; 12:30 to 2:30, fourth through sixth grades; 2:30, clean up. Assign each class a station number to begin the field day. Then have classes move through the stations in sequence. Use a loud horn to signal a change of station every 11 to 12 minutes. At the end of your fitness field day, give each participant a special Fun, Food, and Fitness certificate, pin, ribbon, headband, or button. Ask local businesses to donate incentives such as water bottles, key chains, or T-shirts with a health message to distribute to everyone.

Station 1: Step Aerobics

Ask a local health club for the name of a qualified instructor who may be willing to lead a step aerobics station at your fitness field day. Be sure to observe a few classes that the instructor is teaching before extending an invitation to your school. Once the instructor has agreed to come, arrange a meeting to get to know your volunteer.

Station 2: Cageball Fun

Set two cageballs in automobile tires approximately 30 yards (27 m) from a starting line. Divide the class in half. At the signal, each team runs up to the ball and rolls it back by pushing it with their hands to the finish line and then back to the tire. The first team to place the cageball back in the tire is the winner. Change teams for the second round.

Station 3: Zumba Line Dancing

Using popular Zumba music, organize a line dance. Line dancing is an ideal physical education activity because it requires no partners, the steps are easy, and everyone is moving together, which makes students feel secure (see chapter 13 for details).

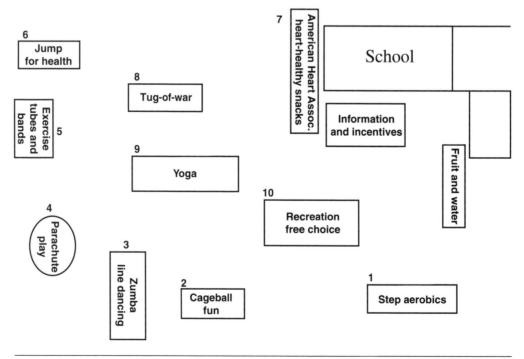

Figure 15.1 Possible setup for the fitness field day stations.

Station 4: Parachute Play

Take a group jog with everyone grasping a large parachute. Then play Pop Out. Divide the group into two teams. Place one or two playground balls in the center. Then have the teams try to pop the balls over the heads of the players on the opposing team to score a point. Three points wins the game.

Station 5: Exercise Tubes and Bands

Incorporate the use of exercise tubes and bands as discussed in chapter 11. Design a large task card describing (and, if possible, demonstrate) the specific exercise you selected for this station. Be certain to provide a variety of exercises and tubes and bands of various tension levels so that everyone will be able to participate and feel successful. Incorporate music to add excitement.

Station 6: Jump for Health

Allow students to jump rope at their own paces or participate in groups. Provide long ropes for small groups of students to use with two students turning the rope and two others taking turns jumping. If you wish, include standard individual ropes and heavy individual ropes to offer a variety of physical activities that enhance arm muscle endurance.

Station 7: American Heart Association Heart-Healthy Snacks

This station will help teach children about healthy snacking. Ask a volunteer from the American Heart Association to set up a display and provide a brief (two- to three-minute) explanation of heart-healthy foods. If you choose, distribute samples of healthy snacks, such as yogurt, low-fat cookies, and rice cakes. Ask the American Heart Association to provide a handout or brochure with recipes for healthy snacks.

Station 8: Tug-of-War

Tug-of-War is a great way to encourage teamwork and cooperation. If possible, use lightweight synthetic fiber webbing ropes to prevent cuts and burns.

Station 9: Yoga

For this station, have an instructor lead students through a series of basic yoga poses and breathing exercises (see chapter 14 for complete descriptions).

Station 10: Recreation Free Choice

Provide a number of recreation options at this station (e.g., hopscotch, jump bands, balance sticks, horseshoes, paddle ball, individual balance boards).

In addition to the 10 basic stations, you may wish to organize a fruit and water station supervised by the PTA, perhaps setting it up as a chance for a break in the field day circuit, in addition to the healthy snacks at station 7. You could also have an information and incentives station as a central organizing and equipment management location. At the end of the fitness field day, have each class walk by to receive participation incentives.

FIT FOR LIFE FAMILY NIGHT

Hold a Fit for Life Family Night (or Day) on a weekday evening or on a Saturday morning for parents, grandparents, and children alike. Advertise at least six weeks in advance so that busy parents can fit the event into their schedules. In the initial announcement, recommend that parents obtain medical clearances before participating in this event. Enlist the help of university students majoring in physical education to assist you with the management and instruction of the family activities. The following is a sample program outline.

Facts About Fitness (10 minutes)

Give each parent a handout listing the health-related benefits of physical activity and printed materials such as brochures from NASPE, the American Heart Association, or the American College of Sports Medicine. Ask a professor of physical education from the local university or another guest to make a few opening remarks about physical activity and its health benefits. The speaker may make specific points about the benefits of physical activity and the importance of a well-balanced physical education program. The speaker also may instruct everyone to take their resting heart rates to get the audience involved. Be sure to review the USDA's dietary guidelines (MyPlate) and make the connection that healthy eating and physical activity go hand in hand.

Warm-Up (5 minutes)

With music playing, have everyone walk in place, do march steps with double-arm reaches, or jog in place while doing arm curls. Have them step sideways foot to foot, left, and then step sideways foot to foot, right.

Fit for Life Activities (45 minutes)

Divide the parents and students into three groups, doing three different activities in three different areas. Set up a circuit course in the gymnasium, including activities such as curl-ups, rope jumping, using exercise bands, and doing basketball activities. Organize aerobic dancing and line dancing in the cafeteria. Discuss heart-healthy eating, and provide snacks in the auditorium or a large classroom. Have groups rotate every 15 minutes.

Cool-Down (10 minutes)

Have everyone meet back in the gymnasium. Lead the entire group in exercises to music, gradually decreasing the activity level. Allow two to three minutes of rest, and then ask all participants to take their heart rates once again. Emphasize the importance of having good heart rate recovery. Their heart rates should be close to the resting heart rates they had at the beginning of the event.

GEOGRAPHY RUN

A Geography Run is an excellent schoolwide walking and jogging program. Students may walk or jog in class, at home, or during recess and report their mileage to you on a trip ticket. Insist that this ticket be signed by the student as well as either a parent or a teacher. Plot the total mileage on a large map of the United States posted in the gym, in a hallway, or in the school cafeteria. For example, students may run from New York to California (Disneyland) or the route of the Oregon Trail. You can also use maps of other countries to tailor the Geography Run to any region.

Meet with classroom teachers about how to integrate math, science, art, and language arts into meaningful, related classroom activities. For example, classroom teachers could design math problems to calculate the miles traveled and the miles needed for reaching the next state or the final destination. They could organize activities to teach the geography of the region your students are traveling through. Encourage the school cafeteria personnel to prepare special lunches or snacks to represent the next state or region the students will enter (e.g., low-fat pizza for New York, red beans and rice for Louisiana, taco salad for New Mexico, barbecued chicken for Texas). It would also be fun to decorate the cafeteria in the style of the state that the children are passing through that week.

When the students have run or walked the miles necessary for reaching the final destination, celebrate by sponsoring a school party. Choose a theme; for example, throw a California Beach Party. Encourage teachers, staff, and students to come to school dressed in their California "cool" attire. Organize students to decorate the cafeteria with a beach theme and play surf music. Serve turkey club sandwiches with sprouts and vegetables. Present each student who participated in the Geography Run with a special reward for a job well done (e.g., a frozen yogurt coupon, a free play pass in physical education, or a participation certificate commemorating the event).

SCHOOL HEALTH FAIR

You can hold a school health fair in the gymnasium or a multipurpose room. Have each class be responsible for a specific health area and have them design a health fair display. Meet with classroom teachers and parents to set up the guidelines for the displays, schedules, and selected topics. Hold a health fair in the fall and the spring by having kindergarteners through third graders develop the fall health fair and fourth- through sixth-graders develop the spring event. Give all grades, however, an opportunity to attend both health fairs. The following are possible topics for displays:

- Cardiovascular health
- No smoking, please
- Back and neck care
- Healthy snacking
- Daily physical activity
- Managing stress
- Reading food labels

- Say "No!" to drugs
- Dancing for fun and fitness
- Cancer prevention
- Weight control
- Muscle up
- I'm OK—every day!

Make it the responsibility of the class that designed the health station to explain its content to visitors. In the younger grades, have children display their individual projects, such as Health Art pictures or other creative experiences. Set aside the last hour of the school day for parents and community members to visit the health fair. And, if possible, schedule hours after school so working parents can attend. (See also chapter 10.)

EARLY BIRD WAKE-UP AND AFTERNOON PERK-UP

Start the day right and perk up those slow afternoons with these fun ideas. For a week in the fall and again in the spring, use these activities to bring attention to physical activity throughout the entire school. Directly following the morning announcements, have everyone in the school (teachers, students, parents, staff, custodians) stand up for an early bird wake-up. Develop an audio recording of exercises and background music to play on the school public address system. At approximately 1:30 p.m., use the same recording for an afternoon perk-up.

JUMP ROPE FOR HEART, HOOPS FOR HEART, AND STEP FOR HEART

Try different events such as Hoops for Heart (basketball) and Step for Heart (step aerobics) for exciting activity alternatives to the traditional, yet still fun, Jump Rope for Heart. These schoolwide events are sponsored by the American Heart Association (AHA) and the American Alliance for Health, Physical Education, Recreation and Dance (AAHPERD). You can obtain a complete package of information, materials, and pledge cards from your local American Heart Association. While waiting for your package, set aside a day for the entire school to participate in one of these activities. Next, have students obtain monetary pledges from the community for the

exercise they perform. The funds are divided among your school, AHA, and AAHPERD. Then, have fun!

ACES: ALL CHILDREN EXERCISING SIMULTANEOUSLY

ACES was created by Len Saunders, a New Jersey physical educator. In May, during National Physical Fitness and Sports Month, one day is set aside each year so that millions of children throughout the world can exercise in unison at their schools—whether they are in physical education class, in the classroom, or having lunch in the cafeteria. To participate, each school organizes its own 15-minute activity, such as walking, jogging, dancing, or doing aerobics. The objectives are to promote fitness, nutrition, and world peace. Project ACES is supported by the Youth Fitness Coalition. Project ACES offers free materials such as certificates, posters, word searches and crossword puzzles, and additional educational materials. For further information, visit Len Saunders' website (lensaunders.com).

RECESS WORKOUTS

Use recess for additional time for physical activity. Set up several activity stations with task cards around the playground. Don't make the stations a requirement; rather, let students volunteer to participate in this opportunity to be more physically active. Volunteer your time to help supervise the activities, or enlist the help of a college student, parent, or senior citizen to support this effort. Take advantage of this extra time to interact with children who have special needs (e.g., obesity, spinal cord disabilities, low activity levels). Recess workouts will also support those students interested in improving their fitness levels.

FITNESS CLUBS

Organize a fitness club for students who have a special interest in exercising. Meet before school, after school, or during recess. Give the club a clever name such as The Physical Activators. Provide each student with a detailed portfolio, including information on exercise principles, practical exercises, and recommended training techniques along with log sheets to keep track of their efforts. Consider taking the club on a field trip each year to an exercise physiology lab at the local university or to a health spa. In addition, you may wish to train the students in this club to help with fitness activities, assist with equipment setup, or help other students enter data on eating and physical activity levels into computers.

PRINCIPAL WALKS

Help your principal get to know the students in the school better. This activity works well for developmental levels I and II, but it may be appropriate for level III as well. For this event, every Friday the principal walks with two classes for about 30 minutes throughout the school building, the outside school campus area, or the neighborhood. If necessary, organize parent volunteers or other assistants to help supervise students during walks in the neighborhood. But stay in the background for this event. Let the students perceive the principal as the professional promoting physical activity for health and social benefits.

HOLIDAY CLASSICS

This schoolwide event, developed by Allen (1996), brings attention to physical activity during certain holidays throughout the year. Provide each classroom teacher with colored slips of paper denoting the holiday (e.g., orange for Halloween). Ask students to write on the slips their names and what, if any, physical activity they participated in outside of school for a total of 30 minutes. Make it clear that each day of adequate activity allows the student to submit additional entries. Then collect the slips of paper and place them in a large box for

a drawing at the end of the month. The more days of physical activity they have, the more chances students have to win. But give each student who enters the drawing a sticker, certificate, or token to encourage continued effort and participation. Explain your program objectives to local businesses, and ask if they would donate the prizes in return for a little publicity. Examples of prizes are a large pumpkin for Halloween, a snowboard for Christmas, an American Heart Association cookbook or heart-shaped pillow for Valentine's Day, and a baseball glove for Easter.

SUMMARY

Integrating schoolwide events into your physical education program benefits everyone by reinforcing the major goals of health-related physical fitness, by raising student spirit, by encouraging positive morale, and by creating more interest in your physical education program. Moreover, these events create effective public relations opportunities to help you build support for your curriculum as well as any innovative program reforms you may have in mind. Indeed, parents and other community members who volunteer to help you run events will see firsthand how exciting your program is and how important increasing physical activity is. Schoolwide events may also help you network with the faculty, staff, and administration, thereby helping you to develop positive, long-term professional relationships as you strive to integrate physical education goals throughout the school curriculum. Study and adapt the examples of schoolwide events in this chapter to your situation, and you'll be off and running!

Sample Personal Active Lifestyle Portfolio

My Physical Activity Pledge

I, _____, pledge that today,

_____, I am determined to change my lifestyle and

become more physically active.

    I acknowledge that I need improvement in the various components of physical fitness and

promise to devote _____ minutes, most days of the week or every day, toward

making positive changes in my fitness level and physical activity habits. I will do this in school

or at home.

    The best time of day for me to work on this change is _____ a.m./p.m.

    I will try my best to fulfill this pledge as I work toward my personal fitness goals to the

best of my ability.

Signed (student) _____

This pledge was witnessed by (parent or guardian)_____

From S.J. Virgilio, 2012, *Fitness education for children: A team approach* (Champaign, IL: Human Kinetics).

Name _____ Sex _____ Age _____

Grade _____ Class _____

My Health and Fitness Profile

Measurement	Date	Date	Date	Comments
Body weight				
Body height				
Body composition (percent fat)				
Resting heart rate				
Flexibility (sit-and-reach, shoulder flexibility)				
One-mile run				
PACER				
Curl-ups				
Push-ups				
Posture				

From S.J. Virgilio, 2012, *Fitness education for children: A team approach* (Champaign, IL: Human Kinetics).

Fitness Graphs

Name _____ Sex _____ Age _____

Grade _____ Class _____

Plot your fitness scores on the correct line on the graph each time you measure a component of physical fitness. Use dots to plot your results. Connect the dots with straight lines to see your progress.

One-Mile Run

Minutes

Improving ↓

	Pretest date	Interim test date	Posttest date
15			
14			
13			
12			
11			
10			
9			
8			
7			
6			
5			
4			
3			
2			
1			
0			

Pretest date _____   Interim test date _____   Posttest date _____

Fitness Graphs

Name _____ Sex _____ Age _____

Grade _____ Class _____

Plot your fitness scores on the correct line on the graph each time you measure a component of physical fitness. Use dots to plot your results. Connect the dots with straight lines to see your progress.

Curl-Ups

Number

75				
70				
65				
60				
55				
50				
45				
40				
35				
30				
25				
20				
15				
10				
5				
0				

Improving ↑

♡

Pretest date   Interim test date   Posttest date

_____   _____   _____

From S.J. Virgilio, 2012, *Fitness education for children: A team approach* (Champaign, IL: Human Kinetics).

Fitness Graphs

Name _____ Sex _____ Age _____

Grade _____ Class _____

Plot your fitness scores on the correct line on the graph each time you measure a component of physical fitness. Use dots to plot your results. Connect the dots with straight lines to see your progress.

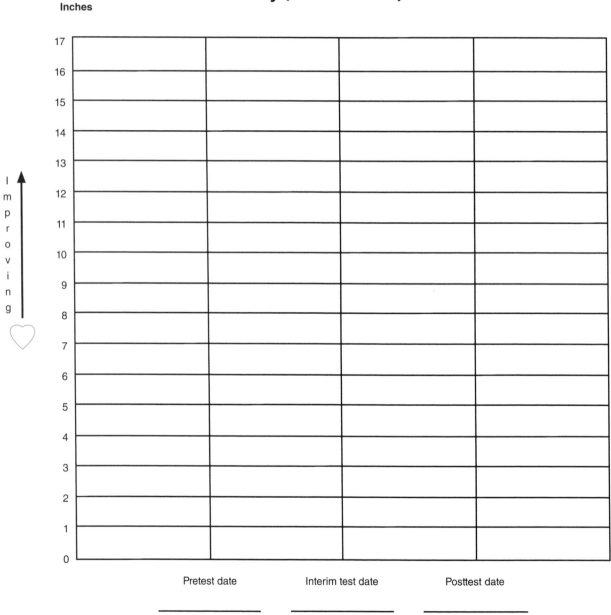

From S.J. Virgilio, 2012, *Fitness education for children: A team approach* (Champaign, IL: Human Kinetics).

Fitness Graphs

Name _____ Sex _____ Age _____

Grade _____ Class _____

Plot your fitness scores on the correct line on the graph each time you measure a component of physical fitness. Use dots to plot your results. Connect the dots with straight lines to see your progress.

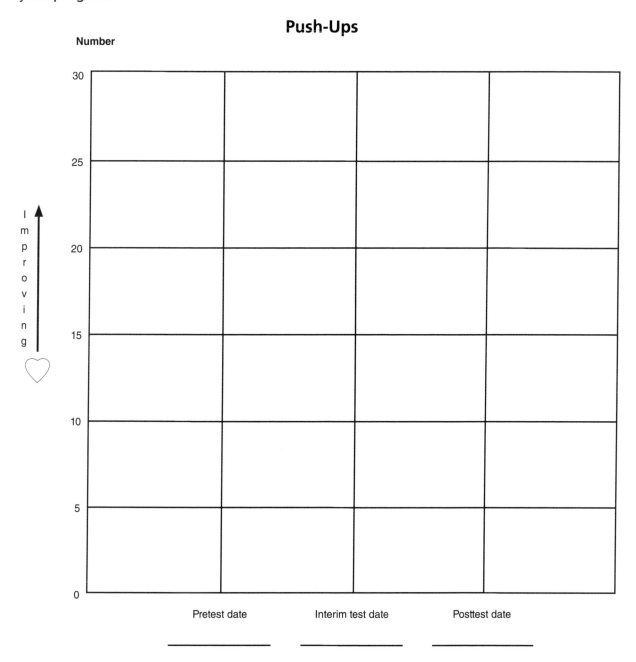

From S.J. Virgilio, 2012, *Fitness education for children: A team approach* (Champaign, IL: Human Kinetics).

My Active Lifestyle Program

Name _____ Grade _____

Class _____

   I. My activity goal is_____

_____

   II. Activities I enjoy to help me accomplish my goal are:

_____

_____

_____

_____

_____

_____

_____

_____

Warm-up activities	*Cool-down activities*
1. _____	1. _____
2. _____	2. _____
3. _____	3. _____
4. _____	4. _____

III. My planned physical activity schedule

   (Plan physical activity on at least five days per week.)

Date	*Day*	*Time of day*	*Activity*
_____	Monday	_____	_____
_____	Tuesday	_____	_____
_____	Wednesday	_____	_____
_____	Thursday	_____	_____
_____	Friday	_____	_____
_____	Saturday	_____	_____
_____	Sunday	_____	_____

From S.J. Virgilio, 2012, *Fitness education for children: A team approach* (Champaign, IL: Human Kinetics).

My Physical Activity Log

Name _____ Grade _____

Class _____

Date	Physical activity	Rating	Minutes	Time of day	How I felt

Ratings of physical activity levels: L = low or easy, M = moderate or midlevel, H = high or vigorous

From S.J. Virgilio, 2012, *Fitness education for children: A team approach* (Champaign, IL: Human Kinetics).

My Daily Nutrition Log

Name _____   Grade _____

Class _____

Date	Breakfast	Lunch	Dinner	Snacks
Monday				
Tuesday				
Wednesday				
Thursday				
Friday				
Saturday				
Sunday				

From S.J. Virgilio, 2012, *Fitness education for children: A team approach* (Champaign, IL: Human Kinetics).

My Favorites

Name _____ Grade _____

Class _____

My favorite physical activity to do in school physical education is _____

because _____

_____

_____

My favorite physical activity to do at home with my friends is_____

because _____

_____

_____

My favorite physical activity to do with my family is_____

because _____

_____

_____

My favorite physical activity to do by myself is_____

because _____

_____

_____

From S.J. Virgilio, 2012, *Fitness education for children: A team approach* (Champaign, IL: Human Kinetics).

Additional Websites

Action for Healthy Kids

www.actionforhealthykids.org

A comprehensive site for information, research, reports, facts, and supporting materials to help schools become healthier places.

Active and Healthy Schools

www.activeandhealthyschools.com

Offers a complete set of program materials to help change the school environment in the areas of physical activity and nutrition.

American Academy of Pediatrics

www.aap.org

Click the link "Health Topics" for information on obesity, nutrition, and general health for children.

American Alliance for Health, Physical Education, Recreation and Dance (AAHPERD)

www.aahperd.org

General information including conferences, events, resources, and membership.

American College of Sports Medicine (ACSM)

www.acsm.org

A national organization to promote and integrate scientific research, education, and practical application. Personal certifications are offered for a variety of interests and levels.

American Dietetic Association

www.eatright.org

A national source for trustworthy, science-based food and nutrition information.

American Heart Association

www.heart.org

A national association for heart disease research; offers up-to-date information and heart-healthy materials including cookbooks, brochures, and school resource materials.

Center for Interactive Learning and Collaboration

www.cilc.org

Teachers can become members of this center (free membership) and collaborate with others on any topic of interest. It allows you to post your ideas for a specific collaboration or respond via e-mail to other teachers who are looking for partners for videoconferencing collaborations throughout the school year.

Centers for Disease Control and Prevention

www.cdc.gov

Information related to research studies, including national reports such as the U.S. surgeon general's statement on physical activity and health.

Create A Graph

http://nces.ed.gov/nceskids/createagraph

This program allows students to create various types of graphs using their own data. Graphs can be saved and used in educational presentations or printed for other purposes.

Discovery Education

www.discoveryeducation.com

School districts can subscribe to this program so that all students can log on. It offers exceptional educational activities for students at both the elementary and middle school levels, including full videos, video segments, reading passages, e-books, and interactive labs on numerous science-related curriculum topics.

Dole Foods

www.dole.com

This site offers nutrition and fitness information and also contains special sections on games, comics, music, recipes, and fitness for children. There is a separate section for educators that includes lesson plans and classroom activities.

Fitness and Kids

www.fitnessandkids.com

Offers fitness equipment, books, and DVDs for children.

Fruits and Vegetables Matter

www.fruitsandveggiesmatter.gov

A CDC initiative to encourage people to have five to nine servings of fruits and vegetables every day.

Health Ahead/Heart Smart

http://tulane.edu/som/cardiohealth/ahead.cfm

A comprehensive health education program (K-6) that includes the Superkids/Superfit physical activity approach, curriculum guide books, general health information, nutrition information, coping skills, and the Gimme 5 nutrition program.

Human Kinetics

www.humankinetics.com

The information leader in physical activity; produces books, journals, videos, and conferences.

KidsHealth

www.kidshealth.org

Comprehensive website for parents, kids, and teens.

Kimbo Educational

www.kimboed.com

An excellent children's music company offering great selections of physical activity music from such artists as Hap Palmer, Greg and Steve, Georgiana Stewart, and Raffi.

Let's Move

www.letsmove.gov

A White House program to combat childhood obesity throughout various segments of our society. It provides separate links for parents, kids, schools, and more.

Moving and Learning

www.movingandlearning.com

Resources for young children, including books, CDs, and instructional materials for motor skill development, music, and creative movement.

MyPlate

www.choosemyplate.gov

This site includes the USDA's dietary guidelines for healthy eating. Specific pages address different audiences such as the general population, expectant mothers, preschoolers, kids, and people who wish to lose weight.

National Association for Sport and Physical Education (NASPE)

www.aahperd.org/naspe/

Offers projects, materials, standards, position statements, events, and services.

National Coalition for Promoting Physical Activity (NCPPA)

www.ncppa.org

A national organization committed to uniting public, private, and industry efforts into collaborative partnerships.

NFL Rush: Play 60

www.nflrush.com/play60

An NFL website designed to tackle childhood obesity through in-school, after-school, and team-based programs.

Parental Wisdom

www.parentalwisdom.com

A website for parents that addresses children's health, parenting strategies, and behavior management approaches; offers a monthly question and answer interactive section.

PBS Broadcasting Service

www.pbs.org/parents/childrenandmedia/

A site that directs parents to information on high-quality children's television, how to combat advertising directed at kids, computers and kids, and video games. Many broadcasts address eating and physical activity behaviors.

PE Central

www.pecentral.org

Activities, lesson plans, assessments, and practical techniques for physical educators.

pelinks4U

www.pelinks4u.org

Up-to-date news, lesson plans, games, and assessment ideas for the physical education teacher.

President's Council on Fitness, Sports and Nutrition

www.presidentschallenge.org

A national council to improve the health, physical activity, and fitness of all Americans; includes information on the Presidential Active Lifestyle Award.

Project ACES

www.lensaunders.com/aces/aces.html

Project ACES (All Children Exercise Simultaneously) takes place during the first week of May; this site includes free materials.

Puzzlemaker

www.discoveryeducation.com/free-puzzle-maker/

This program offers students a variety of puzzle-making activities. Student can input their vocabulary words into many types of puzzles, including word searches and crossword puzzles.

Skillastics

www.skillastics.com

This site offers a number of standards-based fitness and sport skill activity kits.

SPRI Products

www.spri.com

A fitness equipment company that offers DVDs, instructional materials, and an online education center.

Winter Feels Good

www.snowlink.com/winterfeelsgood.aspx

An introduction to snow sports with curriculum materials. The purpose of the site is to keep the entire family active during cold months.

Yoga in My School

www.yogainmyschool.com

A site that offers yoga basics and materials for integrating yoga throughout the curriculum: math, science, language arts, art, music, physical education, and social studies.

References and Resources

Allen, V.L. 1996. The out-of-school fitness connection. *Teaching Elementary Physical Education* 7 (1): 15-17.

American College of Sports Medicine (ACSM). 2006. *ACSM's guidelines for exercise testing and prescription.* 7th ed. Philadelphia: Lippincott Williams & Wilkins.

American Heart Association. 2010a. *Heart disease and stroke statistics.* www.heart.org/HEARTORG/General/Heart-and-Stroke-Association-Statistics_UCM_319064_SubHomePage.jsp.

American Heart Association. 2010b. *Risk factors and coronary heart disease and stroke.* Dallas: Author.

Anderson, K.C., and S. Cumbaa. 1993. *The bones game book.* New York: Workman.

Bandura, A. 1986. *Social foundations of thought and action.* Englewood Cliffs, NJ: Prentice Hall.

Berenson, G.S., ed. 1986. *Causation of cardiovascular risk factors in children: Perspectives on causation of cardiovascular risk in early life.* New York: Raven Press.

Berenson, G.S. et al. 1998. *Health Ahead/Heart Smart curriculum guides K-6.* New Orleans: Tulane Center for Cardiovascular Health.

Bersma, D., and M. Visscher. 2003. *Yoga games for children.* Alameda, CA: Hunter House.

Blahnik, J. 2002. *Full body flexibility.* Champaign, IL: Human Kinetics.

Blair, S.N., H.W. Kohl, R.S. Paffenbarger, D.G. Clark, K.H. Cooper, and L.W. Gibbons. 1989. Physical fitness and all-cause mortality: A prospective study in healthy men and women. *Journal of the American Medical Association* 262 (17): 2395-2399.

Block, M. 2007. *A teacher's guide to including students with disabilities in general physical education.* 3rd ed. Baltimore: Brookes.

Bouchard, C., R.J. Shephard, T. Stephens, J.R. Sutton, and B.D. McPherson, eds. 1990. *Exercise, fitness and health: A consensus of current knowledge.* Champaign, IL: Human Kinetics.

Centers for Disease Control and Prevention (CDC). 2006. *School health policies and programs study (SHPPS).* Atlanta: National Center for Chronic Disease Prevention and Health Promotion; Division of Adolescent and School Health.

Centers for Disease Control and Prevention (CDC). 2010. *Promoting physical activity: A guide for community action.* 2nd ed. Champaign, IL: Human Kinetics.

Centers for Disease Control and Prevention (CDC), and American College of Sports Medicine (ACSM). 1993. Summary statement: Workshop on physical activity and public health. *Sports Medicine Bulletin* 28: 7.

Child Nutrition and WIC Reauthorization Act. 2004. Public Law 108-265, Section 204. June 30, 2004.

Cole, J. 1991. *The magic school bus: Inside the human body.* New York: Scholastic.

Cooper Institute. 2010. *Fitnessgram and Activitygram test administration manual.* Updated 4th ed. Champaign, IL: Human Kinetics.

Corbin, C., G. Le Masurier, M. Greiner, and D. Lambdin. 2011. *Fitness for life: Elementary school.* Champaign, IL: Human Kinetics.

Corbin, C.B., G. Welk, W. Corbin, and K. Welk. 2011. *Concepts of physical fitness.* New York: McGraw-Hill.

Downey, A.M., G.C. Frank, L.S. Webber, S.J. Virgilio, D.W. Harsha, F.A. Franklin, and G.S. Berenson. 1987. Implementation of "Heart Smart": A cardiovascular school health promotion program. *Journal of School Health* 57 (3): 98-104.

Downey, A.M., J. Greenberg, S.J. Virgilio, and G.S. Berenson. 1989. A health promotion model: The university, the medical school, and the public health department. *Health Values* 13 (6): 31-46.

Dowson, A. 2009. *More fun and games.* Champaign, IL: Human Kinetics.

Faigenbaum, A., and W. Westcott. 2009. *Youth strength training.* Champaign, IL: Human Kinetics.

Finkelstein, E.A., J.G. Trogdon, J.W. Cohen, and W. Dietz. 2009. Annual medical spending attributable to obesity: Payer and service specific estimates. *Health Affairs* 28: 822-831.

Freedman, D.S., Z. Mei, S. Srinivasan, G. Berenson, and W. Dietz. 2007. Cardiovascular risk factors and excess adiposity among overweight children and adolescents: The Bogalusa Heart Study. *The Journal of Pediatrics* 150 (1): 12-17.

Gray, C. 2000. *The new social story book.* Illustrated ed. Arlington, TX: Future Horizons.

Hellison, D.R., and T.J. Templin. 1991. *A reflective approach to teaching physical education.* Champaign, IL: Human Kinetics.

Kasser, S., and R. Lytle. 2005. *Inclusive physical activity.* Champaign, IL: Human Kinetics.

Kelly, L.E. 2011. Spinal cord disabilities. In *Adapted physical education and sport*, 5th ed., ed. J.P. Winnick, pp. 311-345. Champaign, IL: Human Kinetics.

Kern, K. 1987. Teaching circulation in elementary physical education classes. *Journal of Physical Education, Recreation and Dance* 58 (1): 62-63.

Lark, L. 2003. *Yoga for kids*. Buffalo, NY: Firefly Books.

Lieberman, L., and C. Wilson. 2009. *Strategies for inclusion*. 2nd ed. Champaign, IL: Human Kinetics.

Lockette, K.F., and A.M. Keyes. 1994. *Conditioning with physical disabilities*. Champaign, IL: Human Kinetics.

Meeks, L., and P. Heit. 2010. *Comprehensive school health education: Totally awesome strategies for teaching health*. 7th ed. New York: McGraw-Hill.

Meinbach, A., A. Fredericks, and L. Rothlein. 2000. *The complete guide to thematic units: Creating the integrated curriculum*. 2nd ed. Norwood, MA: Christopher Gordon.

Miller, P.D., ed. 1995. *Fitness programming and physical disability*. Champaign, IL: Human Kinetics.

Mosston, M., and S. Ashworth. 2002. *Teaching physical education*. 5th ed. San Francisco: Benjamin Cummings.

National Association for Sport and Physical Education. 2003. *What constitutes a quality physical education program?* (Position statement). Reston, VA: Author.

National Association for Sport and Physical Education. 2004a. *Moving into the future: National standards for physical education*. 2nd ed. Reston, VA: Author.

National Association for Sport and Physical Education. 2004b. *Physical activity for children: A statement of guidelines for children ages 5-12*. 2nd ed. Reston, VA: Author.

National Association for Sport and Physical Education. 2008. *Comprehensive school physical activity programs*. (Position statement). Reston, VA: Author.

National Association for Sport and Physical Education. 2009a. *Active start: A statement of physical activity guidelines for children from birth to age 5*. 2nd ed. Reston, VA: Author.

National Association for Sport and Physical Education. 2009b. *Appropriate use of instructional technology in physical education*. (Position statement). Reston, VA: Author.

National Association for Sport and Physical Education. 2011. *Physical education for lifelong fitness: The physical best teachers guide*. 3rd ed. Champaign, IL: Human Kinetics.

National Physical Activity Plan. 2010. www.physicalactivityplan.org.

Ogden, C., M. Carroll, and K. Flegal. 2008. High body mass index for age among U.S. children and adolescents, 2003-2006. *Journal of the American Medical Association* 299 (20): 2401-2405.

Ogden, C., M. Carroll, L. Curtin, M. Lamb, and K. Flegal. 2010. Prevalence of high body mass index in U.S. children and adolescents, 2007-2008. *Journal of the American Medical Association* 303 (3): 242-249.

Ormrod, J.E. 2009. *Educational psychology: Developing learners*. Columbus, OH: Prentice Hall.

Pangrazi, R.P., and L. Beighle. 2009. *Dynamic physical education for elementary school children*. 16th ed. San Francisco: Benjamin Cummings.

Pate, R.R., M. Pratt, S.N. Blair, W.L. Haskell, et al. 1995. Physical activity and public health: A recommendation of changes from the Centers for Disease Control and Prevention and the American College of Sports Medicine. *Journal of the American Medical Association* 273 (5): 402-407.

Powers, S.K., and S.L. Dodd. 2011. *Total fitness and wellness*. San Francisco: Pearson Education.

Puleo, J., and P. Milroy. 2010. *Running anatomy*. Champaign, IL: Human Kinetics.

Ratliffe, T., and L.M. Ratliffe. 1994. *Teaching children fitness*. Champaign, IL: Human Kinetics.

Rimmer, J.H. 1994. *Fitness and rehabilitation programs for special populations*. Dubuque, IA: Brown and Benchmark.

Rink, J. 2010. *Teaching physical education for learning*. 6th ed. New York: McGraw-Hill.

Rink, J., T. Hall, and L. Williams. 2010. *Schoolwide physical activity*. Champaign, IL: Human Kinetics.

Rodgers, C.R. 1994. *Freedom to learn*. 3rd ed. New York: Macmillan.

Rouse, P. 2009. *Inclusion in physical education*. Champaign, IL: Human Kinetics.

Sallis, J.F., and T.L. McKenzie. 1991. Physical education's role in public health. *Research Quarterly for Exercise and Sport* 62 (2): 124-137.

Shear, C.L., D.S. Freedman, G.L. Burke, D.W. Harsha, L.S. Webber, and G.S. Berenson. 1988. Secular trends of obesity in early life: The Bogalusa Heart Study. *American Journal of Public Health* 78 (1): 75-77.

Sherrill, C. 2004. *Adapted physical activity, recreation and sport*. 6th ed. New York: McGraw-Hill.

Simons-Morton, B.G. 1994. Implementing health-related physical education. In *Health and fitness through physical education*, eds. R.R. Pate and R.C. Hohn, pp. 137-145. Champaign, IL: Human Kinetics.

Smith, A.L., and S. Biddle, eds. 2008. *Youth physical activity and sedentary behavior*. Champaign, IL: Human Kinetics.

U.S. Department of Agriculture (USDA). 2011. *MyPlate*. www.ChooseMyPlate.gov.

U.S. Department of Health and Human Services (USDHHS), and Centers for Disease Control and Prevention (CDC). 1997. Guidelines for school and community programs to promote lifelong physical activity among young people. *Morbidity and Mortality Weekly Report,* 46 (RR-6), 1-36.

U.S. Food and Drug Administration (FDA). 2011. *How to understand and use the nutrition facts label.* www.fda.gov/food/labelingnutrition/consumerinformation/ucm078889.htm.

Vacca, R.T., and J.A. Vacca. 1996. *Content area reading.* New York: HarperCollins.

Virgilio, S.J. 1990. A model for parental involvement in physical education. *Journal of Physical Education, Recreation and Dance* 69 (18): 66-70.

Virgilio, S.J. 1996. A home, school, and community model for promoting healthy lifestyles. *Teaching Elementary Physical Education* 7 (1): 4-7.

Virgilio, S.J. 2006. *Active start for healthy kids.* Champaign, IL: Human Kinetics.

Virgilio, S.J., and G.S. Berenson. 1988. Superkids-Superfit: A comprehensive fitness intervention model for elementary schools. *Journal of Physical Education, Recreation and Dance* 59 (8): 19-25.

Winnick, J.P. 2011. *Adapted physical education and sport.* 5th ed. Champaign, IL: Human Kinetics.

Index

Note: Page numbers followed by an italicized *f* or *t* indicates a figure or table will be found on that page. Page numbers followed by italicized *ff* or *tt* indicate multiple figures or tables will be found on that page.

About the Author

© Brian Ballweg

Stephen J. Virgilio, PhD, is a professor of physical education at Adelphi University in Garden City, New York. He has researched and studied childhood obesity and fitness education for over 30 years. He taught elementary physical education for six years before earning his doctorate from Florida State University.

Dr. Virgilio has authored four other books, including *Active Start for Healthy Kids* (Human Kinetics, 2006), which focuses on children ages 2 to 6. He has published over 75 manuscripts and conducted more than 150 presentations and workshops, including several keynote addresses. He is the coauthor of the nationally known Heart Smart Program, a school-based cardiovascular health intervention program.

Dr. Virgilio has been quoted in over 100 major newspapers, magazines, and websites. He has served on the editorial board of *Teaching Elementary Physical Education: Journal of Physical Education, Recreation, and Dance;* and *Strategies*. He has also served on several national committees and projects with the National Association for Sport and Physical Education (NASPE). In 2006, he was elected to the NASPE board of directors. He has been a consultant to school districts throughout the United States as well as Dannon, Fisher-Price, Sport-Fun, and Skillastics. He has also served as senior writer to the PBS children's TV show *Kid-Fitness*. Since 1977 he has been a member of NASPE and the American Alliance for Health, Physical Education, Recreation and Dance.

Dr. Virgilio resides in East Williston and Seneca Falls, New York. In his spare time he enjoys bass fishing, kayaking, boating, traveling, and studying world economics.

You'll find other outstanding
physical education resources at
www.HumanKinetics.com